The Unity of Reason

The Unity of Reason

Rereading Kant

SUSAN NEIMAN

New York   Oxford
OXFORD UNIVERSITY PRESS
1994

Oxford University Press

Oxford   New York   Toronto
Delhi   Bombay   Calcutta   Madras   Karachi
Kuala Lumpur   Singapore   Hong Kong   Tokyo
Nairobi   Dar es Salaam   Cape Town
Melbourne   Auckland   Madrid

and associated companies in
Berlin   Ibadan

Published by Oxford University Press, Inc.
200 Madison Avenue, New York, New York 10016

Oxford is a registered trademark of Oxford University Press

Library of Congress Cataloging-in-Publication Data
Neiman, Susan.
The unity of reason : rereading Kant / Susan Neiman.
p.   cm.
Includes bibliographical references and index.
ISBN 0-19-506768-1
1. Kant, Immanuel, 1724-1804. Kritik der reinen Vernunft.
2. Reason.   3. Knowledge, Theory of.   I. Title.
B2779.N45   1994   121—dc20
93-8434

2 4 6 8 9 7 5 3 1

Printed in the United States of America
on acid-free paper

Preface

This book began as the doctoral dissertation of a student troubled by the dissonance between Kant's stated intentions and the apparent content of his major texts. Few who have read the famous acknowledgment of his debt to Rousseau can fail to be moved by it:

> I am by nature an inquirer. I feel the consuming thirst for knowledge, the restless passion to advance ever further, the delights of discovery. There was a time when I believed that this is what confers real dignity upon human life, and I despised the common people who know nothing. Rousseau set me right. This imagined advantage vanishes, and I learned to honor human nature.

Yet when Kant concludes, "I should regard myself to be far more useless than a common laborer, if I did not believe that my work would contribute to restoring the rights of humanity" (XX,44), the acknowledgment begins to acquire an air of pathos. How could a man of Kant's integrity believe that the tortuous investigation of the limits of knowledge would contribute to restoring the rights of humanity? If this belief is not an expression of unexamined and outworn assumptions of the classical Enlightenment, should it be understood as unhappy confirmation of Kant's claim that self-knowledge is the most difficult of reason's tasks?

There remain, of course, Kant's ethical writings. Here it is possible, though not entirely easy, to see how the philosopher might have hoped to contribute to something like the general improvement of humankind. Humankind's improvement is, however, rather different from its rights. The texts that Kant explicitly devoted to political questions do not suffice to explain how he hoped to achieve this broader and far more problematic goal. Indeed, two centuries of Kant scholarship have been unable to decide even whether his undeniable inconsistencies on the subject of the French Revolution were the result of philosophical unclarity or political caution. We seem to be left with a choice between admitting that the most important philosopher of modern times was a deluded, pretentious fool or ignoring Kant's most poignant and interesting statements of his own goals.

I believe that another alternative can be found by redirecting our attention from the epistemological questions in Kant's work to those concerning the nature of reason. It is the latter concept which allows us to unite Kant's wide-ranging texts and concerns; it is the latter concept which enables us to understand the connection between Kant's immense speculative achievements and his unflagging practical hopes. Whether those hopes can be realized by Kant's—or any other—labors, is a matter which remains outside the scope of the present study. My goal is simply to show how those hopes might be genuinely founded.

While writing the dissertation on which this book was based, I was especially fortunate in receiving the advice and encouragement of John Rawls, whose contributions went beyond the normal duties of a thesis advisor. I owe another debt to the students in my Kant courses at Yale College. Their critical and energetic probing helped to sharpen my thinking about Kant's work, and their enthusiasm for it helped to sustain my own.

New Haven, Connecticut   S.N.
June 1993

Contents

The Unity of Reason

Introduction

How should we explain the fact that no full-length study has been devoted to Kant's conception of reason? Perhaps it is due to the suggestion, furthered by Kant himself, that the subject of his critique of reason is one of magnitude: its guiding question is, *How much* can reason accomplish? This suggests that Kant accepted a notion of reason that was given by his predecessors while simply being more cautious than they had been in determining its powers. This book will argue, instead, that a fundamental aim of the Critical Philosophy is to reconceive the nature of reason. The basis of Kant's reconception is his insistence upon the unity of theoretical and practical reason. The route to that conception is the denial that the rational is, or is centrally concerned with, the cognitive.

We are so accustomed to identify the two that we take Kant's unmistakable attempt to disengage them to be a demonstration of the insignificance of reason. Never supposing that reason's achievement might be something other than knowledge, we take Kant to be asking a question about the extent of reason's ability to know. Upon discovering the answer to be minimal, we believe the role of reason to be negligible. These assumptions have led to a number of misemphases in both the German- and English-speaking traditions of Kant scholarship. Most readers of the *Critique of Pure Reason* have focused on its first two hundred pages, dismissing the "Dialectic," whose subject is reason, as an elaboration of the positive doctrines of the "Analytic," which is of little concern to any but those with an interest in the details of the destruction of scholastic metaphysics. Readers of Kant's works as a whole have tended to treat his ethics separately from his metaphysics, with little systematic probing of their mutual dependence.[1]

Kant himself is partly to blame for misunderstandings that led to readings of his work that are so far from his original goals. It is not only his notoriously difficult style which is at fault here. Precisely concerning the nature of reason, Kant's writings reveal inconsistencies and unclarities that can only suggest that he himself had not yet acknowledged the magnitude of the task he had undertaken. It is well known that creators of conceptual revolutions often lack the tools to grasp their own achievement. How else is one to understand the differences between Kant's various depictions of reason? Many passages of the first *Critique* fairly revel in the "humiliation" of reason's "pretensions." Such passages exist side by side with Kant's stunningly casual praise of reason as "the highest faculty." These differences of tone, when noticed, have been viewed as reflections of the tragic conflicts of an Enlightenment figure attempting to salvage something of the worldview he was too honest, or brilliant, to

3

refrain from destroying. Kant's repeated assertion that reason can be practical does not, by itself, undermine this view. This is partly due to the tendency to discuss Kant's ethics and metaphysics separately. The excellent and growing body of recent work on Kant's moral philosophy has not devoted sufficient attention to the question why Kant holds that only reason can function as the source of moral principles. In the absence of an answer to this question, the fact that reason is the center of moral activity is not treated as a fact *about reason* and hence an avenue to understanding Kant's beliefs about the nature of reason's achievement. Thus, this fact may be viewed as little more than Kant's attempt to lend a kind of legitimacy to moral principles that his own epistemology has rendered obsolete. Kant's claim that reason establishes articles of belief fares even worse. Even most acute scholars have followed Hegel in supposing belief to be a second-rate sort of knowledge and viewing Kant's postulates of reason to be pitiful substitutes for the truths that it failed to establish.

This book will argue that far from undermining traditional belief in the significance of reason, Kant deepens and transforms it. Showing this will require, among other things, a reexamination of Kant's discussion of the pretensions of speculative reason and his insistence that reason's ends are practical. These claims have given rise to a rather natural misunderstanding. This is the notion that somehow, reason ought to have been able to solve its problems by speculation. Humiliated and frustrated in metaphysics, reason turns to practice for an inferior version of the resolution it expected to gain from speculation. Kant's idea is rather, I think, to show that reason's expectations were all wrong. Reason's failure to resolve its problems through speculation is not *accidental*: it is not that reason is prevented from providing metaphysical solutions by some unfortunate considerations about space and time. Reason's nature is thoroughly practical; its problems cannot be solved by attaining knowledge. This is not to imply that reason's problems are irresolvable. Kant states quite clearly that reason is not mistaken as to the objects of its concern, and he repeatedly insists that reason must be able to solve the problems that it poses itself. The doctrine that theoretical and practical reason form a unity entails that the practical resolution proposed by Kant will be a genuine resolution of speculative aims.

There is another sort of misunderstanding that may accompany these considerations. If the first mistake involves the failure to recognize the significance of reason, the second is the failure to capture the rationality of practice. It is easy to suppose that if speculation is resolved in practice, the resolution of speculative questions is not intellectual. Some of Kant's more dramatic statements make this supposition so natural that they were used during his lifetime in an attempt to support the antiintellectual "party of faith."[2] And some recent scholars, acknowledging the importance of Kant's insistence on the primacy of the practical, conclude that he holds the value of critical inquiry to be merely instrumental.[3] Again, it is the doctrine of the unity of reason which is to deny such an option: it is practical *reason* which replaces speculative reason. Hence, the practical is as thoroughly rational as the rational is practical. Here we are hampered by our persistent inability to dissociate the rational from the cognitive. Kant's aim, one may fear, is to produce the well-intentioned Pietist burgher, inured to the illusions of metaphysics and oblivious to its other features. But serious attention to his frequent remarks about enlightenment, culture, and education should help to undermine such a picture. Reason (hence practice, reason's end) is reflective; its tasks require criticism and introspection. Reason is intellectual; its nature is to formulate ideas most distant from the senses. It is simply not knowledge, which is wrongly supposed to be the sole province of these other activities.

Kant's concept of reason, then, must permit him to reject two ways of asking what are, in fact, a single question. Both were posed clearly by Hume, and they continue to fuel doubts whether reason is adequate to play the practical role upon which Kant insists. The first is commonly phrased as the question of whether reason extends its capacities beyond scientific inquiry to other areas of concern. The second is the question of whether the real world of tumult and passion, action and mystery is fundamentally inaccessible to reason. Kant's strategy, I will argue, is to disarm both sides of this question by constructing notions of the rational and the practical that no longer permit the question to be posed.

This construction relies on a fundamental distinction between reason and under-standing, the faculty of knowledge. A number of factors probably play a role in most scholars' decision to underplay a distinction that Kant proclaimed to be crucial.[4] One may be Kant's own carelessness on the subject. After insisting on the importance of distinguishing between the two faculties, he will often use '*Vernunft*' to refer not simply to the faculty of reason but to understanding – or even the entire intellectual process.[5] Where this is not an instance of hasty editing, I believe it is an example of Kant's own inability to appreciate the depths of the changes he had wrought. The ideas he expresses are clear enough; the terminology, often, is not. A more important reason to dismiss the distinction between reason and understanding is the wariness to adopt a philosophically untenable language of faculty psychology. Yet recent scholar-ship has shown that even many eighteenth-century writers held a less reified view of the faculties than their language might suggest.[6] The insistence that reason and understanding be viewed as distinct entities need have no more content than the insistence that they be viewed as distinct capacities. While Kant sometimes writes as if sensibility, understanding, and reason were discrete, identifiable objects, his own assertions that they are activities that take place simultaneously should help dispel the uneasiness with faculty talk. A deeper philosophical reluctance to credit the distinc-tion between reason and understanding must await discussion until the notion of transcendental illusion has been further examined.[7]

Here I wish to use the contrasts between reason and understanding to elicit crucial features of Kant's notion of reason that will be explored in this work. These features may be summarized as follows. Reason provides systematic unity to the cognitions of the understanding. This systematization is necessary to move the most minimal gathering of information to the ranks of science. I will argue that the sense of "system" at issue here entails that understanding is capable of nothing other than the simple recording of what is. Of course, because of the way in which understanding is responsible for the synthesis of experience, this recording is not passive. But it is reason's introduction of ends that introduces a motive to question experience and so to form constructions more interesting than simple aggregates of assertions about the data of experience.

Kant's view of reason as the capacity to determine ends is, of course, in direct opposition to the more common view, held by philosophers as different as David

Hume and Theodor Adorno, of reason as an activity of calculating means to ends that are otherwise determined. Kant's attempt to undermine that view relies on the variety of ways in which proposing ends is fundamental to all human activity and on the insight that this capacity has a radically different character from others. An end is necessarily something beyond that which is already given. In proposing ends, therefore, reason declares its right to make demands upon experience in a manner forbidden to the understanding. The concepts of the understanding give order to experience; the principles of reason are the standard by which it is judged. In a conflict between the two, it is not the principles which require revision, but experience which is inadequate to the principles of reason.

This startling expression of idealism poses no threat to Kant's repeated insistence that significant statements be responsible to the claims of experience. Imposing upon practice the limits that we must impose upon knowledge is an act of moral negligence. The demand that reason set the standards by which experience is to be judged is a reinterpretation, not an abdication, of responsibility. Now reason must have some relation to experience which ensures that its activities are not arid, idle fantasies. Yet unlike the grounding of understanding through sensibility, this relation must enable reason to maintain sufficient independence from experience to function as the creator of ends. So Kant introduces the notion of a regulative principle, which guides the human search to constitute experience without constituting it for us antecedently. Regulative principles ensure that reason's activities are grounded in the world without being determined by it.

The fact that only reason has the capacity to prescribe imperatives to experience means that only the activities of reason are genuinely free. Indeed, Kant often describes the objective justification undertaken by understanding as a kind of compulsion.[8] So the distinction between reason and understanding is sometimes expressed in territorial terms: understanding rules the realm of nature, reason's province is that of freedom. This is acceptable as long as it is clear that freedom is not only a moral idea. Kant's statement that the concept of freedom is the keystone of the whole architectonic of reason rests on his awareness of the ways in which freedom—and reason—penetrate the range of human activity. Of course, the principles of reason are not constitutive: to mistake the right to make demands upon experience for the belief that those demands have been fulfilled is to be engaged in transcendental illusion. Human reason cannot know that its order will be satisfied by experience, and it is bound to acknowledge that it does not. The fact that its power is not equal to its independence is just the fact of its peculiar fate.

Even this general outline of the essential features of reason may suggest that Kant's characterization of reason's activities is far more radical than his conception of knowledge. In particular, if his account of the possibility of knowledge constitutes a Copernican Revolution, his definition of knowledge is rather conventional. This is reflected in Kant's consistent rejection of the suggestion that intersubjective agreement is in any way constitutive of truth or knowledge. Such agreement, he allows, may be useful as a criterion of truth. Truth itself, however, is to be found not in any fact about the subject but in some relation between subject and object—roughly, the rather straightforward one of the former recording the latter. Kant takes his definition of truth—the agreement of knowledge with its object—to be traditional and uncontroversial. Now the first *Critique* will give a revolutionary explanation of the only possible way in which knowledge can agree with its object (or, better, in which knowledge can become knowledge of objects). But Kant's attempts to answer the charges of idealism all involve his rejection of the imputation that he has changed the notions of truth and knowledge themselves.

The success of Kant's effort to distinguish coherently between transcendental and subjective idealism is an issue that this book will avoid.[9] I am concerned with Kant's discussion of knowledge only insofar as it is needed to give content to the contrast between knowledge and reason. For these purposes, it suffices at present simply to point out that Kant strenuously resisted every charge that his epistemology placed the justification of knowledge on subjective grounds. Concerning the activities of reason, however, he is willing to make precisely the opposite claim. The postulates of rational faith, for example, are based upon a notion of subjective interest and, Kant argues, can only be justified as such. Knowledge of the objects of belief would not only be insufficient for our needs but would be positively undesirable. In thus separating the activities of knowledge and reason, Kant introduces a notion of justification that is, he suggests, grounded not upon the determination of an object but solely on the nature of a subject.

The foregoing sketch may lead the reader to wonder whether Kant's conception of reason is not revolutionary but simply empty. If sense can be made of the claim that Kant believes something he calls reason to be distinct from something he calls knowledge, with the revision of the notion of justification such belief must entail, what remains to ensure that it is reason that is under discussion? The problem of determining whether to describe a body of work as the transformation of a given concept or as a change of perspective so immense that it no longer makes sense to speak of the concept as the same is a general one. It becomes particularly acute when, as in the case of reason, the concept in question is partly normative. We do not possess a neutral conception of the reasonable, to which Kant's view could succeed or fail to correspond. Hence, the task of this book is a double one: to exhibit and justify Kant's view *as a notion of reason* at the same time and in the same way in which it is shown to be a radical departure from other views.

This justification will involve two sorts of enterprises. The first places Kant's notion of reason historically, demonstrating its continuity with earlier views of reason while showing Kant to be offering solutions to problems those views left unsolved. The second examines Kant's notion of reason itself by examining the activities that Kant attributes to reason. In each case, I seek to provide a coherent account of the elusive notion of a regulative principle. According to Kant, it is the regulative principles of reason that shape our actions in science, morality, religion, and philosophy itself. Examining the nature and the mode of justification of each should, in turn, support the general claims made about reason, which are given content by the examination itself. In each case, it must be possible to discover fundamental differences between the work of reason and the achievement of knowledge; this will show Kant's notion of reason to be genuinely new. In each case, it must be possible to show the presence of some process of public justification; this will show Kant's notion of reason to be still recognizably a notion of *reason*.

In cases where they conflict, I have given preference to the systematic reconstruction of a compelling philosophical view over strict historical fidelity. Kant's writing on reason, as on other subjects, is often inconsistent and unclear; and while certain ideas were more fully developed as the Critical Period wore on, he nowhere argues for the positions he created as clearly as I hope I have here. Where it has been necessary to depart from his texts in order to do so, I have noted it and justified this departure in the attempt to give philosophical credence to his views as a whole.

Notes

I am indebted to Larry Herrera for checking references and standardizing citations, and to Jeremy Bendik Keymer for extensive help in compiling an index. For forms of citation, see p. 207.

1. Happily, exceptions to this claim are becoming more frequent. Most recently, Richard Velkley's *Freedom and the End of Reason* (1989) has made extensive use of the pre-Critical writings to argue that in Kant's work after 1765, "nothing less is at stake than the meaning, status and content of reason as a whole" (1989, 5). Yirmayahu Yovel's *Kant and the Philosophy of History* describes "the creative autonomy of human reason" as Kant's most important single principle (1980, 275). The opening chapters of Onora O'Neill's (1989) *Constructions of Reason* explores the political metaphors involved in the first *Critique*'s discussion of theoretical reason. Surprisingly, Klaus Konhardt's (1979) dissertation, *Die Einheit der Vernunft*, is the only contemporary German study to treat these questions at length. Despite some tendency of the neo-Kantian movement to focus on purely theoretical questions, some earlier scholars, too, emphasized elements of the reading here proposed. Much of Hermann Cohen's work, in particular, contains many points of departure for those concerned with the role of ideas of reason in theory and practice; see, especially, his *Kants Begründung der Ethik* (1910). Cohen's student Ernst Cassirer wrote that "only through a critique of the entire faculty of reason could Kant . . . create that wider and deeper idea of 'reason' which could do justice to Rousseau's ideas" (1945, 59). Hannah Arendt's (1977) *Life of the Mind* stresses the revolutionary nature of Kant's distinction between reason and understanding.

I have learned from all these sources. What I hope to provide that they do not is a general account of Kant's critical philosophy in terms of the goals stated. If statements such as those just quoted are correct, how did Kant construct, in detail, an account of reason that would fulfill them?

2. See the account of Jacobi's conduct during the *Pantheismusstreit* in chapter 4.

3. See Henrich 1976, 13.

4. See, for example, Kant's judgment in the *Prolegomena*: "Had the *Critique of Pure Reason* done nothing but first point out this distinction, it would thereby have contributed more to clear up our conception of, and to guide our inquiry in, the field of metaphysics than all the vain efforts that had hitherto been made to satisfy the transcendent problems of pure reason" (IV, 328–29).

5. Konhardt counts seventeen different uses of the word 'reason' in the *Critique of Pure Reason* alone (1979, 49). Kemp Smith notes, generally, "there is hardly a technical term which is not employed by [Kant] in a variety of different and conflicting senses. As a writer, he is the least exact of all the great thinkers" (1962, xx).

6. See Bencivenga 1987, 78, 117.

7. Kemp Smith's otherwise valuable commentary may stand as a good example of an approach to the subject that begins from assumptions so misleading that Kant might hold them to be instances of the error against which he warns. Kemp Smith charges that Kant has failed to answer the main question of the "Dialectic," since he has not proved that the ideas of reason are

altogether distinct from the concepts of the understanding. The objection assumes that reason could not be anything but another cognitive faculty, whose distinction from the understanding can only be established by determining whether its particular contributions to cognition are unique. Why Kant would attempt to clear a space for some cognitive activity that reason could claim as its own and that, equally mysteriously, the understanding was unable to perform are questions that remained unasked by those who viewed knowledge as the only possible goal of rational activity (see chap. 2).

8. See chap. 2, secs. II–III.
9. See Allison 1983 for a defense of Kant's distinction on this score.

1

Historical Sources

A revision of our understanding of Kant's project requires a revision of our understanding of his relation to his predecessors. The task of this chapter is to provide one. My goal is not to present a detailed study that would trace historical influences on Kant's thought, though I have often drawn on such studies.[1] The aim, again, is systematic reconstruction. If Kant's goal is to provide a reinterpretation of the notion of reason, what philosophical problems led him to do so? What was the conceptual background against which his revolution can be placed and understood? In answering these questions I will draw on the familiar schema that places Kant as mediator between rationalists and empiricists, but will describe this relation in less familiar terms.

The *Critique of Pure Reason* itself provides the basis for doing so. Its final, brief, and programmatic chapter, "The History of Pure Reason," describes three issues that Kant holds to be the basis of the most noteworthy revolutions in philosophy. The third issue concerns philosophical methodology. The second is the issue of whether knowledge is derived from experience or from concepts independent of it. Here Kant presents himself in terms familiar from any introductory philosophy course, as providing the middle ground between empiricists like Locke, who held all our knowledge to come from experience, and rationalists like Leibniz, who sought its origin in reason. But the issue that Kant designates as first is the one that has received the least attention. To be sure, he describes it misleadingly as the question of "the object of all our *knowledge* through reason." But the problem he sketches can be stated quite clearly. Sensualists, he says, maintain that reality is to be found solely in the objects of the senses and that all else is fiction. Those whom Kant here calls intellectualists maintain, on the other hand, that everything given through the senses is illusion and that only ideas have genuine reality (A853/B882). Kant holds Epicurus to be the best representative of the former position, Plato the outstanding defender of the latter. The positions, he believes, have been maintained in unbroken continuity since earliest times — and they remain even long after Kant proposed a resolution between them. The problem that he designates as of first significance is one that he also describes as subtle, and Kant's own interests have often been misread. His primary concern is not to answer the skeptic's question of the reality of the external world, but to determine what sort of reality we can meaningfully ascribe to the ideas of reason.[2] The extended analysis of the nature of objects in the "Transcendental Analytic" is intended to provide a basis for claiming that unlike ordinary things, ideas of reason are not objects of experience. The rest of the first *Critique* and many of

Kant's later works try to show how the ideas, though not things in the world, nevertheless play a role in it.

Kant, I will argue, is the first philosopher to give equal weight to the claims of reason and the demands of the natural world. Rationalism, he believes, succeeds only in projecting the needs of reason onto the world of nature. Empiricism, by contrast, claims to restrict its interests to the analysis of the world as it is, and hence has no place for a claim of reason independent of the demands of nature. Kant's notion of a need of reason is a way of stating this problem; his notion of a regulative principle is a means of resolving it. But this resolution is hardly a reconciliation between rationalism and empiricism, for the concessions that it makes to the truths contained in these positions are less significant than the demand it makes upon both: to recognize a fundamental disunity in our experience that both had attempted to deny.

Kant's insistence upon a fundamental gap between nature and reason – between the way the world is given to us and the way it ought to be – has far-reaching consequences. Many of them are political. For it is only by recognizing the distance between the ideals of reason and the demands of nature that we can begin, in some measure, to overcome it. With this distinction Kant seeks to provide a metaphysical basis for the Enlightenment's conviction that the reigning order of custom and tradition must be replaced by "natural" laws of human reason. Kant's discussion takes place in terms of the power and scope of reason: both rationalist and empiricist conceptions of reason are inadequate to fulfill what he holds to be reason's true task. Hume, we know, described reason as inert, inactive, and even impotent. The inadequacy of the rationalist conception of reason, though less apparent, is equally significant. While Kant often attacks the rationalist vision for having an overweening view of reason's capacities for knowledge, his deeper critique involves the charge that the rationalist's conception of reason as knowledge leaves reason powerless to perform its real function.

This chapter will argue for these claims in some detail. In presenting a Kantian view of the problems inherent in the notions of reason held by his predecessors, I shall concentrate on understanding the rationalist position embodied by Leibniz. This is in keeping with Kant's own emphasis. He did not regard empiricism to be a coherent philosophical position; anyone who rejected reason as thoroughly as Hume did had also, for Kant, rejected philosophy. The two alternatives against which Kant places his work are the positions of rationalism and skepticism. This means that his position cannot be an attempt to combine the virtues of each, as he may be seen to do in discussing the theory of knowledge. Skepticism's sole virtue, for Kant, is methodological. It can be used as an aid to uncovering the defects of rationalism, but should never be considered a final resting place (A761/B789). Accordingly, when discussing the history of philosophy, Kant is far more concerned with uncovering the problems within rationalism that could lead to skepticism than with attacking the skeptics themselves. This is most evident during the *Pantheismusstreit*, which will be treated in chapter 4, but it is a strategy that Kant repeats throughout his work. Only the difficulties in the rationalist conception of reason could, he believes, make the skeptical rejection of reason appear plausible.

Section I will outline the difficulties in Leibniz's use of the principle of sufficient reason. Sections II – IV will examine his claim that the universe is thoroughly without a trace of arbitrariness. Section V will discuss Leibniz's descriptions of the intellectual faculty that is supposed to discover that order before turning to examine, in section VI, the problems in these accounts from a Kantian point of view. Section VII will sketch Hume's conception of reason and Kant's grounds for rejecting it.

I. Leibniz and the Principle of Sufficient Reason

Let us begin by gathering the most general elements of Leibniz's conception of reason. This is not as easy as one might suppose. Although Leibniz represents the apogee of rationalist thought, he devotes little time to an analysis of the process or nature of reasoning. The absence of such analysis is particularly surprising in view of the fact that descriptions of the different components of human intellectual activity were common philosophical projects in Leibniz's day.[3] Still, it is possible to reconstruct his most basic assumptions about reason by examining the uses to which they were put.

In outline, those assumptions are quite familiar. Norman Kemp Smith wrote that the most important idea that Kant found in Leibniz was the view of thought as unlimited in its powers and absolute in its claims (1962, 601). Leibniz describes the scope and power of reason in a manner that has seemed to be unequaled by any other philosopher. He believes that reason is both able and obliged to obtain knowledge of "the very highest things." Human reason, Leibniz holds, is capable of proofs of the existence of God and the immortality of the soul that give us immediate insight into their nature. Such proofs, he writes, are required for human morality and happiness. At the same time, he insists that the very highest things are governed by, or subject to, reason. Nothing in or out of nature may violate what Leibniz calls the principle of reason. In particular, God must act according to laws of reason, which are fixed independently of his will. These general ideas, conveyed in many different ways throughout Leibniz's work, are repeatedly expressed in the claim that Leibniz calls his "great principle"—the principle of sufficient reason.

The claim that nothing happens without a reason has rightly been the subject of some bewilderment. Leibniz's formulations of the principle vary a great deal. They can, I think, be grouped into three main classes. The first and most general simply asserts that everything has a reason (L 142, 227, 337). The second class states that nothing ever happens without a cause (W 94, L 268, T 147). The third class seems to explicate these claims by reference to God's capacities, as in "Nothing ever happens without the idea that an omniscient mind could give some reason why it should have happened rather than not" (W 95; see also L 639). While all of these types of formulations occur in Leibniz's statements of the principle, he never seems to have distinguished or, therefore, related them. More generally, the question whether anything more than a normative tone is common to all his uses of the word 'reason' does not seem to have troubled Leibniz. Sometimes 'reason' seems to be synonymous with 'efficient cause' and sometimes with 'final cause.' Sometimes 'reason' refers to an intellectual faculty, human or divine, and sometimes to an order existing independently of all such faculties. Occasionally, it is simply equivalent to 'God.' This variety leaves the reader convinced of Leibniz's belief in the importance of the thoroughgoing rationality of the universe, but with little way of knowing how that belief could be given content.

In trying to understand Leibniz's insistence on the primacy of reason, it is important to distinguish two ideas. The first is the claim that the world as it is given to us is rationally ordered, where this means that events in the world are neither random nor arbitrary. This is the claim expressed in Leibniz's assertions that the world is subject to or governed by reason, which permeates the universe and subjugates even God's will. The second is the idea that reason—the intellectual faculty we possess in common with God—is, at least in principle, capable of fully discovering this order that exists in the universe as it is. From these descriptions, the first claim would appear to be one about ontology, while the second concerns epistemology. Yet it is often extremely difficult to separate these claims; Leibniz himself does not adequately distinguish them. Often they appear to be converse statements of precisely the same idea. Thus, the first idea can be stated as the claim that the universe is such as to be accessible to reason, while the second can be stated as the claim that reason is capable of understanding everything in the universe.

For some Absolute Idealists, these claims would indeed amount to assertions of the same point. Leibniz, however, insists that there must be more content to the claim that everything is subject to reason. This is, as we shall see, because his concern to avoid arbitrariness leads him to conclude that reason must be determined from without. For Leibniz, if everything is subject to reason, this must be because there are eternal truths manifesting themselves in everything, independently of anyone's intellectual faculty. 'Reason', that is, must not only refer to the possibility of understanding but to an order existing in the universe that is the ground of any such understanding.[4]

These facts will drive Leibniz to a neo-Platonist view, according to which truths (including the essences of all possible things) exist as supernatural objects of contemplation. The world is subject to reason because God created it in accordance with these eternal truths. And the task of both human and divine reasoning, as intellectual processes, is to trace or discover these truths. The Platonist account of truths and of reason as a discoverer of truth is the means by which Leibniz maintains a distinction between the ontological and the epistemological aspects of the principle of sufficient reason. At the same time, it begins to suggest the dependence of the ontological idea on the epistemological one. As will be seen more fully later, the demand for total intelligibility stands behind much of Leibniz's most fundamental work. I shall argue that many aspects of his metaphysics are, in large measure, determined by the requirements that Leibniz takes such a demand to involve.

It was Kant who first made explicit, while transforming, what I have described as the twofold aspect of the principle of sufficient reason. Thus, the ontological statement, for Kant, is the argument that the (experiential) world is subject to causal uniformity.[5] The second part of the principle is not an assertion of knowledge but a regulative demand that we make the world intelligible to ourselves in a variety of ways. Because of the interdependence of the ontological and epistemological aspects of the principle in Leibniz's work, any attempt to divide them is anachronistic. For the purpose of trying to specify Leibniz's general remarks about the scope and power of human reason, however, it is helpful to treat them separately.

II. Against Skepticism

Hegel's *Lectures on the History of Philosophy* tells us: "Leibniz's philosophy appears like a string of arbitrary assertions, which follow one another like a metaphysical fairy-tale; it is only when we see what he wished thereby to avoid that we learn to appreciate its value" (1974, vol. 3, p. 330). The use of the word 'avoid' is acute. Leibniz's metaphysics, which often seems to lack the positive, unified force of that of Kant or Spinoza, gains a great deal of coherence when seen together with the conclusions against which it is directed. In considering the principle of sufficient reason, two general targets stand out: the idea that the universe is unfathomable and the idea that the universe is necessary. I shall discuss Leibniz's treatment of each of these ideas in turn and will argue that for Leibniz, these ideas are not so opposed as they initially seem. In so doing, I hope to show that Leibniz's statements about the power of reason—although not ultimately fully coherent—constitute a genuine and interesting view.

Leibniz directed the principle of sufficient reason against many views that, he felt, led to the conclusion that the universe is arbitrary. His foremost opponent in these matters was Pierre Bayle. Bayle's *Dictionary*, the target of Leibniz's *Theodicy*, was a work of unparalleled influence, although the meaning of its doctrines remains a matter of some dispute. For Leibniz, who always spoke of Bayle with respect, they represented the most formidable defense of a Christian skeptical tradition. The claim that human reason can provide nothing but empty sophisms and that it should therefore be rejected entirely in favor of simple faith, is an old one. Bayle's brilliance, wit, and erudition were put in service of its defense; the *Dictionary* forms a powerful attack upon the capacity of the human intellect to grasp the central doctrines upon which Christianity is based.

Though its ambiguous attempts to prove that the Gospel could not be a product of reason were the source of much of the controversy surrounding the *Dictionary*, Bayle does not rest his case against reason on its inability to comprehend the mysteries of Christian faith. The "theory of the incomprehensibility of all things" is attributed to Pyrrho in one of the *Dictionary*'s most famous entries, and Bayle held it to be confirmed by every reflection on reason's capacities. For more proof of the claim that the nature of things is hidden from us, Bayle directs his readers to turn their attention from the absurdities of theology to the new, Cartesian science. From the Cartesian claim that the real properties of the universe can be described in terms of extension and motion, Bayle derives further basis for the distinction between things as they are and things as they appear and hence for the conviction of the uselessness of attempting real understanding of either. Significantly, Bayle writes that this skepticism cannot harm anyone but the philosopher. The useful aspects of scientific inquiry can, he thinks, exist without knowledge of the nature of things. But a glance at his argument for this claim should make us question his conclusion.

> It does not matter much if one says that the mind of man is too limited to discover anything concerning natural truths concerning the causes producing heat, cold, the tides, and the like. It is enough for us that we employ ourselves in looking for probable hypotheses and collecting data. I am quite sure that there are very few good scientists of this century who are not convinced that nature is an impenetra-

ble abyss and that its springs are known only to Him who made and directs them.
(1965, 194)

Bayle's description of a subject that modestly foregoes the attempt to discover such
natural truths as the causes of heat and the tides is not a description of a subject we
can recognize as natural science. Thus, it unintentionally serves to show us just
how thoroughgoing is his rejection of the possibility of human comprehension of
the world.[6]

In emphasizing that Bayle's skepticism extends from religious matters to questions of the structure of reality, it is important to remember that neither Bayle nor
Leibniz would have drawn this distinction in anything like the way we do. It is
impossible to deny the pervasiveness—though we may have no access to the sin-
cerity—of Leibniz's concern with religious concepts. It has often been noted that
Leibniz makes few distinctions of principle, and his cheerful assumption that all
questions are to be treated equally is likely to shock the post-Kantian reader.[7] Leibniz
will often appeal to the latest research in physics or biology to support an argument
for God's existence or goodness, and conversely, will argue that the existence of
immortal souls of animals is a matter that can be resolved by the right kind of
experiment (L 190). This should be no more surprising than his use of a variety of
religious premises in arguments about the structure of the natural world. As will be
seen more fully later, Leibniz holds reason to be the same everywhere. Hence, one
cannot demarcate some subjects as inaccessible to human reason without rejecting the
supposition upon which all inquiry is based. *Any* unintelligibility in the universe is
unacceptable, for it bespeaks a fundamental arbitrariness of the whole. Because of the
way in which religious concepts, such as God's purposes, are embedded in the
structure of explanation, it would be impossible for Leibniz to give a reason why
some part of inquiry should be distinguished (by its impossibility) from the rest.
Thus, if it were simply declared to be impossible, the universe as a whole must be
intelligible. Trying to understand the world piecemeal is not an alternative. Particularly given the existence of Bayle's complete denial of the possibility of inquiry,
Leibniz thinks that the doctrine of incomprehensibility can only be rejected as
a whole.

Because of the generality as well as the power of Bayle's views, Leibniz's concern
to assert the necessary intelligibility of the universe is clearest in the *Theodicy*, which
can be seen as a sustained argument against Bayle's statement that "one must
necessarily choose between philosophy and the Gospel" (T 429). So the *Theodicy*
contains Leibniz's most general assertions of the principle of sufficient reason, as
well as many of its applications. But while only Bayle went so far as to assert the
incomprehensibility of the universe, Leibniz thought this doctrine to be the consequence of a number of other views.

Leibniz's attack on both Descartes's and Locke's theories of primary and secondary
qualities is one of the more interesting applications of the principle of sufficient reason
to questions about the natural world. As Bayle held Descartes's account to support his
own views, it is not surprising that Leibniz attacks that account because it posits an
"arbitrary" relationship between a thing and its properties. Such a relationship, Leibniz
argues, is impossible because it violates the principle of sufficient reason:

> For [Bayle] is persuaded, with the modern Cartesians, that the ideas of the percept-
> ible qualities that God gives [according to them] the soul, occasioned by movements
> of the body, have nothing representing those movements or resembling them.
> Accordingly, it was a purely arbitrary act on God's part to give us the ideas of heat,
> cold, light and other qualities which we experience, rather than to give us quite
> different ideas occasioned in some other way. I have often wondered that people so
> talented should have been capable of relishing notions so unphilosophic and so
> contrary to the fundamental maxims of reason. (T 329)

The fundamental maxims of reason—particularly the most fundamental, the principle of sufficient reason—dictate that there must be a reason why we experience each
object as we do. This reason must be grounded in the nature of the object. Leibniz
tries to explicate this thought in the *New Essays*, where he writes that sensible
qualities "depend naturally on shapes or motions," which are precisely expressed
through mechanical processes that science has not yet detected (NE 403). Leibniz's
success in specifying this natural relation, a task that occupied him at many times, is
not our present concern. Important is the assumption on which that task was based:
the idea that every relation in the universe must be fully explicable, which requires the
thoroughgoing intelligibility of the world as a whole.

It is interesting to note that Leibniz often put an assumption most thinkers regard
as antiquated to uses that may be seen as very modern. So the *New Essays* accuses
Locke's theory of primary qualities of opening the back door to scholastic occult
powers, and uses the principle of sufficient reason to spur the discovery of mechanistic explanations of phenomena that Locke was content to leave mysterious (NE 382).
On other occasions Leibniz uses the principle of sufficient reason to attack Newton's
postulation of gravity as a lazy, nonexplanatory appeal to occult qualities—a criticism
that is consonant with Newton's own programmatic views. More generally, the
principle served as a means of attacking both empiricist and Cartesian appeals to
direct experience as the cornerstone of objective judgment. Unless accompanied by
instructions telling others how to produce the same experience, Leibniz wrote, the
appeal to direct experience is merely an appeal to the authority of its author (L 168). It
is important to emphasize, however, that while the principle of sufficient reason *can*
function as a regulative demand that human reason refuse to rest until it finds
unquestionable order in the universe, Leibniz could not have allowed such an
interpretation of it. The principle of sufficient reason, in his hands, must be a claim
about the way the world is: the world contains order and harmony because it was
created by God in accordance with the eternal truths. This claim, as well as the
epistemological one that human reason will be able to discover that order, is regarded
by Leibniz to be crucial in answering the threat of unintelligibility posed by his
contemporaries.

This insistence upon the autonomous status of the order that must exist in the
world, which I have called the ontological component of the principle of sufficient
reason, depends upon Leibniz's account of certain features of truth. Most essential is
the idea that truth be independent of any act on the part of the truth seeker. No act of
will or judgment, human or divine, can play a role in determining the truth (NE 66).
Leibniz takes the idea that truth must be fixed and determinate prior to any truth
seeker's relationship to it to be the only possible conception of truth. A commitment

to truth in this sense, he implies, is the only alternative to conceding the incomprehensibility, hence randomness, of all things (T 329).

These ideas are most clearly and dramatically seen in Leibniz's attack upon Descartes's account of God's creation of the eternal truths. Descartes had argued that necessary truths about essential natures must be the free creations of God's will. His argument appealed to traditional demands that God be prior to everything else: if anything were to exist before him or to constrain him in any way, he would not possess the omnipotence ascribed to him. Hence, if statements had truth values independently of God's will, God could not be the omnipotent Being upon whom all else is dependent. Leibniz's argument against Descartes's view takes place in traditional religious terms: only a God whose actions were comprehensibly benevolent could (rationally) be the object of devotion (T 236−39). At the same time, Leibniz's insistence upon just this idea is simply a reassertion of the claim that nothing in the universe is arbitrary. God's actions must be as fully subject to the principle of sufficient reason as our own. In arguing this, Leibniz thinks it sufficient to appeal to the idea that the truth or falsity of a statement cannot be a matter of will: the divinity of God's will confers upon it no special creative relationship to truth.

> I know it is the opinion of Descartes that the truth of things depends on the divine will: this has always seemed absurd to me. . . . The principle of necessary truths is only this: that the contradictory implies a contradiction in terms. Since then the incompossibility of contradictories does not depend on the divine will, it follows that neither does the truth depend on it. Who would say that A is not non-A because God has decreed it? (L 181)

Leibniz's efforts to explicate this intuition led to enormous difficulties. His assertion of the absolute independence of truth from judgment leads him to describe God's relations to truths in a neo-Platonic vein. From most of Leibniz's writings emerges the picture of an eternal and distinct realm of essences that God contemplates when he wants to learn a truth.[8] On occasion, Leibniz even uses Platonic terminology to describe this process: "Evil springs rather from the Forms themselves in their detached state, that is, from the ideas that God has not produced by an act of his will, any more than he thus produced numbers and figures, and all possible essences which one must regard as eternal and necessary; for they are in the ideal region of the possibles" (T 326; see also 242, 353 and W 557). This picture, which seems to have been left deliberately vague, is as theologically unsound as it is philosophically unsatisfying. It involves the very theological problems that drove Descartes to the opposite view, for it threatens to restrict God's power to that of a minor functionary of limited means. And it contains more than a usual number of the fairy-tale elements to which Hegel objected in Leibniz's philosophy, as well as more fundamental difficulties that will be discussed later. Yet it was the only picture that Leibniz found available to express his insistence on the independence of truth, an insistence that was fundamental to the meaning of the claim that nothing ever happens without a reason.

The idea of a world subject to the principle of sufficient reason is the idea of a world permeated with law, whose every corner is ruled by order and harmony. For Leibniz, this is not merely a desirable ideal. The existence of a radical skepticism such as Bayle's−which, both Leibniz and Bayle agreed, simply drew conclusions implicit in more popular views—lends urgent necessity to the assertion of thorough-going universal order. Lovejoy describes the consequences of radical skepticism for Leibniz:

> It meant placing Caprice on the throne of the universe—under however venerable a title. It implied that nature, having no determining reason in it, flouts and baffles the reason that is in man. A world where chance-happening had so much as a foothold would have no stability or trustworthiness; uncertainty would infect the whole; anything (except, perhaps, the self-contradictory) might exist and anything might happen, and no one thing would be in itself even more probable than any other. (1936, 168)

This threat of a world in which anything might happen can only, for Leibniz, be countered by the rigorous application of the principle of sufficient reason.

III. Against Spinoza

The radical skeptics form one major target of Leibniz's conception of reason; Spinoza forms the other. Leibniz's concern to assert the rationality of the universe is always accompanied by the desire to do so in a manner that avoids Spinozism. Spinoza, too, had insisted upon the necessary intelligibility of the world as a whole, and Leibniz praised his insistence upon the universal applicability of the principle of sufficient reason. But Leibniz's published and unpublished work is full of attempted refutations of Spinoza's writings, which he described as being dangerous to anybody who takes the trouble to understand them (L 195). The nature of the relationship between Leibniz and Spinoza became an issue in Leibniz's lifetime, and many questions about it remain unresolved. It is clear both that Leibniz devoted a great deal of effort to distinguishing his views from those of Spinoza, and that his success in doing so is very much in doubt. So many aspects of their metaphysics are similar that Buchdahl writes: "It is a mystery why Leibniz stopped at 'many substances' or a plurality of substances, where atomicity momentarily reappears, only to be made a unity again through the principle of pre-established harmony, and why he did not end—like Spinoza—with just one substance" (1969, 402). Russell's explanation of this mystery was simple: Leibniz, he thought, was in fact committed to Spinozism but refrained from saying so for political reasons.[9] The fact that Leibniz himself says that many of his most important and characteristic views were developed in order to oppose Spinozism does not, by itself, undermine Russell's charge. Leibniz's work indeed reveals an ongoing preoccupation with Spinozism. This is easily seen in his account of freedom, his reintroduction of final causes, and his claim that this world is the best possible one. More surprising may be his claim that Spinoza would be right if there were no monads and his remark that theism depends on possibility, suggesting that both monads and possible worlds were created in order to refute Spinozism (L 663, T 234). But Russell and Lovejoy, who develops Russell's criticism, are quite willing to grant that many of these conceptions are both characteristically Leibnizian and anti-Spinozistic. What they deny is that these features of Leibniz's work are either sound or genuine. Insofar as Leibniz is a good philosopher, the objection runs, he contributes to the development of a Spinozistic view; the rest of his work is a superstitious or venal attempt to avoid Spinozism's more heterodox consequences. Thus, it is believed that Leibniz found Spinoza's most basic philosophical assumptions to be congenial but its practical consequences unacceptable.

Two connected consequences of Spinozism have been thought to be particularly objectionable to Leibniz. Most obviously, Spinoza's doctrine of necessity denies the possibility of that freedom of the will which Leibniz holds to be necessary for morality. A less familiar but equally important reason for Leibniz's anti-Spinozism is expressed in the unpublished "Refutation of Spinoza," where he writes: "What Spinoza says about the intellectual love of God is only trappings for the people, since there is nothing lovable in a God who produces without choice and by necessity, without discrimination of good and evil. The true love of God is founded not in necessity but in goodness" (W 496−97). Spinoza's doctrine of the universe as a single substance is not merely in conflict with crucial tenets of revelation (such as the doctrine of creation). A God who acts only from necessity is not a recognizable (Judeo−Christian) God and cannot, Leibniz believes, serve as an object of devotion at all. If Descartes's God was too unconstrained to be the God of tradition, Spinoza's is far too determined; the one is hardly more contrary to reason and piety than the other (T 238). Hence, Spinoza's denial of freedom, human and divine, undermines traditional foundations of morality and theology.

Leibniz's discussion of freedom has thus been a particular focus of the charge that he is, at bottom, a Spinozist. It is argued that Leibniz cannot simultaneously attack Spinoza's fatalism and a radical skepticism such as that of Bayle. Lovejoy gives an excellent version of this view. By accepting and developing Spinoza's insistence on the necessary intelligibility of the world, he thinks, Leibniz commits himself to Spinoza's fatalism. Leibniz's attempt to develop a notion of free choice by describing the will as being inclined but not necessitated by sufficient reason is so gross a failure that it shows the absence of a genuine position in opposition to Spinozism. So Lovejoy concludes:

> The distinction which Leibniz here attempts to set up is manifestly without logical substance; the fact is so apparent that it is impossible to believe that a thinker of his powers can have been altogether unaware of it himself. *Without abandoning all that is most essential in the principle of sufficient reason*, he could not possibly admit that a sufficient reason "inclines" the will without necessitating its choice, and least of all in the case of a will supposed to be enlightened by an infinite intelligence. (1936, 320; my italics)

The success of Leibniz's account of free will is not my present concern. Recent work has suggested that this account is much more plausible than traditionally supposed.[10] Without attempting to determine whether the traditional criticism of Leibniz's view is ultimately correct, I wish to challenge a major premise upon which it is based. This will prove crucial for an understanding of Leibniz's conception of reason.

What Lovejoy and others take to be "most essential to the principle of sufficient reason" is its commitment to a belief in the thoroughgoing intelligibility of the universe. Both Spinoza and Leibniz, indeed, maintained this commitment in express opposition to the threats of radical skepticism of their times. Lovejoy assumes, however, that Leibniz believed Spinozism to fulfill this commitment. On this assumption, Leibniz's problem is to show how a (Spinozistic) commitment to universal intelligibility can coexist with a coherent notion of freedom of choice. This suggestion appears extremely plausible because Leibniz never denies that if Spinozism were true, the world would be fully determinate. For Spinoza, all God's actions—and therefore every event in the universe—follow necessarily from the divine essence. It may seem natural to suppose that if Leibniz grants that a Spinozistic world would be necessary, he would also assume it to be intelligible. Even if understanding an event is not taken to be equivalent to discovering that it follows necessarily from a necessary series, the first has been thought to be implied by the second. Once we provide a demonstration that something follows necessarily from a necessary truth, we may seem to have done everything conceivable by way of explaining it. This assumption supports the idea that Leibniz has no choice but to abandon either the demand for intelligibility or the need for freedom.

But the view that seeing a thing to be necessary entails the understanding of it is denied in Leibniz's claims that Spinozism makes everything appear arbitrary. This charge, which suggests a great deal about Leibniz's conception of the arbitrary, should strike the reader as surprising. Leibniz's grounds for finding a view such as Bayle's to result in universal arbitrariness are fairly straightforward: Bayle repeatedly proclaims that the world as a whole is fundamentally mysterious, inaccessible to human reason. If the threat of caprice and randomness represented by this view is Leibniz's real fear, why should he object to the attack upon all such possibilities that Spinoza's demonstrations provide? How can the greatest of rationalists pose as serious a problem for the attainment of intelligibility as do the greatest skeptics?

Spinozism is arbitrary, Leibniz holds, because it denies the existence of final causes. After 1682, Leibniz devoted much effort to arguing for the need to appeal to final causes in scientific explanation. This reintroduction of a notion already under attack in Leibniz's day was motivated by a number of grounds. Crucial for our purposes is the fact that Leibniz takes them to be necessary for the full application of the principle of sufficient reason. This fact is often obscured by Leibniz's misleading formulation of the principle of sufficient reason as the claim that every event has a cause. But while some of Leibniz's texts are equivocal, many others make clear that he does not hold a statement of efficient causality to be either necessary or sufficient to fulfill the principle of sufficient reason.[11] For Leibniz, understanding the reason for an event *means* stating its end or purpose.

Discoveries of efficient causes, he thinks, do nothing to answer the deepest questions that drive us to seek scientific explanation. These questions go beyond issues of technology and practice to search for the ultimate reason (which here means purpose) of an event. As he explains:

> When one pushes forward his inquiry after reasons, it is found that the laws of motion cannot be explained through purely geometric principles or by imagination alone. That is why some very able philosophers of our day have held that the laws of motion are purely arbitrary. They are right in this if they take *arbitrary* to mean coming from choice and not from geometric necessity, but they are wrong to extend this concept to mean that the laws are entirely indifferent, since it can be shown that they originate in

the wisdom of their Author or in the principle of greatest perfection, which led to their choice. (L 478)

Explanations containing only statements about efficient causes are arbitrary because they operate only in what Leibniz calls "the realm of power," where causal connections are a matter of simple, brute force (L 479). In "the realm of wisdom," by contrast, everything is explained "architectonically": particular causal connections must be seen to have meaning as part of a fully connected, purposeful whole. Only "an empiric or a beast," Leibniz thinks, whose concerns go no further than learning a sequence for technical purposes, would be satisfied with an explanation which remains at the level of the realm of power (NE 271, 475).

Leibniz's belief that an explanation consisting solely of a chain of efficient causes leaves the world appearing arbitrary reflects the very deep assumption that true understanding can only be had of things which function on the model of our own actions. Only a universe and a God that we can explain on our own terms—terms we reserve for behavior that seems most intimate and natural to us—will be fully comprehensible. This is why Spinozism, for Leibniz, involves as much arbitrariness as does the outright denial of the possibility of explanation. In abandoning final causes, Spinozism (as well as other more popular views) abandons the only kind of category that could be genuinely explanatory.

Spinoza's attack upon the use of final causes had explicitly addressed these issues. He regarded the appeal to notions of end and purpose in scientific explanation as a primitive projection of our own categories—themselves deceptive—onto the natural world.[12] Leibniz does not directly discuss Spinoza's critique of the use of categories of human action in explaining nature; his work exhibits, but does not assert, the idea that to understand something at the very deepest level is to understand it as functioning as we do. Yet the belief that complete understanding is fundamentally empathic is present in many of Leibniz's most important ideas. In addition to providing a basis for his belief in the necessity of final causes, it fuels, for example, his assertion that there is "nothing fallow, sterile, or dead in the universe" and hence that self-generating monads must be postulated in order to explain the deepest levels of reality. The genuine order must be monadistic: mechanical explanations are left at the phenomenal level because they are not, Leibniz thinks, sufficiently deep to express the nature of reality. Buchdahl elaborates this claim in his discussion of Leibniz's attempts to distinguish true unity from a mere aggregate. Noting Leibniz's dependence on what Buchdahl calls the "analogy" of the self, he writes:

> The crucial question is whether such a narrowly conceived model of reality, viz., mind, can make contact with the world of physical relationships. This is what Leibniz believed, despite the fact that there is considerable uneasiness in his writings whenever he has to explain the status of the phenomenal world, its own relationships, and its relationships to the substances" (1969, 414).[13]

It is not surprising, then, that many of Leibniz's attacks on Spinoza's notion of substance express the idea that full intelligibility requires viewing substances as being constructed like us (T 359; L 478, 502, 583, 663).

Leibniz's accusation that Spinoza's denial of final causes leads to arbitrariness suggests that his criticism of Spinoza is much more central to his most basic philosophical assumptions than was often believed. The traditional suggestion was that Leibniz accepted Spinoza's attempt to show the world to be explicable as the only possible defense against fanaticism, while trying to maintain a sense in which this intelligibility was compatible with freedom. I have argued that Leibniz attempts to avoid Spinozism at a much more fundamental level. Leibniz holds that Spinoza, far from being overzealous in his application of the principle of sufficient reason, has instead misconstrued it: by denying the existence of final causes, Spinoza deprives himself of the means of achieving intelligibility.[14]

The idea that Leibniz's discussion of free will is not (primarily) an attempt to reconcile a Spinozistic conception of intelligibility with a morally necessary notion of freedom is confirmed by the fact that divine, rather than human, freedom is the focus of Leibniz's attention. Leibniz's treatment of human freedom largely follows traditional attempts to reconcile human freedom with divine foreknowledge. Human action is contingent only in the sense that it takes place in a world that God freely chose to realize from all the possible worlds that might have become actual; that is, the free choice in which Leibniz is most interested took place at the creation. This event is of primary importance to Leibniz because he holds it to be necessary for universal intelligibility. God's freedom is not even in prima facie conflict with the application of the principle of sufficient reason: rather, it is required for it. Only because God chose to create this world by a certain procedure can we find it comprehensible. This will be shown more fully in later discussion.

IV. Intelligibility

Having seen some of the uses to which the principle of sufficient reason was put by briefly examining the major targets against which it was directed, we are now in a position to state its content more clearly. To say that everything has a reason, for Leibniz, is to say that a final cause exists for everything in this world as it was created. Two major points are to be emphasized in this formulation. The first, that the ultimate reason for anything can only take the form of a final cause, is seen most clearly in Leibniz's attack on Spinoza. The second, that this reason must be given as a fact about the world as it exists outside us, is most evident in Leibniz's attack on Bayle and on Descartes's account of God's creation of the eternal truths.

This explication of the principle of sufficient reason is very much at odds with what Russell called the most revolutionary conclusion of Couturat's major work *La logique de Leibniz*. That conclusion, in Russell's words, is "that the principle of reason, for all its trappings of teleology and divine goodness, means no more than that, in every true proposition, the predicate is contained in the subject, i.e., that all truths are analytic" (1972, 366). Couturat argued that the principle of sufficient reason could be given a purely formal interpretation. This interpretation—that every truth is analytic—allows Couturat to say that the principle of sufficient reason has "no moral or teleological significance" (1901, 36) Many difficult issues raised by Couturat's argument have been well treated elsewhere.[15] Here I wish to address a major motivation that has made such claims seem attractive.

By giving a purely formal interpretation of the principle of sufficient reason, Couturat and Russell hoped to disentangle that principle from the claim that this is the best of all possible worlds. Recall that in the line of reasoning just discussed, these principles must be thoroughly intertwined. The insistence that the principle of sufficient reason be applied to divine as well as other actions has the immediate consequence that this world is the best of all possible ones. Otherwise, its omnipotent, omniscient creator would have acted in violation of the canons of reason. As Leibniz writes in the *Monadology*, "[The sufficient reason for God's choice] can be found only in the fitness or in the degrees of perfection that the several worlds possess, since each possible thing has the right to aspire to existence in proportion to the amount of perfection it contains in germ" (L 648). At least since Voltaire, this claim, as it stands, has seemed to express an optimism that is at best empty and at worst cruel. The claim that this world is the best one is not subject to confirmation or refutation of any kind. As the *Theodicy* makes clear, any fact, however awful, can be incorporated into Leibniz's view: no knowledge of how a fact is compatible with a world that is the best possible one is required to assert that it is so. Many readers have found this to leave Leibniz's view intolerably empty. Russell summarizes this charge: Leibniz "seems to imply that existence *means* belonging to the best possible world; thus Leibniz's optimism would reduce itself to saying that *actual* is an abbreviation which it is sometimes convenient to substitute for *best possible*. If these are the consolations of philosophy, it is no wonder that philosophers cannot endure the toothache patiently!" (1972, 377). The point behind Russell's charge seems undeniable: as a justification of God's ways to man, Leibniz's discussion leaves much to be desired. His a priori assurances may even seem to miss the motivation which drives people to seek a theodicy; and in doing so, they have struck readers as the most superficial aspect of his work. It is natural, then, for readers such as Couturat, Lovejoy, and Russell to seek an interpretation of the principle of sufficient reason that is unconnected to this assertion of universal optimism.

But although the motivation for a purely formal interpretation of the principle of sufficient reason is understandable, such interpretations cannot succeed in explicating the nature of the thoroughgoing intelligibility of the world that Leibniz's statements proclaim. To see this we need to consider Couturat's claim that the principle of sufficient reason can be reduced to the assertion that there is an a priori demonstration of every truth (1972, 20). We must ask what it would mean for Leibniz to assert that there is such a demonstration. For Leibniz, something must explain the possibility of demonstration: unless grounded in the right way in the eternal truths of reason, any purported proof would be meaningless. As we saw in discussing his attack on Descartes, the only way which seemed right to Leibniz was found by viewing a proof as a matter of referring to objects that exist outside of all subjects. The demand that truth be independent of judgment led to an account of truths as supersensible objects existing prior to God's will. Section VI will show in detail how Leibniz viewed all reasoning to be a matter of referring to those truths.

This view is required by the fact that the principle of sufficient reason, for Leibniz, contains two claims. The first is the idea that the universe is fully ordered, while the second is the idea that human reason is capable of discovering that order. The formal interpretation of the principle conflates these two claims, with the result that the crucial issue, for Leibniz, of what grounds a proof is ignored.[16] The idea that there are grounds in a universal order of eternal truths that animate the existing world is essential to Leibniz's assertion of the principle of sufficient reason. The bare claim that there is an a priori demonstration of every truth fails to express Leibniz's insistence that *there is reason in the world*: without this, he thinks, no act of reasoning could be meaningful. To say that there is a sufficient reason for everything that exists means more than that an omniscient being could demonstrate every truth; for in order for any being, however omniscient, to be able to give a demonstration at all, something must be true of the world as its basis—and it is this thing that appears to Leibniz to be crucial.

But what could it mean to say that there is reason in the world? To understand this claim, we need to employ just the sort of teleological description that seems suspect. To give a sufficient reason for anything requires, eventually, an answer to the question why this world exists at all. Without an answer to this question, the series of reasons that can be given to explain particular events stops arbitrarily. Now the answer cannot be given by the eternal truths themselves, for they are not sufficient to determine the existence of the world. God's choice, constrained by his knowledge of the eternal truths, is required to do that. This idea explains Leibniz's excitement over his discovery of the otherwise abstruse notion of compossibility, which he held to be necessary to refute Spinozism. A Spinozist would hold that the eternal truths by themselves *do* determine the occurrence of everything that happens. Leibniz's response is that the eternal truths, which include every possible essence, cannot themselves rule out the existence of incompossible entities. For this, God's choice to create the world is needed. It is this choice that ensures that there is reason in the world, actualized and embodied, linking the eternal truths with particular facts. God's decision to create this world because it was the best of all possible ones (a fact that God saw by examining all of them) is what constitutes the existence of reason in the world.

This account should make clear the interdependence of the two claims that I have said are integral to the principle of sufficient reason: that reason must be given in the world independent of human reasoning and that giving ultimate reasons involves giving final causes. For Leibniz, the second claim is the only way of realizing the first. The first claim is crucial to the possibility of reasoning at all. That there is reasoning is a function of the existence of the eternal truths, to which every correct act of reasoning must correspond. These truths, which exist prior to the creation and hold for every possible world, are the foundation of the existence of reason at all. For reason to exist in the world, however, something further must take place: God must, as it were, put it there at the creation, by choosing to create the world in the right way. To put the point another way: if there is one thing that is *constitutive* of the world, it is God's choice to create it, and that is, precisely, something teleological.

Note that the optimism involved in this way of stating the claim that this world is the best possible one can be regarded primarily as an optimism about our capacity for understanding. Leibniz says nothing about the goodness of the world as we know it; this, indeed, is what made his optimism so disturbing. Viewed as an assertion about the necessary intelligibility of the world, however, it takes on a somewhat different caste. Leibniz's idea seems to be that once granted that giving a sufficient reason involves answering the question why this world exists as it does, no other answer than the one he has given could count as intelligible. To admit that a world that is not the best could, nevertheless, be the one we inhabit is to give up the possibility of understanding it, leaving a mystery at the heart of things that no amount of mechanistic explanation could ever solve. To say, on the other hand, that the world as a whole is the product of a conscious agent who, limited by the laws of logic, used means—end reasoning to produce what he took to be the best outcome is to say that the world is the sort of place we can understand.[17]

It has long been apparent that Leibniz insisted on the necessity of final causes in opposition to most of the major thinkers of his day. What I have wished to stress is that this insistence is intrinsic to the meaning of the principle of sufficient reason, for it tells us what it is, for Leibniz, to give a reason for something. To give a sufficient reason for something is to understand it in terms of our own organization. Everything that exists is the product of a creator who functions, roughly, as we do.[18] Those objects themselves, at the noumenal or monadic level of reality, must be truly understood as functioning like us as well.[19] A world governed by reason is thus doubly permeated by reason: it is the product of a creator whose behavior is a more powerful version of our own, and its ultimate constituents are structured like we are. Leibniz's creator only creates in his own image.

The anthropomorphism implicit in Leibniz's notion of intelligibility is as ubiquitous as it is unexamined. Yet an understanding of his use of the principle of sufficient reason must acknowledge its commitment to the use of intuitive models of human reasoning as the right sort of categories with which to comprehend the nature of reality. It is this commitment that explains why Leibniz's targets—the claim that the universe is inexplicable and the claim that the universe is necessary—are not, as they seemed, in opposition to one another. Leibniz did not attempt to find a middle way between the options of accepting an arbitrariness that allows for freedom and proclaiming an intelligibility that entails determinism. Both these options are equally unintelligible, equally arbitrary for him. This is most clearly to be seen in Leibniz's criticisms of Cartesian and Spinozan theology. Descartes thought it impious to put any constraints upon God, whose omnipotence requires that nothing, including truth, exist prior to his decision. Spinoza's account might seem to be just the opposite: for him, all of God's actions follow necessarily from the divine essence. As we have seen, Leibniz has a single objection to both these views: indeed, he goes so far as to argue that they are at bottom identical (T 244). Only a God who "does things for reasons" is a God we can worship, not merely fear—just as only the creation of such a being is a world we can understand.

Leibniz's expressions of this anthropomorphism are often so crude as to obscure whatever is interesting about the idea; the spectacle of God as a master watchmaker violates too many convictions of every discipline, including theology. But Kant will develop the intuition that Leibniz found no means to express plausibly: showing an event to be the necessary consequence of a series still leaves something to be explained. Reason seeks comprehension of the world as a whole. Without the hope that such comprehension is possible, Kant believes, neither science nor morality can be sustained. Where the statement of a series of efficient causes leaves room for further questions, providing another one may still leave an investigator experiencing the event as mysterious or arbitrary. At that point, only the statement of a final cause—the end toward which an event is directed—will satisfy human reason's demand for intelligibility.

The naïveté of Leibniz's discussion lies not in his insistence on reason's need for a world in which it is, transparently, at home but in his failure to ask whether that which satisfies reason's needs might *not* be constitutive of the world. Leibniz simply assumes that these must coincide and proceeds to argue that reason's need for intelligibility cannot be fulfilled without employing final causes, that is, that Spinozism cannot satisfy the principle of sufficient reason. For Kant, it will be shown, the posing of this question proves fundamental, leading to his rich and central distinction between regulative and constitutive principles.

V. The Process of Reasoning

The last three sections were devoted to the first component of Leibniz's principle of sufficient reason, the claim that the world as a whole is rationally ordered, its events neither random nor arbitrary. The present section will examine the second claim embedded in that principle: human reason is an intellectual faculty capable in principle of discovering the order that exists in the universe. The most fundamental feature of the second claim is a consequence of the first. I have argued that for Leibniz, there must be a rational order in the world existing independently of any particular act of reasoning. Otherwise such reasoning would be arbitrary, that is, no act of reasoning at all. This means that reasoning, for Leibniz, is a process of recognizing truths that exist independently of human or divine understanding. Two ideas are contained in this assumption. The first, that reasoning is a matter of minds fastening onto independent entities, is far more controversial than the idea that reasoning is a matter of obtaining truth. Yet it is this idea that will prove to provide the most interesting point of difference between Leibniz and Kant. Although for Leibniz, as for others, the idea of reasoning as a process of obtaining truth was thought to be too self-evident to require even statement, much less argument, it follows plainly from his insistence upon the necessity of the existence of reason in the world, most clearly stated in his arguments against Descartes's conception of God's relationship to the eternal truths.

Leibniz uses two models to express the process by which reason makes the world intelligible to itself through the recognition of independent truths. Nowhere do his remarks about this process cohere sufficiently to be called an account of it. But Leibniz surely knew he was drawing on a long tradition in employing both models and perhaps, therefore, felt no need to explicate the intuitions involved in them. We can begin to do so by examining a variety of his statements about reasoning.

One major source of such statements may be found in Leibniz's descriptions of the universal characteristic, which express his vision of a perfected reason. Though Leibniz never actually developed a satisfactory example of the project that remained his lifelong ambition, his discussions of it reveal more about his conception of reasoning than any of his other texts. The universal characteristic, as conceived by Leibniz, embraced a number of projects that had long been of great interest.[20] Least ambitious among those was a universal language that would further human communication by composing "an alphabet of human thoughts." By constructing a language that would exhibit the order and connection of concepts as ordinary languages do not,

Leibniz hoped to repair the confusion that develops through the existence of different languages. A major motivation for systematizing communication was, Leibniz said, the propagation of the Christian faith, insisting that a universal language would ensure conversion as it would prevent apostasy (W 25, L 262).

Leibniz's assurance on this point is explained by the difference between his project and that of, say, latter-day proponents of the universal language Esperanto. Both have the rationalization and improvement of human communication as a goal. For Leibniz, however, this rationalization cannot be imposed from without, by human decision; communication can only be furthered by uncovering the rationality that is intrinsic to the relations between words and things. For Leibniz, this entails that false belief arises through the use of languages in which words do not truly denote the truths they are meant to denote. The discovery of the "real connections" between words and objects would leave no room for false belief. Animating Leibniz's interest in the practical goals of such a project was his conviction in the principle of sufficient reason, which dictated the necessity of a language in which the connections between signs and the signified would be both real and manifest. This "natural language," as he sometimes calls it, was that spoken by Adam and his descendants until other languages were introduced at the tower of Babel (Couturat 1901, 77). This aspect of Leibniz's project is to be seen in his criticisms of earlier attempts to construct a universal language. Those attempts, he complained, maintained a merely arbitrary and artificial correspondence between word and object (Couturat 1901, 54). What Leibniz thought a "real," intrinsic correspondence could be is difficult to determine, for his attempts to give examples are unconvincing. An early work assigns numbers to simple ideas, while symbolizing the combination of ideas by multiplication. At a later stage, Leibniz thought the natural relation between words and things to be capturable by hieroglyphs rather than numbers. Neither this idea, nor further attempts to create a universal language through mathematics, was ever completed. The goal of constructing a language that revealed the intrinsic connections between word and object remained, however, unchanged throughout Leibniz's lifetime.

As this conception of the universal characteristic suggests, Leibniz was much less interested in an improved means of communication than in a method of discovery and proof. His major criticism of earlier attempts to construct a universal language was precisely that they had failed to attend to the latter task. And Leibniz thought little of previous efforts, both informal and mathematical, to find a universal method: their alleged proofs of known truths were flawed, and their instructions for discovering unknown ones were too empty to provide real guidance.

Leibniz's goal, then, was to improve upon these earlier efforts by providing a universal characteristic that would be at once an improved version of Aristotle's logic of demonstration, a greatly refined version of Descartes' logic of discovery, and a logic of probability. With the tasks of these three projects served by a single method, everything, Leibniz assures us, could be discovered and judged. Through this method, Leibniz looked forward to the construction of a unified science, which, beginning with rational grammar and logic, would ascend through arithmetic and geometry to mechanics, cosmography, psychology, and finally history and theology. Leibniz's conception of the ordering of the different branches of science within the unified science was subject to change. What remained stable was the vision of a science in which every dispute was resolvable as simply and automatically as equations are solved. So unified and systematic would be the encyclopedia of this science that it would contain an empty place for every unproven truth so that all the scientific work that remained to be done could be seen at a glance (Couturat 1901, 155). Within such a science, Leibniz wrote, some thought would need to be given to satisfying the amour propre of future scientists: discovery and proof would be such child's play that the motivations for undertaking them would surely diminish. (Couturat 1901, 151). "Given a few selected men," once the characteristic is invented, most of this science could be created within five years; the doctrines most useful for life—those of morality and metaphysics—could be developed within two. It is not surprising, then, that Leibniz typically described the universal characteristic in terms such as these:

> Once the characteristic numbers for most concepts have been set up, the human race
> will have a new kind of instrument which will increase the power of the mind much
> more than optical lenses strengthen the eyes; and which will be as far superior to
> microscopes or telescopes as reason is to sight. The magnetic needle has brought no
> more help to sailors than this lodestar will bring to those who navigate the sea of
> experiments. (L 224)

Leibniz's invention of the integral calculus, in the context of the general euphoria over the mathematization of science that was widespread in his day, virtually ensured that the universal characteristic would be conceived as mathematical. Leibniz's praise for mathematical reasoning is as frequent as it is extravagant. By clarifying figures and motions, he writes, geometry gives us civilization instead of barbarism; clarity in things is simply reducing them to numbers; things can be rendered intelligible only by the rules of mathematics; the art of discovery is unknown outside of mathematics (W 24, 49, 59; L 583). Although Leibniz's model for a perfect method seems to be ordinary mathematical reasoning, he criticizes both a purely geometrical, and a purely arithmetical, conception of method (Couturat 1901, 177−78). The foundation of the universal characteristic must be, rather, what Leibniz sometimes calls "universal mathematics"—a yet-to-be-discovered formal science that provides the foundation for the basic concepts of arithmetic and geometry. It is this subject that "gives words to languages, letters to words, numbers to arithmetic, notes to music" (W 4). The universal mathematics is to form the cornerstone of the universal characteristic, in which concepts are to be replaced by signs, propositions by the relations between signs, and reasoning by a calculus.

In assuming that the yet-to-be-discovered foundation of a universal science must take a mathematical form, Leibniz relied on the traditional idea that mathematics is the only science that had achieved both the certainty and the universality that were taken to be the criteria of any genuinely scientific method. Occasionally, he states these claims explicitly. Mathematics is the only science that could form the basis of a *universal* science because "there is nothing which is not subordinate to number. Number is thus a basic metaphysical figure, as it were, and arithmetic is a kind of statics of the universe by which the powers of things are discovered" (L 221). And though his efforts to explain the certainty of mathematical reasoning are confusing and even bizarre,[21] his conviction that only mathematics is absolutely certain remains clear. In one of many examples, Leibniz urges that the universal characteristic is of greatest importance for the fate of religion; once it is constructed, "apostasy will be no more feared in the future than would an apostasy of men from the arithmetic and geometry which they have once learnt" (W 25).

The hope of constructing a universal method, mathematical in form, that would share the spectacular successes of the calculus led Leibniz naturally to the view that errors in reasoning are largely formal. This, in turn, presupposes a conception of reason that is predominantly deductive. Reasoning, on this model, is not a matter of directly intuiting truths but of performing transformations on truths that are otherwise obtained. So Leibniz sometimes defines reasoning as the linking together of truths (T 73, 107), which may themselves come from sensory perception or the kind of intellectual insight he then calls the natural light. Leibniz uses the deductive model of reasoning when arguing against Descartes and his followers (who had ridiculed the scholastic emphasis on syllogisms) for the necessity of a mathematical method. Leibniz charged that the Cartesian appeal to properties of intuition—be they clarity and distinctness or anything else—was at worst an appeal to one's own authority and at best remained esoteric and unreliable (L 389). Certainty, he urged, could only be achieved by the formal procedures of logic. His discussion in these matters suggests a conception of reason as indifferent to content. Reasoning, on this model, concerns only formal relations between ideas. Using the rules of Aristotelian logic and perhaps other kinds of operations (see L 487, 639), reason's task is to provide transitions from one member of a series to the next. The members of the series themselves are given by direct intuition, either intellectual or sensual, in a wholly distinct procedure.

But in addition to the model of reason emphasizing the linking and ordering procedures that characterize logical inference, Leibniz draws on another model, in which reason attains knowledge by a simple and immediate act of intuition. This model too has a long tradition,[22] and its most striking feature is the degree to which it is derived from the experience of vision. Leibniz makes extensive use of the visual model even when discussing the method that is to provide a purely formal solution to reason's problems. We have already seen him claim that the universal calculus will strengthen the capacity of reason even more than the telescope and the microscope have improved the capacity of the eye. Indeed, the telescope is Leibniz's favorite metaphor for the universal calculus. Use of this metaphor to describe the instrument that is to perfect reason goes naturally with the description of reason itself as a "natural" or "inner" light (L 549, 552; NE 89). The picture of reason as light of the mind, which Leibniz inherited from Descartes, is carried to extremes in passages like the following, where Leibniz discusses innate truths: "These writings in the inner light would sparkle continuously in the understanding, and would give warmth to the will, if the confused perceptions of the senses did not monopolize our attention" (NE 100). Less dramatic but no less telling are Leibniz's remarks that reason is better than eyesight (W 49). In explaining the superiority of reason to vision Leibniz sometimes appeals to the idea that reason sees essences, while eyesight is limited to the apprehension of accidents (W 17, T 119). More important than the differences between reason and vision in such passages is the suggestion that they are analogous, a suggestion that is often made explicit (NE 361, T 98–99). In the universal calculus, he wrote, all thoughts will be pictured (L 193); and some versions of the calculus took this metaphor literally, proposing that the signs of the calculus should be hieroglyphs, which "would literally speak to the eyes" (Couturat 1901, 113). Therein, Leibniz continues, would lie its success, for pictures are "inherently significant," while "our letters and Chinese characters, on the other hand, are significant only through the will of man" (NE 399). Here again, we see Leibniz searching for the intrinsic relation that the principle of sufficient reason dictates must exist between signs and things; only pictures, he here concludes, could adequately and naturally provide this relation.

Leibniz's heavy reliance on a visual model to explicate what he calls the most perfect form of knowledge may seem ironic in view of his constant insistence that knowledge gained through the senses is vastly inferior to that gained through intellection. Yet the inclination to construct an analogue of eyesight to portray the source of knowledge that would supersede that gained through eyesight—rather than describing a wholly different sort of process altogether—is an old one.[23] Such an idea is a natural way of understanding the kind of requirements that Leibniz has placed upon adequate knowledge. First and foremost is the requirement that knowledge involves apprehension of truths that exist independently of, and are unaffected by, the truth seeker. The second is that adequate knowledge involves a simple act of mind (L 593). This very Cartesian premise is said, by Leibniz, to be crucial for avoiding Cartesian skepticism. Leibniz explains this in terms that are almost spatial. A simple act of perception leaves no room for error; mistakes are made as mental operations grow more complex, adding judgments and inferences whose possible errors are the subject matter of logic. An act of mind consisting in one step simply cannot fail (NE 361). The combination of these two requirements—which make the highest form of knowledge a matter of simple, immediate relation to an object outside of the understanding—may have seemed to make the temptation to a visual model of reasoning nearly unavoidable.

Leibniz's texts provide few direct clues as to how these two very different conceptions of reasoning are to be related. Indeed, he rarely acknowledges that he appeals to disparate models; in discussing each, he tends to write as if reason could only be a process of the kind he is currently describing. There are some indications that Leibniz conceived the relations between the deductive and the intuitive model according to the account given in Descartes's *Rules*.[24] For the purposes of contrasting Leibniz's conception of reason with Kant's, however, the differences between the intuitive and deductive models of reason are less important than the features that they share in common. These features can be seen in the following quotations:

> [God's] own wisdom is the greatest judge that he can find, there is no appeal from its judgments; they are the decrees of destiny. The eternal verities, objects of his wisdom, are more inviolable than the Styx. (T 194–95)

and, earlier, writing to Oldenburg,

> Nor ought we to believe in such concepts until they have been tested by that criterion I seem to recognize, and which renders truth stable, visible, and irresistible, so to speak, as on a mechanical basis. (L 165)

Three related ideas are of interest in these quotations. The first is the claim that truth is completely determinate, independent of any reasoning, human or divine. The statement that the eternal verities are more inviolable than the Styx gives dramatic expression to this idea, emphasized in my discussion of Leibniz's formulation of the first part of the principle of sufficient reason. A stronger claim is also implicit here. Not only is truth, the object of reason, determined independently of reason; Leibniz holds that truth determines reason. That is, once we understand the truth, we cannot help but accept it. Recognizing truth is equivalent to following it: there is neither psychological nor logical room between perceiving a truth and acknowledging it. Ignorance and passion may obscure the truth, but only ignorance and passion stand in its way. Truth itself commands reason's assent. Leibniz's frequent descriptions of reasons as weights in the balance of the mind expresses this point (T 321, L 696). Not only is the weight of a reason fixed independently of the intellect; a reason affects the intellect as immediately and automatically as weights determine the balance when placed in a scale. This is as true for God's intellect as it is for our own. The point is summarized in Leibniz's statement that "one must always yield to proofs" (T 89). Leibniz seems to view the idea of truth as automatically determining the intellect to be presupposed by the idea that the intellect in no way determines truth. Hence, the claim is, for him, so much a part of the nature of truth that it is rarely discussed as expressly as in the two quotations. Nevertheless, it is clearly embedded in his elucidation of the principle of sufficient reason, where the measure of a nonarbitrary judgment is an act of assent free from every act of will. Such assent can only be produced by the perception of an object that is inherently commanding. This exclusion of any possibility of choice guarantees the validity of judgment, rendering it independent of the subject and thus free from the possibility of error.

Now given these two claims and given Leibniz's optimism about the (potential) powers of human reason, a third claim seems to follow: reason is mechanical. This is a formulation that Leibniz himself uses, as we have just seen. I take this to mean that the correct use of reason involves a simple procedure that can be followed without choice or embellishment to reach the truth that is reason's goal. The discovery of this procedure is the object of Leibniz's work on the universal calculus. Russell laconically described the universal calculus as "obviating the necessity of thinking" (1937, 169). For Leibniz, the automatic character of this procedure is nothing but a virtue, ruling out the possibility of disagreement, which he believes to be a function of passion and will.

Couturat cites a number of passages to show that Leibniz was fully aware of the mechanistic character of the universal calculus, and by extension, of human reason.[25] This conception is familiar from Leibniz's frequent statements that all disputes are resolvable by calculation and his determination to create a method of proof from whose results dissent would be impossible. The mechanism of Leibniz's account is even more striking, Couturat argues, as embodied in the idea of a universal calculus as a method of discovery. This is due to Leibniz's claim that the investigator using the universal calculus will be unable to err, or even to fail to discover the truth, *should he desire to go astray*. His hand, Leibniz says, will refuse to write an error. Independently of—even contrary to—the will of an investigator, the universal calculus will force assent to the truth. Couturat's discussion deserves full quotation:

> In effect, all false reasoning is expressed by an error of calculation; and consequently it will be obvious, for it will violate an intuitive and mechanical rule, becoming a habit of the eye and the hand. It will be just as shocking as a solecism or a barbarism

for us, a mistake in spelling or syntax. Likewise any calculator who is the least bit trained will hardly be able to commit errors even if he wanted to. His hand will refuse to write a nonsequitor, or his eye will discover it as soon as it is written. One will not even be able to formulate a false or absurd proposition: for in trying to do so, the author will be immediately warned by the incongruity of the signs; he will catch himself in time, and the rules of the calculus will dictate the unknown or unrecognized truth in place of the error he was going to write. (1901, 99)

Couturat later describes this conception as the abandonment of the spirit to blind mechanism, while recognizing that it is just this blindness and mechanicity that, for Leibniz, guarantees the validity of reasoning and that is therefore the goal of the construction of the universal calculus.

Couturat's discussion of the mechanical nature of Leibniz's conception of reason is confined to the deductive model of reason, which predominates in the discussions of the universal calculus. It is not difficult to see why the word 'mechanical' should be applied to this model. Indeed, the idea that reasoning could be carried out without human agency was foreseen and desired by Leibniz, who hoped that a machine could be built that would be capable of performing the formal transformations involved in the universal calculus. (Couturat 1901, 115–16). The mechanical character of Leibniz's other model of reasoning may seem less obvious, for it is never suggested that intellectual insight is something that could literally be performed by machine.

Nevertheless, the central feature of this mechanical character—the idea that correct reasoning takes place automatically, without human choice—is as present in the intuitive as in the deductive model of reasoning. The former model includes not only the idea of reason's determination by an object outside of itself but also the idea that this determination takes place by a simple and immediate process. No room is left between reason and its object in which human agency can play a role: intellectual insight is a matter of reason's direct contact with supersensory truths, which command assent as soon as they are fully glimpsed. Here it is important to remember that the conception of vision upon which this model of reasoning draws is a pre-Kantian one. For Leibniz, human faculties play no constitutive role in perception. Hence, just as the normally functioning eye is directly determined from without to see the object placed in front of it, so reason has no choice in assenting to the truths that the universal calculus uncovers. The very simplicity of the automatic character of this process makes, for Leibniz, further explication unnecessary.

The differences between Leibniz's characterizations of the two parts of the principle of sufficient reason are striking. I have argued that the first component must be construed in a manner that is fundamentally teleological: the world is rational because God chose it in a certain way. The component of the principle that concerns our ability to reason seems, by contrast, as nonteleological as could be imagined. Even when discussing the content of our reasoning directly, Leibniz suggests that our scientific explanations should always be stated mechanistically. Though the principles of mechanics themselves have a teleological basis, we may never expect to get closer to this basis than Leibniz did in the *Theodicy*. We need the assurance that everything functions according to "more sublime principles" of order and wisdom, but we will never have access to these. The reasons for God's choice—and hence the final ends of creation—must remain hidden from us.

The differences between the teleological and the mechanical aspects of the principle of sufficient reason suggest a flaw in Leibniz's account but not, I believe, a contradiction. The mechanical form of human reason's procedures is the consequence of Leibniz's insistence that reasoning be a matter of discovering independent truths that are the only possible basis of the order in the world. Kant's procedure, we might say, is to reverse the two components. For him, the order in the world is mechanical, while reasoning itself is teleological. While sharing Leibniz's conviction that mechanistic explanations do not satisfy reason's need for full intelligibility, Kant insists that further intelligibility is to be constructed rather than discovered. The consequences of this reversal will be seen in later discussion.

VI. The Heteronomy of Rationalism

Let us return to the statement that the crucial aspect of Leibniz's thought, for Kant, was "the view of thought as absolute in its powers and unlimited in its claims." The foregoing discussion should make this claim appear problematic: if there is a sense in which Leibniz holds reason to be absolutely powerful, it is not a sense in which reason is autonomous. Leibniz's own designation of a perfected reason as mechanical only makes explicit the consequences of the central elements of his conception of reason. Having declared that reason is in the world, Leibniz is stuck with the fact that reason is *in the world*—to be read off of, rather than put into, the objects of experience. Naturally, those objects are not the everyday ones to which empiricists appeal but the supersensible truths of an intelligible world. For Kant, however, the determination of reason by eternal truths is as fundamentally heteronomous as its determination by any other object.[26] It is important to note that this charge of heteronomy is quite distinct from a more traditional one. It is not the claim that following the principle of sufficient reason will lead us to know things, such as the determining reasons for all events, which reveal that we are not free.[27] For Leibniz, reasoning is itself a heteronomous process, so that insofar as we are rational, we are not autonomous, whatever the outcome of our reasonings may be. Thus, Kant's assertion to have denied knowledge in order to make room for faith should not be read as an attempt to prevent access to truths which might show our freedom to be limited. In so speaking, Kant is, rather, pointing the way toward a kind of thinking that is itself more autonomous than the acquisition of knowledge.

The heteronomy of Leibniz's conception has its source in the idea that there is reason in the world, as well as in the assumption that reasoning is a matter of obtaining knowledge. In denying both these claims, Kant may well be seen as "all-destroying," as Moses Mendelssohn complained. Mendelssohn's remark was prescient: Kant's work *is* the destruction of a vision of complete intelligibility, of fundamental harmony between reason and the world. Yet the only alternative to the destruction of this vision is the assertion that the world as we know it is the best of all possible ones or, to put the point differently, that the real is rational.[28]

If the principle of sufficient reason is the fundamental law governing the universe, and if divine as well as human reasoning is a matter of knowledge, then Leibniz is necessarily driven to the conclusions of the *Theodicy*. Those conclusions, I have argued, are an expression of reason's need for intelligibility: it is inconceivable to human reason that the present state of reality be the final word. Like many traditional theologians, Leibniz attempted to satisfy reason by positing an order hidden behind the apparent one. All the assurances of the *Theodicy* take us no further than the assertion of its existence. Leaving the details of that order forever obscure to everyone but its creator may seem to be a restatement rather than a resolution of the problem reason posed. In this, Kant was right to suggest that the comfort that reason derives from such assertions is no better than the comfort Job might have derived from those of his friends. It is, however, the only comfort available to a conception of reason that conceives its task as one of knowledge.

Kant categorically denies that the order reason seeks can be found in the world. Such order is manifestly absent in the realm of appearance, and we have no access to another. But his transformation of the principle of sufficient reason prepares the ground for another possibility: the order that cannot be found may yet be constructed.[29] Kant's version of that principle may seem, at first glance, to be an enfeebled version of Leibniz's. The vision of rational order permeating the universe becomes the bare statement of efficient causality of the Second Analogy; the confidence in reason's capacity to discover that order becomes the regulative injunction to seek it. Yet Kant's work is not the evisceration of the application of the principle of sufficient reason but the insistence that it apply *as a demand*. With the construction of science and through the creation of a moral order, reason can make an obscure world into an intelligible one. Kant's conception of reason's tasks will prove, finally, to be more powerful than that available to any rationalist.

Before turning to articulate that conception, it is important to examine, briefly, its other sources.

VII. Hume's Challenge

If the impotence of reason is an unexpected consequence of Leibniz's views, it is the starting point of David Hume's. His *Enquiry* begins with a description of the picture of reason usually attributed to classical rationalism:

> Nothing, at first view, may seem more unbounded than the thought of man, which not only escapes all human power and authority, but is not even restrained within the limits of nature and reality, . . . while the body is confined to one planet, along which it creeps with pain and difficulty; the thought can in an instant transport us into the most distant regions of the universe. . . . What never was seen, or heard of, may yet be conceived; nor is anything beyond the power of thought, except what implies an absolute contradiction. (1975, 18)

Hume's theory of ideas is but the first step in undermining this view of the power of human reason. According to Kant, Hume denied the concept of cause "in order to deny to reason any judgment concerning God, freedom, and immortality; and he knew very well how to draw conclusions with complete cogency when once the principles were conceded" (V, 13). Those conclusions were drawn in such unforgettable phrases as "Reason is, and ought to be the slave of the passions" and " 'Tis not contrary to reason to prefer the destruction of the whole world to the scratching of my little finger" (1978, 415, 416). Kemp Smith calls the principle of the subordination of reason to the passions the central one of Hume's philosophy (1966, 154).[30] Hume's exposure of the pretensions of reason seemed unanswerable: not only was reason unable to travel unaided in the empyrean realms that it sought but it proved incapable of establishing the simplest of assumptions on which our lives are based.

The threat implicit in Hume's writing was that contained in those of every great skeptic, from the Sophists to Bayle. The claim that human reason is unable to demonstrate anything of substance is an old one. Refuting it had often been held to be necessary in order to block the path to relativism which could undermine the established order of religion and morality. Hume's skepticism was troubling not simply because of the brilliance and rhetorical persuasiveness with which his claims seemed to defy such refutation. What was new about Hume was less something that was present in his arguments than in the forefront of the minds of those who were impressed by them. This was the new, or Newtonian, science, which seemed to present a model of intellectual activity that was free of contradiction and uncertainty. The existence of such a model sharply distinguished Hume's skepticism from that of a predecessor such as Bayle. Earlier skeptical attacks on metaphysics could be more easily dismissed with the thought that metaphysics was a science that, like any other human creation, was susceptible to error. After Newton, metaphysics was no longer a science like any other; for at least one science seemed free of mortal failings. Devastating in Hume's skepticism was the claim that most of the ordinary judgments on which we rely, as well as the extraordinary claims of metaphysics, could not measure up to the new standard that finally commanded general agreement.

Among the judgments that did not seem to meet the criteria set by Newton's achievement were, of course, the two parts of the principle of sufficient reason. Hume's reduction of the notion of causality to the observation of constant conjunction was a denial of the thoroughgoing order thought to pervade the universe; his rejection of the principle of induction denied reason's capacity to discover any more superficial order that might exist, since any connections reason might uncover could be purely accidental.

Kant's response to Hume on both these matters involves a crucial move that is repeated throughout much of the Critical Philosophy. Its first step is to agree with Hume's critique of traditional metaphysics: many of the notions upon which we rely are not to be found in the world but in ourselves. Thus, the concept of cause is derived neither from things in themselves nor from our experience of nature; so reason does not find laws of nature in the world as it is given to us.[31] The second step in Kant's response is to show that these notions, though found in ourselves and not in the world as it is given, are not subjective in the sense in which Hume charged. Our experience of causal connections is not a subjective habit of mind but a necessary condition on the possibility of experience of any kind. Our conviction that the sun will rise tomorrow is not derived from useful custom but from regulative principles of reason. Like many other principles, the two parts of the principle of sufficient reason are not a part of nature. This does not, Kant insists, entail that they are merely a matter of custom and habit. Kant's answer to Hume requires a development of the notions of reason and understanding to show that these principles are not psychological or accidental but carry general and necessary validity. Having accepted Hume's charge that these notions are to be found in us, Kant's task is to provide an understanding of "in us" that avoids Humean subjectivism.

In accepting Hume's critique of rationalism, Kant accepts the idea that what is needed is an "active" principle. The picture of reason expressed by Leibniz limits reason's task to passively reading off experience notions that, Hume and Kant agree, cannot be found there. Hume had used this discovery to condemn reason tout court as "utterly impotent," "perfectly inert," and "wholly inactive." (1978, 457–58) Kant's response, I have claimed, is to limit this condemnation to a traditional conception of reason, and to devote a great portion of his work to constructing an alternative one. Here one might naturally ask after the point of Kant's effort. Both Kant and Hume agree that it is not sheer experience, but an active principle that we contribute, which is the source of our conviction that one event causes another, or that the sun will continue to rise every morning. What issues turn on the nature of that active principle? They cannot, I suggest, be purely theoretical ones. It hardly matters whether custom or reason is responsible for validating what was never a matter of doubt even to David Hume, as soon as he left the confines of his study. Hence, as long as we view Kant's main goal to be proving the truth of something that Hume denied, we will never be able to determine the real differences between them. Had Kant's central concern been to establish the legitimacy of the notion of cause or even the everyday use of certain ethical principles, he might well have agreed that the nature of the source of that legitimacy was a matter of relative indifference.

The Hume-inspired Jacobi, in an effort to assimilate Kant's position to his own, used the following quotation from a work by Kant's student Herder:

> We have a friend inside us—a sensitive sanctuary in our soul where God's voice and intention clearly resound. The ancients called this the *Daimon*; Christ conceived it as the *clear eye*; David entreats it as the good, joyful *spirit of life*, which leads him to the right path. Whether we now call it *conscience, inner sense, reason*, or the *logos* in us, or whatever we choose; enough, it speaks loudly and clearly. (*Hauptschriften* 1916, 196)

Kant's effort to distance himself from a Humean fideism with regard to religion will be discussed in chapter 4. Here I wish to address the more general question why it mattered to Kant, as it did not to Herder, that the "voice inside us" that guarantees our most general convictions be clearly attributable to reason. To put the question more ominously, as did Jacobi and other Humeans following him: Did Kant's insistence that this active principle is reason carry more than a merely nominal weight? It is true that Kant wished, as Hume did not, to affirm certain traditional propositions of morality and religion, but this could be done within a Humean framework, as Jacobi showed. Are there substantive matters at issue between them that could not be so easily handled?

The answer to this question is easily found by turning to the third major figure most commonly mentioned when discussing Kant's antecedents. We know that Kant's discovery of Jean-Jacques Rousseau preceded his reading of Hume.[32] We know that it was Rousseau, rather than Hume, whom Kant described as "the Newton of the mind" and to whom he attributed the revolution in his philosophical aims. Velkley's excellent book *Freedom and the Ends of Reason* has amply described Kant's debt to Rousseau and persuasively argued for the need to understand Kant's critique of reason as motivated by a Rousseauean vision of human emancipation. I shall not repeat his arguments here but simply urge that it is only such considerations that give weight to the contrast between Kant's and Hume's views of the active principle that grounds our beliefs. For it is only in regard to a project of political emancipation that the nature of that principle receives significance.[33]

Hume's political conservatism confounded traditional fears that skepticism regarding metaphysics and morals would undermine the foundations of established social order. His conservatism seems to have been a matter of philosophical principle rather than political pragmatism: Hume was a fearless atheist at a time when challenging religion seldom went further than criticizing the clergy and subscribing to Deism and an incipient utilitarian in an age when an attack on morals meant inveighing against corruption. Hume's skepticism was equally skepticism about the possibility of radical improvement in human nature or society. Without a legitimate standpoint from which our experience could be evaluated and judged, whence could such improvement be expected to spring? If custom and habit are all we have to rely on in grounding our most basic assumptions about the nature of reality, custom and habit must suffice to guide us in the more complex realms of political and social organization.[34]

Heine's comparison of Kant and Robespierre may sound puzzling to contemporary ears, but the view of the stolid sage of Königsberg as the philosophical foreman of the French Revolution is an old one.[35] It is only this view that explains the urgency with which Kant worked to show that the active principles that order our lives are principles of reason and understanding rather than custom and habit. The question whether reason or custom has primary authority is an academic one in the realm of metaphysics and even in the ordinary moral dilemmas that occur in the course of our lives. Only in the political sphere could it be a matter of import for Kant to show that the principles of reason were primary, for only such a demonstration could validate the Enlightenment conviction that traditional custom and habit should be overthrown by newly discovered ideas of "natural law." Without a basis for the claim that ideas of reason are the primary source of authority, there is no point from which to make reasonable demands on the world. Animated by the vision of human emancipation expressed by Rousseau, Kant strove to create a foundation on which this point could rest. If Kant believed the creation of a society based on principles of justice to be the greatest problem facing the human race (VIII, 22), his own problem was to develop a metaphysics that supported its possibility.

With this in mind, we may return to the question raised at the beginning of this chapter concerning Kant's relation to rationalism and skepticism. As I said, this relation is misleadingly viewed as one of reconciliation; Kant views both parties to be deeply mistaken about the nature of thought and its place in the world. Neither of them leave room for an independent standpoint from which reason could challenge the world as we know it. Rationalism's conception of reason as an instrument of knowledge left reason a passive spectator, reduced to projecting the order it desired onto an imagined reality. Hume's skeptical attack on those projections left him without a basis from which given experience could be evaluated and transformed. In very different ways, both positions require — and validate — an acceptance of the order existing in the world that must lead to political quietism. Kant's struggle to construct a conception of reason whose task is to set the goals and determine the standards by which experience is to be judged is the first metaphysical foundation for political action. So we can understand the excitement with which the generation following Kant could speak of his rescue and revitalization of reason.[36]

That rescue may easily go unnoticed by those whose reading of Kant's metaphysics is centered on the "Transcendental Analytic." For its dominant tone is one of humility, its primary lesson, one of acknowledging limits. The "Analytic" suggests that traditional metaphysics seeks a standpoint that could only be appropriate to God and urges us, instead, to be content with a far more modest one. The recognition that we cannot know what things that appear to us may be in themselves — because things are given to, not created by, us — is the first step in recognizing what it means to be human.[37]

Yet the theory of reason expressed in the "Transcendental Dialectic" and amplified in later works makes clear that this step is only the first one. Human reason may not create objects, but it does create ideas, whose force and glory stand in sharp contrast to the message contained in the "Analytic." The bulk of the "Dialectic" is devoted to examining the errors reason makes when it attempts to gain knowledge of those ideas. Since they are not objects of experience, Kant repeats, they cannot be objects of knowledge. But recognizing the limits of our knowledge allows us to realize our real power: to use the ideas of reason to judge, evaluate, and transform experience.

The present chapter has argued that no traditional account of reason was adequate to allow for this power. Let us turn to examine Kant's own account.

Notes

1. In particular, I am indebted to Frederick Beiser's work, and to conversations with him about eighteenth-century philosophy. Although I disagree with many aspects of his reading of Kant's views, I have learned much from his understanding of the issues at stake in them.

2. See, among other things, Kant's scathing remarks in Bxxxii – xxxv. In light of such passages, Kant's description of the absence of a definitive refutation of skepticism as a "scandal to philosophy" conveys a sense of disgust: if philosophy cannot even cope with these "scholastic" problems, how can it hope to resolve difficult and crucial ones concerning humankind's essential ends? This is surely the reason for Kant's barely concealed rage at the Garve-Feder review and in his subsequent discussions of Berkeley. Kant had classified Berkeley as a rationalist who failed to appreciate the reality of things of the senses. He repeats that none but "the schools" would be so foolish as to deny the reality of ordinary objects; the problematic question is that of the reality of ideas. To have been classified together with someone who denied the reality of ordinary objects of the senses must have seemed, to Kant, the result of perverse or willful misreading.

3. Arnauld's *Port Royal Logic*, Descartes's *Rules for the Direction of the Mind*, and Locke's *Essay Concerning Human Understanding* are only the best known of the many taxonomies of human thought. Leibniz's lack of interest in such a project may stem from his conviction of the importance of the universal characteristic, whose success would obviate the need for differentiated accounts of human thinking. Perhaps it also signals his dissatisfaction with his own very problematic conception of reason.

4. It might be thought that Leibniz's meaning would be plainer had he used two different words to discuss these two claims. For example, the German *Grund* could be used to refer to the order which exists in the universe, letting *Vernunft* denote the intellectual faculty whose function is to discover this order. The French use of *raison* for both these meanings helps to obscure Leibniz's views. But this obscurity, while it can be meliorated, is far from accidental. The order in the universe that Leibniz insists must be independent of any intellectual faculties is crucially characterized by reference to them. Its essential feature is that it be nonarbitrary, which amounts to being intelligible, or fully accessible to the faculty of reason. It must, somehow, have this feature prior to its ever having been found accessible; but Leibniz has no other terms with which to characterize the universal order.

5. See A201/B246.

6. Even the most charitable reading of such a passage, which would construe it as proposing a positivistic account of science along the lines of Mach, would be wholly unsatisfactory to Leibniz, who held that the knowledge of the empirics, which does not attempt to uncover the principles underlying phenomena, is no better than that of beasts (NE 273, 476). Bayle's skepticism about our capacity to discover the causes and foundations of natural phenomena precludes, for Leibniz, the possibility of any genuine inquiry.

7. See, for example, Mates (1986, 5) For an interesting discussion of relations between Leibniz's metaphysics and his views about language see Mates (1986, 178–87).

8. There are passages in which Leibniz describes the eternal truths as existing in God's understanding (L 647, T 243). This should not be taken to suggest, as Russell believes, that Leibniz holds God's thought to constitute the eternal truths. In these passages, Leibniz borrows a solution to the problem from the theologian Suarez, which relies on a sharp distinction between God's understanding and God's will in order to preserve, simultaneously, God's ontological priority and the nonarbitrary nature of God's actions. This solution, too, is beset with theological difficulties; for a real distinction between God's faculties would deny the fundamental unity of the divinity. More importantly for Leibniz, it cannot have served as a sufficiently strong ground for the independence of truth—so that even when using this solution, Leibniz writes that God is not the author of his understanding (T 353). For these reasons, I think, Leibniz fails to develop this solution; the suggestions that the eternal truths inhabit God's understanding remain occasional, isolated remarks.

9. Russell gives a succinct summary of this common idea in the preface to the second edition of his *Philosophy of Leibniz*: "There are abundant texts to support the view which I took. This is an instance of Leibniz's general duality: he had a good philosophy which (after Arnauld's criticisms) he kept to himself, and a bad philosophy which he published with a view to fame and money. In this he showed his usual acumen: the bad philosophy was admired for its bad qualities, and the good philosophy, which was known only to the editors of his manuscripts, was regarded by them as worthless and left unpublished" (1937, vi).

10. See, e.g., Adams (1977).

11. That it is not necessary is stated in the passages where Leibniz distinguishes between 'reason' and 'cause', where the latter clearly means "efficient cause" (L 486). Eternal things—God and the necessary truths—cannot, by definition, have efficient causes. This does not suggest that the principle of sufficient reason fails to hold. Leibniz always insists that God is fully subject to that principle. In saying that there must be a reason even where there is no cause, Leibniz suggests that the idea of full intelligibility is universally applicable and that it is satisfiable by a statement of final causality.

The idea that a statement of efficient causality is not sufficient to fulfill the principle of sufficient reason is expressed in many passages. One of the more straightforward occurs in a discussion of Spinoza's assertion of the principle of sufficient reason, namely, "For the existence or nonexistence of anything, it must be possible to assign a cause or a reason" (*Ethics*

1, 2). Leibniz comments that he agrees with Spinoza's observation, namely, that nothing exists unless a sufficient reason of its existence can be given, which is easily shown not to lie in the series of causes. While claiming to be in agreement with Spinoza, Leibniz here interprets the principle of sufficient reason in a way that is fully at odds with Spinoza's ideas concerning explanation. A different sort of expression of the insufficiency of efficient causes may be seen by recalling Leibniz's attack on the Cartesian–Lockean account of primary and secondary qualities. In arguing that this account violates the principle of sufficient reason, Leibniz does not claim that the account leaves secondary qualities uncaused but that it leaves them without the right sort of cause. This can only be a cause that is "rooted in the nature of the object" and therefore not "arbitrary" (NE 382). Leibniz insists not simply that the occurrence of an idea of a secondary quality be caused but that it be caused in such a way that we can understand why it was caused to occur as it did. Tracing the series of mechanical causes is part of an account of the events in the world, but an account confined to this task will still leave the world appearing mysterious. The question of ultimate interest will always be to determine why the series was caused to occur in just these particular ways. Leibniz expresses the relationship between final and efficient causality as follows: "The true middle term for satisfying both truth and piety is this: all natural phenomena could be explained mechanically if we understood them well enough, but the principles of mechanics themselves cannot be explained geometrically, since they depend on more sublime principles that show the wisdom of the Author in the order and perfection of his work" (L 478).

12. See Spinoza, *Ethics* 1, appendix.

13. Of course, many other considerations, such as investigations of the concept of force, are involved in Leibniz's notion of the monad. But to cite Buchdahl once more, "The interesting point is indeed that the influence does not just operate from the side of physics on metaphysics, but also in reverse, for Leibniz's 'metaphysical needs' (if the expression may be permitted) in their turn evidently did much to dictate the direction of his enquiries into the foundations of physical science, in particular, dynamics" (1969, 407).

14. Spinoza, of course, also denies that final causes are appropriate for explaining human behavior. Final causes, he claims, are projections of (false) human beliefs about human freedom of the will. It could be argued that this makes the central issue between Spinoza and Leibniz, indeed, a question about free will. Leibniz applies final causes to everything, not simply persons; but since both Leibniz and Spinoza are fundamentally monists, the issue must be raised in all-or-nothing terms. I do not wish to deny the possibility of this way of viewing the debate but to emphasize that Leibniz's case for the necessity of final causes rests not on moral considerations but on the assertion that the use of certain categories is necessary for comprehending the world.

15. See, e.g., Curley (1972) and Mates (1986, 162).

16. Although, as previously mentioned, the claims are always so formulated as to be easy to conflate.

17. Cassirer makes a similar claim in arguing that "the true task of [Leibniz's] theodicy is the defense of reason against pessimistic skepticism" (1962, 480). Rather than functioning primarily as a justification of God's ways to man, in Leibniz "theodicy becomes logodicee, the justification of reason" (474).

18. Leibniz's claim that a complete understanding of the world requires an infinite analysis of all truths that only God can perform marks, of course, a difference between God's reasoning and our own. While this difference is undeniable, I do not believe it to be fundamental. First, Leibniz suggests that the difference between our reasoning and God's is a matter of time: if we were immortal, we could also perform the same sort of infinite calculations that God can perform. Second, a number of Leibniz's discussions of the universal characteristic suggest that he often believed even this difficulty to be surmountable. Excited by his discovery of the integral calculus, Leibniz notes in the *Theodicy* that the recently acquired human ability to

comprehend the infinite provides grounds for optimism about human reason's ability to reach nearly divine heights. See also Cassirer (1962, 474).

19. For further discussion see Mates's claim that for Leibniz, "reality consists of individual minds" (1986, 10) and Buchdahl (1969, 414).

20. For a full discussion of the universal characteristic, see Couturat's (1901) *La logique de Leibniz*, on which I have relied heavily in the following discussion.

21. Sometimes he seems to argue that because mathematics is based on the principle of noncontradiction, its propositions can be resolved to identities that can be checked at a glance, requiring no external proof of certainty (W 51, L 236). On other occasions, however, he seems to hold that mathematics is more certain and simple because its "experiments," unlike those of natural science, require little labor and expense (NE 371–72). Given that Leibniz's goal is a completely unified science, he cannot acknowledge the distinctions that others have drawn between empirical and a priori sciences. The interpenetration of the notions of reason and experience at stake here includes, but is even wider than, that of which Kant complained (B62). Kant's charge, while correct, fails to acknowledge that this blurring of distinctions is necessary for Leibniz. The assumption that the universal calculus can successfully resolve all scientific questions entails the absence of a principled distinction between pure and empirical knowledge; and this assumption is probably the most important – and certainly the most continuous – of Leibniz's work. Its consequence will be a certain vagueness at the heart of Leibniz's notion of reason itself. The resonances of that notion are sharp and dramatic: it is impossible to forget Leibniz's image of all questions of reason being solvable through the demand, "Come, let us calculate!" Yet again and again, Leibniz's efforts to specify this image reveal a fluctuating range of conceptions.

22. So Jacobi perfectly summarized the conception of reasoning as intellectual insight, which Leibniz shared: "We maintain that two different powers of perception in men have to be accepted: a power of perception through visible and tangible and consequently corporeal organs of perception, and another kind of power, viz., through an invisible organ. . . . This organ, *a spiritual eye for spiritual objects*, has been called by men – generally speaking – reason. He whom the pure feelings of the beautiful and the good, of admiration and love, of respect and awe, do not convince that in and with these feelings he perceives something to be present which is independent of them – such a one cannot be argued with." (Quoted in Hegel 1974, vol. 3, p. 418; my italics). For an excellent discussion of the use of the visual metaphor to describe the act of reasoning, see Arendt (1977, 104–13). Taylor (1989) also examines this tradition in his *Sources of the Self*.

23. Leibniz himself refers to Plato as the source of the idea that the highest form of knowledge is a kind of vision, involving direct apprehension of a special realm of truths.

24. Leibniz owned an original copy of the *Rules*, which he annotated with great care. According to Descartes's account, both intuition and deduction are processes of reasoning, each of which is required at different stages of the acquisition of knowledge. Knowledge of simple truths takes place via intuition, the direct apprehension of an object by the pure intellect. In more complicated cases, deduction, which is compared to a chain, is required to connect successive intuitions. Whether deduction is a simple and unique operation in its own right or is itself a kind of intuition that serves to provide connections between other intuitions is left unexplored. This unclarity in Descartes's account is certainly exploited by Leibniz. Rather than committing himself to Descartes's description of these two models of reasoning and their relation to one another, Leibniz draws alternately on the two strands of thought that these models represent. I believe that this kind of openness about the process of reasoning reflects Leibniz's preoccupation with method. His primary goal is the construction of the universal calculus: once this is achieved, our conflicting intuitions about the nature of the instrument it is to perfect may be resolved to fit the form that is actually constructed.

25. Couturat and Beck argue that Leibniz derived the conception of reasoning as a mechanical process from Hobbes.

26. For further discussion of this point, see Rawls 1980, 558–60.

27. This is roughly the charge made by Jacobi during the *Pantheismusstreit*. Like Leibniz, Jacobi held that the principle of sufficient reason, used as Spinoza did, led to fatalism and thus concluded that the "fundamental law of reason's use" leads to nihilism. Jacobi held Leibniz's attempt to escape this conclusion by making final causes integral to the principle of sufficient reason to be a failure and claimed that Leibnizianism was nothing but "new, muddleheaded Spinozism." For further discussion, see chapter 4.

28. Arendt expresses the exclusive character of these alternatives: "Finally we shall be left with the only alternative there is in these matters—we can either say with Hegel: *Die Weltgeschichte ist das Weltgericht*, leaving the ultimate judgement to success, or we can maintain with Kant the autonomy of the minds of men and their possible independence of things as they are or have come into being" (1977, 216).

29. For a similar discussion, see Yovel (1980, 133–34).

30. For a contemporary elaboration of Kemp Smith's claim, see Stroud (1977, 11–16).

31. For a fuller account of Kant's discussion of induction, see chap. 2.

32. See Velkley (1989, 206) and Gulyga (1985, 59).

33. For some (occasionally problematic) further discussion, see Danford's *David Hume and the Problem of Reason* (1990), which argues that "what has been forgotten in the case of Hume is that he was a political philosopher" (168). Beiser shows the degree to which conservative German political thinkers made explicit use of Hume's skepticism about the powers of reason in order to undermine what they clearly viewed as Kant's attempt to provide a philosophical underpinning for the revolutionary doctrines of Rousseau (1992, 306–7). For a discussion of the political implications of alternate views of practical reason within the Scottish Enlightenment, see MacIntyre (1988, chap. 12).

34. For a discussion of the peculiar nature of Hume's conservatism see Wolin (1976).

35. See Heine (1981). The view was little questioned in Kant's day and has remained a commonplace of Kant scholarship in the formerly socialist countries. For a full discussion, see chapter 3 and Ley, Ruben, and Stiehler (1975).

36. Cassirer, for example, writes, "Goethe extols as Kant's 'immortal service' that he . . . 'brought us all back from that effeminacy in which we were wallowing' " (1981, 270). Kant's own expression of such an impulse can be found in VII, 340.

37. See, e.g., A277/B333.

2

Reason in Science

All our knowledge starts with the senses, proceeds from thence to understanding, and ends with reason, beyond which there is no higher faculty to be found in us for elaborating the matter of intuition and bringing it under the highest unity of thought.
                                          —Kant, *Critique of Pure Reason*

Kant continues the introduction to the "Transcendental Dialectic" with an uncharacteristically personal expression of perplexity: "Now that I have to give an explanation of this highest faculty of knowledge, I find myself in some difficulty [*Verlegenheit*]" (A299/B356).

The difficulty becomes clearer when we consider the conclusions of the previous chapter. There I argued that Kant's task was to develop an autonomous notion of reason capable of judging and ordering experience in a manner unavailable to rationalist or empiricist models. Doing so, I claimed, required rejecting the rationalist assumption that reason's task is to provide knowledge of the world. Yet if Kant's conception of reason abandons all relation to the acquisition of knowledge, it cannot retain more than a nominal connection to the notions of reason that preceded it. We cannot, that is, make sense of the idea that Kant's notion is indeed a notion of *reason* unless it maintains some continuity with the conception of reason as an instrument of scientific inquiry.

These difficulties are reflected in his failure to produce a work demonstrating that unity of practical and theoretical reason he insisted must exist. Originally, he seems to have planned to do this in the first *Critique* itself.[1] Later, he wrote that the exhibition of this unity would be the requirement of a completed critique of practical reason (IV, 391); but the second *Critique*, too, fails to address the problem directly. The importance of doing so had been clear to Kant at least since the first *Critique*, where he wrote that showing the connection between practical and speculative reason would give support to the moral ideas themselves (A329/B386). The claim that moral principles can be given public, objective justification, that is, that they are principles of practical reason, depends upon their recognizability as the work of an intelligible notion of reason. Such a notion must encompass many traditional features of reason even as it transforms them. It must, at the least, include a theoretical as well as a practical function: practical reason cannot be all there is to reason.

Yet Kant's discussions of theoretical reason often appear to leave little scope for its activity. At most, it may seem that theoretical reason has the negative function of preventing error by limiting the dogmatic claims of both skeptics and rationalists to knowledge of things they cannot know. Many passages in Kant's writings support this idea while leaving obscure the means by which reason could perform even this limited function. For valid claims to knowledge, tested and constrained by experience, seem to be the work of the understanding, whose structure is set out in the "Transcendental Analytic." What need does it have of another faculty to do what looks like little more than to apply its general conclusions? Matters seem to be made even worse by passages in which Kant states that the principles of pure reason have objective reality in their practical, but not their theoretical, employment (A 808/B836). Such texts lend weight to the idea that the theoretical use of reason is entirely negative and that reason has a real use only in the moral sphere.[2] But if this is the case, what is reasonable about practical reason save its name? No wonder that Kant confessed to finding himself in difficulty when faced with the task of giving an account of reason in general.

Most earlier scholars paid scant attention to that account, confining their discussion of Kant's theory of the construction of knowledge to the study of the understanding in the "Analytic." Kant's remarks that reason is needed to direct the employment of the understanding, when discussed at all, were treated as a sentimental afterthought or simply a mistake.[3] Recent work on Kant's philosophy of science has changed this situation considerably, for only attention to Kant's description of the principles of reason reveals that his account of the construction of science has considerable interest in its own right.[4] In the present chapter, I will draw on much of this work to present the foundations of a systematic view of reason that meets the requirements just suggested. I shall argue that the principles of reason are absolutely necessary for the construction of science, although they can never be known, nor do they directly provide knowledge. Showing their foundation to be necessary—and necessarily regulative—will provide a conception of theoretical reason that makes possible the claims of its unity with a practical one.

This will also prove useful for understanding Kant's motivations in undertaking to examine the foundations of knowledge in the first place. Earlier scholars' accounts of Kant as primarily moved by the need to prove the existence of the external world in the face of Humean or Berkeleyan skepticism are hard to reconcile with the passages in which Kant refers to such positions as dangerous only to the Schools and their targets as cobwebs whose loss will hardly be felt (B xxxiv). More contemporary descriptions of the issues at stake in Kant's metaphysics and epistemology raise equal problems. To characterize Kant's metaphysics as an attempt to show that Newtonian science rests on secure foundations not only runs counter to Kant's own descriptions of his aims but also ignores the question why Kant should be concerned about the foundations of the one thing he and his contemporaries take to be a *standard* for certain and solid intellectual achievement. If his works fairly trumpet the idea that it is not Newton's work but other fields that need to be put on the sure path of a science, why should he go to the trouble of uncovering the foundations of the very effort by which all others are to be judged? The *Prolegomena* raises this question explicitly: "Our laborious Analytic of the understanding would be superfluous if we had nothing else in view than the mere knowledge of nature as it can be given in experience; for reason does its work, both in mathematics and in the science of nature, quite safely and well without any of this subtle deduction" (IV, 330−31).

The view of Kant's metaphysics as an effort to expose the foundations of Newtonian science can only be understood on the assumption that this effort is undertaken with another goal in mind, namely, to show that the foundations on which it rests are also the bases of something that seemed less secure.[5] If Kant could show that the revolutionary achievements of natural science were grounded in the same regulative principles of reason that support our actions in morality, religion, and philosophy, he would provide crucial support for the latter. This would turn the tables on Hume, who sought to discredit metaphysics — and all it includes — by showing that it could not measure up to the scientific standards upon which all were agreed. Accepting Hume's use of Newton's work as a standard, Kant sought to show that it permits us to ground far more than Hume thought, without requiring any return to Leibnizian metaphysics. Thus, Kant's efforts to expose natural science as being founded not on the empiricist models upheld by Bacon, Newton, and Hume but on a notion of reason that is fully applicable in less certain areas will prove to be the cornerstone of his defense of reason in general. The centrality of these efforts is signaled by the famous passages concerning reason and science that were added in the preface to the B edition of the first *Critique* (Bxiii—xiv). The present chapter's account of reason's role in the construction of science should be read with these broader aims in view.

Section I uses Kant's discussion of mathematics to show how far removed his notion of reason is from a notion of knowledge. Section II examines the inadequacies of the account of experience given solely from the perspective of the understanding. Sections III — V offer a general account of reason's part in the construction of science, while section VI examines the teleological version of that account. Section VII argues that regulative principles cannot be items of knowledge as a prelude to discussing, in section VIII, the justification of regulative principles in general.

I. The Denial of Knowledge

Before examining Kant's view of reason's function in scientific activity, it is important to show what reason does not do. Therefore, I shall begin by showing that reason is not, for Kant, the instrument of scientific knowledge, where this is construed as an organ for obtaining theoretical insight, according to any of the rationalist models described in chapter 1. Nowhere is this idea more strikingly exhibited than in his views concerning the nature of mathematics. By looking briefly at those views, then, we can begin to measure the extent of his break with tradition. Philosophers from Plato to Frege have held mathematics to be the paradigm instance of a production of pure reason. To what extent this was due to the fact that mathematics exemplifies features believed essential to reason — certainty and universality, in particular — and to what extent the importance of these features is itself derived from the mathematical paradigm may be left an open question. It is clear, however, that both those who emphasized the importance of reason in human experience and those who denied it were agreed in the assumption that mathematical knowledge was the most characteristic product of reason. Hence, philosophers belonging to the former group conceived part of their task to be one of assimilating the rest of human inquiry to mathematics as thoroughly as possible. Leibniz's universal calculus is the best-known instance of this conception. Whether or not this task was held to be possible – whether *all* of human knowledge was seen to be derivable from reason – the idea that mathematical knowledge was so derivable was taken for granted.

Kant first denies this assumption in the early *Prize Essay* of 1763. There he insists upon the distinctness of the methods of metaphysics and mathematics and introduces the claim that mathematical principles must be constructable in intuition. This claim, repeated with further refinement throughout Kant's work, is discussed most thoroughly in the first *Critique*, where it is connected with the claim that mathematical truths are synthetic, that is, not derivable from the law of noncontradiction, as Leibniz had argued they were. Both of these claims drew a great deal of fire from traditional commentators. The objections to Kant's claims may be summarized by the charge that Kant's insistence upon the constructability of mathematics derived solely from his use of Euclidean geometry as the paradigm of mathematical reasoning. Further developments in geometry, the critics continue, show constructions to be unnecessary even in geometry, while Kant's attempt to assimilate arithmetical to geometrical reasoning results in the barely intelligible idea that arithmetical proofs cannot be justified without reference to physical objects.[6]

A number of recent philosophers have, however, made considerable efforts to reconstruct and defend Kant's position in a variety of ways. Since my concern is not with the justification of Kant's philosophy of mathematics but with the consequences of Kant's views for his notion of reason, I shall not consider their arguments here.[7] For these purposes, it suffices to consider the systematic grounding of Kant's insistence that mathematical concepts be constructed in intuition. This insistence is the product not simply of attention to obsolete proofs of Euclidean geometry but of a general thesis about the theory of knowledge. Kant's idea is that mathematical principles, by themselves, are empty of content. In order to yield knowledge they must fulfill the requirements for doing so to which every concept is subject: they must be given an object in intuition. Intuition is demanded not for the application, but for the very sense and meaning, of mathematical concepts (A240/B300). Without construction in sensible intuition, Kant writes, we could not know mathematical truths to be other than "mere phantasms of the brain" (IV, 292). The difficulties in understanding Kant's doctrine of the construction of mathematical concepts in intuition are compounded by unclarity as to whether Kant is referring to pure or empirical intuition.[8] We need not resolve these questions in order to view Kant's assertion of the reliance of mathematics upon intuition as an attempt to make his account of mathematical knowledge consistent with the dictum that concepts without intuitions are empty. Only the full cooperation of sensibility and understanding – of the given matter of appearances and discursive concepts – can produce a claim of knowledge.

Looking briefly at Kant's views about the nature of logic will help to clarify his position on mathematics. Neither mathematics nor logic is derived from experience; rather, both are conditions of it, although mathematics is only valid for those creatures possessing our form of sensibility. Logic is the more universal, holding a priori for every rational being as such. Unlike mathematics, logic is the work of pure reason alone. It requires no intuition, pure or empirical, and is analytic; that is, its truths consist of subject – predicate judgments in which the predicate asserts no more than what is contained in the subject. Through logical judgments, therefore, our knowledge is in no way extended. For this reason, Kant states in the introduction to the *Logic*, logic cannot serve as an organon for scientific knowledge, although mathematics can do so. In several places Kant goes so far as to say that logical principles are not genuine principles: "Some few fundamental propositions, presupposed by the geometers, are indeed, really analytic, and rest on the principle of contradiction. But as identical propositions, they serve only as links in a chain of method and not as principles; for instance, A = A; the whole is equal to itself; or (A + B > A), that is, the whole is greater than its parts" (B16). The *Prolegomena* describes identical propositions as a "method of concatenation" rather than actual principles (IV, 269). And in the first introduction to the *Critique of Judgment*, logic is said to offer a "principle for progression" (XX, 204). Two different but related points can be distinguished in these statements, although Kant does not seem to do so. The first is that logic is not knowledge because it is empty of content. The second is that logic is not knowledge because it is not really made up of statements, but of links between or ways of transforming other statements. It is worth reminding ourselves of the remarkable character of these claims. While we may have become accustomed to views that hold analytic statements to be empty of content, Kant's immediate predecessors had hoped to deduce the whole of knowledge from them. The view that analytic truths do not really form part of knowledge but, at most, constitute some of the principles necessary for ordering and systematizing knowledge elsewhere derived marks a real break with much of the past.

In constructing a conception of reason that is not cognitive, Kant must somehow account for those bodies of knowledge whose necessity and nonexperiential character made them seem paradigmatically productions of reason. The bold solution adopted for logic — Kant's outright denial that logic forms a body of knowledge, rather than a small set of methodological principles — seemed unavailable for mathematics. For Kant, it was clear that mathematical principles lead to the increase of knowledge, forming truths in the full, objective sense. His solution was to invoke the idea that mathematical concepts are constructed in intuition, in order to account for the objectivity of mathematical truths in a way that was consistent with his account of the objectivity of knowledge in general. The result of that account is the startling claim that pure reason alone cannot provide mathematical knowledge.

That Kant is fully aware of the blow this idea renders to traditional notions of reason is suggested by the fact that his fullest discussion of mathematical knowledge occurs in a chapter of the first *Critique* entitled "The Discipline of Pure Reason." The word 'discipline', Kant tells us, is to be used in a negative sense: his intention is to humiliate reason's pretensions to knowledge. A key step in doing so is to cut off the traditional attempt to model metaphysics on mathematics, presuming that the methods used in one field will assure success in the other. This attempt proceeded on the assumption that the successes of mathematics were due to pure reason alone, an assumption that Kant emphatically denies: it is intuition in mathematics that "keeps reason to a visible track," giving content and meaning to its concepts and principles (A711/B739). Every systematic metaphysician had tried to follow, or develop, a method based on principles of mathematics or logic. If mathematics only becomes knowledge through the mediation of intuition and logic is not knowledge at all, then all attempts to imitate them within philosophy are doomed to failure. The damage thereby rendered to traditional conceptions of philosophy will be discussed in chapter 5. For the present, we should underline consequences that are even more significant. If even the a priori science most unquestionably assigned to pure reason relies on something else to become knowledge, we can safely assume that pure reason cannot give us knowledge at all. So Kant concludes the "Discipline" in the satisfaction that he has shown reason's search for knowledge to be fruitless and compelled it to look elsewhere for its proper function.

II. The Inadequacy of Understanding

Reason's function in theoretical inquiry is not, then, to provide a priori knowledge of the kind available in mathematics or logic; for, we have seen, it cannot even provide the former by itself, and the latter is not sufficiently substantial to be regarded as knowledge at all. Determining what reason's correct function may be will depend on determining what functions are left unfulfilled by the other faculties available. Before proceeding to this task, it is important to say a little about Kant's use of the notion of 'faculty' itself.

The development of a taxonomy of the human mind was a common project of seventeenth- and eighteenth-century philosophy; both empiricists and rationalists developed detailed, albeit fluid, distinctions between activities variously described as judging, deducing, reasoning, understanding, and so on. Most of those writers viewed these distinctions in modal rather than ontological terms: to say that the mind has a faculty to do something is simply to say that it is able to do it.[9] Kant's division of the mind into three faculties is, in part, a continuation of these projects, whose purpose he holds to be almost self-explanatory. Before determining what can be built, we have to take stock of the available materials; examining the nature of the powers we have for knowing things before determining the extent of our knowledge is equally a requirement of common sense (A707/B735). A metaphor Kant uses less frequently compares his procedure to that of a chemist, who isolates particular elements in an attempt to exhibit each in a pure state (B xxi; A842/B870; V, 291). This metaphor will prove particularly important when it is remembered that much of the chemical analysis of Kant's day was "rational" rather than "real": the chemist expected analysis to reveal the composition of mixed bodies but not to isolate elements as concrete substances that he could handle.[10] This procedure served Kant as a model for separating the faculties that contributed to making up experience. Without ever supposing that one might be found operating independently of the others, he could proceed to examine the distinctive contributions made by each in a separation clearly intended to be artificial.

In addition to providing an inventory of the elements that compose our experience, Kant's separation of the faculties plays a role in his answer to Hume. It is this separation that allows Kant to distinguish features of experience that are valid only because of the human constitution from those which are valid for experience in general, without requiring features of such experience to be part of the nature of things in themselves. Put somewhat paradoxically, Kant avoids psychologism by constructing transcendental psychology. Thus, sensibility will be shared by all human beings; but those inhabitants of other planets on whose existence Kant is willing to bet may well perceive the world in different spatiotemporal terms. The truths of understanding, by contrast, hold for all created beings, while reason is shared by everyone, including God.[11]

At least as important as the increasing scope of these faculties is the increasing degree of activity characteristic of each. Sensibility is the passive capacity of being affected by objects, contributing nothing to experience but the pure forms of space and time. Understanding is characterized as spontaneous and capable of generating and applying its own concepts but dependent on sensibility for content and meaning. Only reason, Kant says, is fully autonomous; it does not "follow the order of things as they present themselves in appearance, but frames for itself with perfect spontaneity an order of its own according to ideas, to which it adapts the empirical conditions" (A548/B576).

Equating spontaneity with autonomy, many of Kant's readers have missed the difference between the degrees of activity available to understanding and reason and thus underestimated the importance of the distinction between reason and understanding itself. The categories of the understanding are spontaneous in that they are applied to, rather than derived from, experience. Thus, they are distinguished from Hume's laws of association, which are empirical generalizations formed through a purely passive, receptive process. The understanding provides the conditions under which anything can be perceived as an object, yet it does so in a way Kant describes as reactive, dependent on the sensible world as the occasional cause of its activity (VII, 71). Its operations are routine, automatic, and mechanical: understanding "merely spells out appearances according to a synthetic unity, in order to read them as experience" (A314/B371). In later works, the mechanical nature of this process becomes increasingly explicit. The way in which the understanding connects the manifold is compared to a lever, which can be used purposively but whose possibility is not dependent on such use (XX, 219). The fact that the workings of the understanding are automatic is the ground of the fact that its concepts are fully determinate: there is no need to invoke an external decision procedure to determine whether, and how, a category of the understanding is to be applied. That is, the heteronomy of the understanding is just the other side of the transcendental deduction. Were the procedure by which the categories applied not automatic, without room for choice or decision, there could be no argument that their application was a necessary condition of experience. This necessity, however, has its price:

> Understanding—although it too is spontaneous activity and is not, like sense, confined to ideas which arise only when we are affected by things (and therefore are passive)—understanding cannot produce by its own activity any concepts other than those whose sole service is *to bring sensuous ideas under rules* and so to unite them in one consciousness: without this employment of sensibility it would think nothing at all. Reason, on the other hand—in what are called "Ideas"—shows a spontaneity so pure that it goes far beyond anything sensibility can offer. (IV, 452)

We may read this passage as a commentary on the first *Critique*'s statement that concepts without percepts are empty. Though the concepts of the understanding are not culled from experience, they are dependent upon experience for all significance. If the categories are constitutive of nature, they are in a very real sense constituted by it; unlike the ideas of reason, they have no meaning whatever in the absence of the material of the sensory world. Sensibility and understanding belong together, limiting nature as they are limited by it.[12] Precisely because their role is to determine experience, they are restricted to it in the strictest sense; unlike reason, they are incapable of measuring, judging, or making demands on experience:

> We note two wholly different kinds of parts in human beings, namely, on the one side sensibility and understanding, and reason and free will on the other, which are very essentially different from one another. In nature everything *is*, there is no question of *should* in it; sensibility and understanding only aim to determine what and how it *is*, thus they are destined for nature, for this world, and thus belong to it. . . . Understanding is limited to this world through its very form, for it consists merely of categories, that is, modes of expression which can only be related to sensual things. Understanding comes to an end where the categories come to an end, because they form and compose it. (VII, 70)

Kant concludes that it is reason—the capacity freely to prescribe its own principles to experience, not understanding's capacity to know it—that makes us human. While the absolute value of freedom is a fundamental presupposition of Kant's entire work, this is not simply a moral question. As I will argue, it is just the capacity to function independently of experience that gives us the possibility of constructing a science of experience. The move to increasing degrees of autonomy is at issue in the process by which knowledge, Kant tells us, begins with the senses, and proceeds through understanding to reason.

In examining this process it is important to remember that Kant's use of 'begins' signals logical, not temporal, priority. In human beings, with the possible exception of Adam and Eve before the Fall, all three faculties operate simultaneously; Kant's attempt to separate them is solely for the purpose of analysis. Following this artificial separation, which corresponds to the division of the first *Critique* itself, we may nevertheless ask about the knowledge of experience described by the end of the "Transcendental Analytic." What is missing in the product of understanding and sensibility which leads Kant to introduce the third of his elements, the faculty of reason?

What is missing, I will argue, is any but the most general of natural laws. The transcendental laws of the understanding abstract from all the variety of possible empirical laws; thus, the categories alone guarantee us little of what we need to comprehend nature. The third *Critique* states this point most explicitly:

> We saw in the *Critique of Pure Reason* that the totality of nature as the sum of all objects of experience forms a system according to transcendental laws, which the understanding itself gives a priori to appearances, insofar as their connection in one consciousness is to constitute experience. . . . But it does not follow from this that nature is a system comprehensible by human cognition through empirical laws, or that the common systematic unity of its appearances in one experience (hence experience as a system) is possible for humankind. For the variety and diversity of empirical laws might be so great that . . . we were confronted by a crude, chaotic aggregate totally devoid of system, even though we had to presuppose a system in accordance with transcendental laws. (XX, 208; see also V, 179–80, 185)

Despite the fact that the transcendental laws of the understanding ensure a very general uniformity among objects, the variety of objects leaves open the possibility of an infinite number of laws in which we could discover no order that would permit us to "make a coherent experience out of such confused material" (V, 185). Far from supposing that experience must be thoroughly law-governed in order to be possible, such passages assert that an experience subject to the categories could be one of enormous chaos, "totally devoid of system." While this point is stated most clearly in the third *Critique*, it is fully available in the first. The "Analytic" itself denies that the understanding is the source of laws of nature or serves as a sufficient condition of the possibility thereof (A127, B135, B165). In particular, nothing about the concept of cause that is proven there implies that we know that any particular causal regularities will continue to hold. Even further, the necessity of the very general transcendental laws does not require that we be able to discover any empirical laws whatsoever (A653/B682). The knowledge that every event must be caused does not guarantee us the possibility of knowledge of the cause of any event at all, nor does it demand a uniformity of nature more thoroughgoing than is involved in the bare requirement that every event be caused by something or other.

In explicating the poverty of the experience generated by the combination of understanding and sensibility, it is useful to refer to the distinction made in the last chapter between the two aspects of the principle of sufficient reason. There I argued that Leibniz's failure to make this distinction was the source of his surprisingly heteronomous conception of reason. Kant's insight lies not only in having distinguished between the claim that the given world is subject to order and the claim that human reason is capable of discovering that order but also in insisting that the second claim cannot be proven but must be held as a regulative principle, with all that this will be seen to entail. The Second Analogy proof that the principle of sufficient reason is the ground of possible experience is a proof that every appearance has some cause that precedes it in time (A201/B247). Kant's attribution of the principle of causality to the understanding not only serves to answer Hume by asserting that the notion of cause is not a habit of inference but a necessary condition of our experience of objects. At least as important is the fact that Kant's placing the source of causal order in the understanding eliminates all the problems that Leibniz faced in trying to explain the origin of that order. Assuming this order to be present in things in themselves, Leibniz, as we saw, had to claim that God put order into the world at the creation, a claim that turned out to be neither philosophically nor theologically viable. Kant requires no such claims: for him, it is simply a condition of our experiencing the world that this part of the principle of sufficient reason holds or that all our experience is constructed according to this (causal) order. The order that is thereby assured is, however, very thin, guaranteeing only that every event has some cause that precedes it. There is, Kant holds, no a priori proof of the second aspect of the principle of sufficient reason: the world we experience might be such that we were unable to discern its order:

> The objects of empirical knowledge are, except for this formal time-condition, determined or, as far as one can judge a priori, determinable in such a variety of ways, that specific-different natures could have causes in an infinitely variable way, besides that which they have in common as belonging to nature in general. . . . In

this respect we judge the unity of nature according to empirical laws, and the possibility of the unity of experience (as system according to empirical laws) to be contingent. (V, 183)

When the Analogies and the Transcendental Deduction(s) are reread with this framework in mind, it seems clear that most of Kant's own statements of intention support the idea that the conditions of the possibility of experience provided at the end of the "Analytic" are very far from being conditions of the possibility of science. The A Deduction concludes by stating that the synthesis of the manifold through the categories *precedes* all empirical knowledge. (A130). That this synthesis is not sufficient for science but is merely preliminary to it is emphasized in the B Deduction in passages like the following:

> Nature, considered merely as nature in general [*Überhaupt*] is dependent upon these categories as the original ground of its necessary conformity to law [*natur formaliter spectata*]. Pure understanding is not, however, in a position, through mere categories, to prescribe to appearances any a priori laws other than those which are involved in a nature in general, that is, in the conformity to law of all appearances in space and time. . . . To obtain any knowledge whatsoever of these special laws, we must resort to experience. (B165)

As the "original ground" of the lawfulness of nature, the categories provide what Buchdahl describes as the framework for a public language (1969, 475). This requires an account of what it means to be an object at all. To achieve knowledge of the laws governing the behavior of particular objects, Kant says, we must resort to experience. The same point is made in the Second Analogy: "How anything can be altered and how it should be possible that upon one state in a given moment an opposite state may follow at the next moment – of this we have not, a priori, the least conception. For that we require knowledge of actual forces, which can only be given empirically" (A207/B253).

Now everything in these passages turns upon what Kant means by resorting to experience. As will shortly be argued, Kant holds this to be a complicated affair, involving the use of reason in numerous and crucial functions. Thus, the advance from the very basic knowledge guaranteed in the "Analytic" to a system of scientific explanation cannot be an automatic one; for the Second Analogy, Kant says, has merely given the formal condition of every alteration, thereby anticipating our own apprehension (A210/B256). This condition is nothing but the fact that appearances of past time determine all existences in succeeding time. (A199/B244). Kant's concern here is not the grounding of a system of causal laws but a prior task, the grounding of the notion of causality itself. Melnick explains this by saying that the Second Analogy is primarily concerned to show that the concept of necessary connection is not subject to the difficulties Hume claimed:

> The point is, for Hume, we are only justified in asserting that, given x, y has always occurred in our experience. For Kant, we are justified in asserting that, given x, y must always obtain (not just at the times in the past when we have actually experienced y) *if* indeed x is the cause of y. Now we can never be sure that we have got it right that x is the cause of y. . . . But whatever the specific cause of y turns out to be (though this can only be determined empirically and is subject to correction) that cause is necessarily and universally connected with y. (1973, 132)

In arguing that the determination of every alteration according to a rule in time is a condition of possible experience, Kant grounds the principle that Hume held to be merely a matter of habit. Without this a priori grounding, Kant says, the principle of causality would be merely subjective and fictitious (A196/B241). With this a priori grounding, Kant has begun to introduce the possibility of determining whether or not *x* is the cause of *y*, as opposed to whether or not *x* happens to have preceded *y* in experience. What else is required before we are in a position to discover a particular cause or system of causal connections will be discussed later.

A conflation of the two aspects of the principle of sufficient reason has often been responsible for a traditional misreading of Kant's intentions in the "Analytic," according to which he was thought to prove—or more often, to attempt to prove—that objectivity requires being subject to empirical law. In particular, it was frequently claimed that the Second Analogy attempted to prove the a priori validity of a principle of induction. A recent statement of this view is summarized in the following: "If the concepts of object and cause are 'reinstated', then we know in advance that changes will be law-governed, that induction will 'work'. If induction does not 'work', there will be no objective world, hence no unity of consciousness" (Brittan 1978, 205). The conflation of the two aspects of the principle of sufficient reason entails a conflation of the two problems Hume raised concerning causality. He claimed both that any concept of cause apart from observed causal conjunction is incoherent and that we have no way of knowing that the causal regularities we observe in nature will continue. The Second Analogy is concerned solely with the first problem. Kant fully grants Hume's second charge, arguing that a principle of induction must therefore be a regulative principle of reason. The conflation of these two charges may result from the supposition that the concept of cause requires the existence of some causal regularities. Yet the questions are distinct. On the one hand, Hume's charge that we cannot know the future to resemble the past assumes that all nature's laws are causal laws but it need not do so: any principle of induction would be subject to the same problem. On the other hand, the notion of one thing's causing another is fully intelligible apart from the assurance of specific causal regularities, although there are, of course, difficulties concerning our knowledge of causes that are not repeated. The meaning of the concept of cause—whether it involves necessary connection, or merely consists in constant conjunction—can be determined independently of the question whether we are in a position to discover any causal laws. Hence, Kant's proof that the concept of causality is constitutive of experience does not require the guarantee of the existence of any empirical laws. The Second Analogy assures us that the future will resemble the past only in the very weak sense that the future will continue, somehow or other, to be determined by the past.

In one passage, Kant suggests that Hume's own error regarding the meaning of the concept of cause arose from a similar confusion. Hume, he writes, correctly observed that no causal regularities can be universally and necessarily given but must be derived from experience (A765/B793). From this, he wrongly concluded that the concept of cause itself was derived from experience and was hence without universal and necessary validity. The Transcendental Logic, Kant continues, has shown this to be false:

> If, therefore, wax, which was formerly hard, melts, I can know a priori that *something* must have preceded (for instance, the heat of the sun), upon which the melting has followed according to a fixed law, although a priori, independently of experience, I could not determine, *in any specific manner*, either the cause from the effect or the effect from the cause. Hume was therefore in error in inferring from the contingency of our determination *in accordance with the law* the contingency of the *law* itself. (A766/B794)

Most recent interpretations have tended to separate the two problems.[13] This is the result of two considerations. First, Kant's arguments in the Second Analogy clearly do not suffice to prove a principle of induction. Rather than continue to fault him for failing to prove a thoroughgoing lawlike quality of experience that the "Analytic" does not support, it seems wiser to view his task as a more limited one. Second, the detailed attention to Kant's philosophy of science sparked by Buchdahl's work makes the conclusion unavoidable that Kant holds the principles of reason to be responsible for *some* aspects of scientific law. Unclear is the question of how many.

The strongest version of this claim holds that the understanding plays a severely limited role in the construction of science, restricted to mechanically recording particular events and guaranteeing the existence of some causal order or another. Genuine scientific thinking, and with it, the possibilities of the uniformities of experience on which we rely, are, then, products of reason. The most important consequence of this view is that the level of certainty guaranteed within experience is rather minimal. Only a few transcendental laws—no empirical ones—can be known with necessity; and the order required to comprehend experience is thin indeed. The scantiness of this order has led some scholars to suggest a weaker interpretation, according to which some empirical laws, or their foundations, are guaranteed by the understanding.

Both versions acknowledge that a great deal of the work of scientific theorizing must be left to the regulative principles of reason so that even the weaker view would suffice to make the claims with which I am concerned.[14] Since I believe that the stronger view is the correct one, I would like, however, to answer the principle objections that have been made against it.

Some of these are textual; there are a number of passages in the "Analytic" in which Kant claims to have shown, though his arguments fail to prove it, that nature is subject to universal law. Now even Buchdahl, who introduced the strong interpretation, acknowledges that the texts are inconclusive (Buchdahl 1967, p 356; 1986, 213). For reasons that I shall suggest shortly, it is possible that Kant himself may have been subject to just the sort of slide he accuses Hume of. Yet so many passages, like the ones just quoted, clearly state that the understanding does not give any but the most formal conditions for natural science, that Kant's first *Critique's* suggestions to the contrary might be overlooked as instances of ambiguity.

More serious problems are presented by the *Metaphysical Foundations of Natural Science*, where Kant discusses the philosophical grounding of basic principles of Newtonian mechanics. Many passages of this work suggest that Kant hoped to provide a priori deductions of Newton's laws from the transcendental laws of the understanding, with the addition of the empirical concept of matter. Thus, the *Metaphysical Foundations* could be regarded as the completion of the metaphysics of experience whose basis is provided in the "Analytic." Even if the latter work fails to give us the concepts needed to construct science, it is argued that Kant thought they could be derived from it. If this were the case, Kant must be seen to propound a view according to which fundamental scientific laws are as necessarily conditions of experience as the categories themselves. The level of chaos and uncertainty that seemed to be allowed in an experience subject to the categories would thereby be greatly reduced, and the role within science left to be played by regulative principles of reason would be minimal.

We need not resolve the problems raised by this difficult work in order to determine the claims that are relevant to this inquiry.[15] Most important, the a priori conception of science sometimes suggested in the *Metaphysical Foundations* is thoroughly at odds with the empiricist tendencies expressed throughout Kant's work. Far from supporting a rationalist vision that would deduce the laws of science from other necessary truths, Kant's statements about the importance of observation and experiment, as well as his insistence on the incompletability of natural science, suggest a very modern view, to which the hope of an a priori deduction from transcendental principles is completely foreign.[16] Such a deduction would be lacking in content so fundamental that it lies at the heart of his distinctions between concept and intuition, self and nature. In contrast with the "pure rational sciences" of ethics and mathematics, he writes, "In natural science there is endless conjecture, and certainty is not to be counted upon. For the natural appearances are objects which are given to us independently of our concepts, and the key to them lies not in us and our pure thinking, but outside us" (A480/B580). It is important to recognize that such sentiments are expressed not only in the first and third *Critiques* but in the *Metaphysical Foundations of Natural Science* itself, which states that natural science can be infinitely extended, even if its foundations can be provided a priori (IV, 473). Indeed, recent work suggests that the *Metaphysical Foundations* makes clear not only the empirical character of specific scientific laws but the use of regulative principles to characterize the concept of matter itself.[17] Thus, even without accepting Buchdahl's claim that the *Metaphysical Foundations* makes *no* attempt to prove the actuality of physical laws but only their possibility, we need not regard it as undercutting Kant's essentially empiricist vision of science. The role of the a priori in Kant's account of science remains disputed; yet even those who view the *Metaphysical Foundations* as attempting to provide deductions of some of the principles of natural science allow that these are very few, insufficient to account even for the laws of physics, not to mention the other sciences.[18] Obtaining these will require, on any interpretation, a resort to the uncertainties of experience.

A more troublesome objection to the strong interpretation has been most forcefully articulated by Michael Friedman.[19] While acknowledging that the attempt to separate the concept of cause from the existence of any particular causal laws has strong textual support, Friedman questions, most importantly, the philosophical coherence of such a separation:

> The problem is that, for Kant, to say that events occur in a determinate objective sequence — and hence fall under the concept of causality — *is* to say they are subject to a general causal law or uniformity. Kant is quite explicit in the Second Analogy that events acquire determinate position in time only in virtue of a general rule or law

asserting that all events of the same kind or type as the preceding event are followed by events of the same kind or type as the succeeding event. . . . It follows that if the understanding is in fact to guarantee the existence of particular determinate sequences of individual events, it must somehow guarantee the existence of particular causal laws as well. (1991, 79)

Thus, Friedman argues that the proof of the necessity of the principle of causality in the Second Analogy is already a proof of the existence of causal laws; the very meaning of the concept of cause depends on the possibility of causal regularity. Thus, the separation of the two aspects of the principle of sufficient reason may appear artificial: How could one coherently use the concept of order in the world if human reason had not been able to discover some of it? Similarly, we might conclude that the slide Kant accused Hume of is nothing but a correct conclusion: if there are no necessary causal laws but merely observed uniformities, then the notion of cause itself seems highly questionable. From considerations such as these, Friedman concludes that the strong interpretation introduced by Buchdahl cannot be maintained. Instead, he claims, Kant must be seen to argue for both the existence and the necessity of particular causal laws as part of his argument for a transcendental principle of causality. Consequently, Friedman proposes an account whereby particular causal laws would be accorded a mixed status and the sharp dichotomy between regulative and constitutive principles would have to be withdrawn.

The thrust of Friedman's point is undeniable: while the distinction between the necessity of the concept of cause and the necessity of any particular causal law is clear enough in principle, we can hardly use the concept of cause without appealing to the existence of causal regularities. In the sense that permits us to raise philosophical problems about the nature of causality, inquire about partial or simultaneous causes or unique causal sequences, or even search for particular causes and integrate our findings into the rest of our experience, it is clear that we could not be said to possess the concept of cause had we never discovered a single causal regularity. Perhaps one could imagine a faculty of understanding that applied the principle of causality— succession in time according to a rule—to the sensible manifold, but we could hardly be said to be conscious of this process or, hence, to find the concept of cause intelligible. Yet this insight need not lead us to Friedman's conclusions but may point in another direction entirely.

To see this, it must be emphasized that Kant's separation of the faculties is an artificial one for the purpose of analysis; within actual experience, he holds, all faculties operate simultaneously. Once Kant's project of describing individual faculties' contributions to experience is taken seriously, the temptation to forget this and to imagine them as autonomous, reified entities is strong. When it is remembered, however, that understanding and reason operate together while performing separate functions, the claim that there is no coherent notion of causality without the experience of particular causal laws becomes an argument for the need for reason in anything we could recognize as full systematic experience. Indeed, these considerations help to explain a key passage that has often proved puzzling: "Without reason [we would have] no thoroughly coherent employment of the understanding, and in the absence of this no sufficient criterion of empirical truth. In order, therefore, to secure an empirical criterion we have no option save to presuppose the systematic unity of nature as objectively valid and necessary" (A651/B679).

Nothing Kant says in the first *Critique* seems to warrant so strong a claim. He tells us that reason is needed to direct the employment of the understanding and that reason introduces systematicity into experience. But even those who interpret these claims so as to give reason the greatest possible number of tasks have found it difficult to explain the idea that reason is required for any coherent employment of the understanding at all. The problems Friedman raises provide a solution. Since we need to presuppose the existence of certain causal uniformities in order to apply the concept of causality, we need the regulative principles of reason in order for understanding to function "coherently." We need the assumption that nature's order is intelligible to us in order to give meaning to the notion of order itself. These considerations are properly understood not as an objection to Kant's proceedings but, precisely, as a confirmation of his most general goal, namely, to demonstrate the need for regulative principles of reason in every crucial aspect of our experience. Establishing this goal requires, first, an understanding of the other elements of experience, which requires a *logical* separation between the law of causality and the existence of particular causal laws.

It may be asked why a separation so artificial ought to be preserved. The answer must be not only that (most of) Kant's texts insist on it but also that it needs to be maintained for precisely the reasons that make it seem so disturbing. The final objection to the strong interpretation is more often evinced than argued, yet it is that which fuels the others.[20] For what is at issue in the separation of causality from particular causes is the question of certainty. Kant has given us a transcendental deduction; we should like it to prove as much as possible. We should like to have a guarantee of particular empirical laws, not only abstract transcendental ones. The unity of experience that Kant wishes to demonstrate in the Deduction seems undermined by the absence of such a guarantee; the security of science seems in jeopardy if left to rely on "merely" regulative principles. Understanding confers certainty, only its principles can be *known*; so the more ingredients of experience that can be attributed to the understanding, the more certain our experience as a whole will be.

It must be noted that this objection goes to the heart of the regulative/constitutive distinction itself. In leaving so much of experience grounded on nothing but regulative principles, Kant's view does guarantee us less than we had hoped. Kant himself seems at times unable to accept the radical lack of certainty entailed in his own position: this is the source of his occasional speculation on the possibility of giving a transcendental deduction of the regulative ideas and perhaps also the source of some of the formulations in the *Metaphysical Foundations* that seek to provide the laws of science with a greater degree of certainty than he finds available. But this is just to say that Kant is no more immune than the rest of us to the possibility of transcendental illusion, reason's constant attempt to exchange regulative principles for constitutive ones. If Kant is right about the persistence of this illusion, the objection can never be fully dispelled. It can, however, be partially answered by a full account of the notion of a regulative principle, which examines the source of our dissatisfaction with the absence of certainty. Section VIII will begin to present such an account. Its completion is, of course, the task of this book as a whole; for only a full account of Kant's notion of reason can give sense to the notion of its regulative principles.

* * *

A complete reading of Kant's theory of knowledge would be required to establish the strong interpretation proposed; in the foregoing discussion I simply hope to have made it more plausible. Let us turn to describe the character of the experience that, on the strong interpretation, would be available at the conclusion of the "Analytic," before reason was introduced to the product of understanding and sensibility. Because such experience is in fact unavailable to us, this description must be purely speculative. Kant himself devotes little space to conjectures of this kind. The *Conflict* suggests that this is the experience of animals:

> Understanding must belong merely to nature, and if the human being only had understanding without reason and free will, he would be in no way different from animals, and would perhaps merely stand at the peak of their scale; since he is now, on the contrary, in possession of morality, as a free being, thoroughly and essentially distinct from animals, even the most intelligent (whose instinct often works more clearly and decisively than the understanding of human beings). (VII, 70–71)

But neither here nor elsewhere does Kant attempt to give a detailed description of animal experience. Somewhat more suggestive is Kant's "Conjectural Beginning of Human History," which describes the process by which the human being distinguished himself from animals through the use of reason as most likely to have been a gradual one. Reconstructing the story of Adam and Eve, Kant sees the exit from paradise as the transition from merely natural functioning to the use of reason. Kant describes the first acts of reason as involving the capacity to resist natural drives. More interestingly, he designates the "third step" of reason to have been the considered expectation of the future:

> This capacity not merely to enjoy the present moment but to make the coming, often very distant time present, is the most decisive sign of human advantage, in order to prepare for distant purposes in accordance with his determination—but at the same time the most unfailing source of care and affliction, which the uncertain future causes, and from which all animals are exempt. (VIII, 113)

This passage goes even further than Kant's general claim that reason is required to set ends and purposes (discussed in section III). Without the faculty of reason, he says, we would be unable to form a notion of the future that first provides the possibility of having ends. Understanding and sensibility are merely capable of recording what is and what has been.

Hence, it is conceivable that without the interjection of reason, we might experience the world causally, as young babies and animals do. Since understanding and sensibility record particular causal sequences, we could, presumably, observe that one billiard ball caused another to roll. This observation would not be a fully conscious one; for the reasons just discussed, the sense of causality thus experienced would be very minimal, leaving us incapable of testing whether the next collision of billiard balls would have the same result, of inquiring as to what factors in the first situation produced such an outcome, and in general, of incorporating the observation into anything else in the body of our experience. Indeed, we could hardly speak sensibly of having a body of experience, as opposed to a simple aggregate of occurrences.

Understanding is incapable of anything other than this meager performance because it lacks autonomy, and its mechanical nature is inseparable from the abstractness of its results. Routinely and automatically, understanding applies the twelve categories to the given manifold. This is its sole function, and there is no means within it for doing anything else, for "understanding . . . is nothing but the faculty of combining a priori, and of bringing the manifold of given representations under the unity of apperception" (B135). It must be repeated that it is precisely the automatic character of this process that allows Kant to argue that the categories are necessary conditions of possible experience. Conversely, the autonomy of reason—the fact that its principles are not automatically applied—means that they will have no transcendental deduction.

Now it is clear that the outcome of this automatic procedure is knowledge, but it is equally clear that it is not science. This is true first, I have argued, because no empirical laws are yielded: the laws of the understanding are transcendental. Second and even more generally, the product of understanding contains no possibility of *explanation* of any kind. Melnick writes, "How far phenomena can be understood, beyond what is required for them to be objects of judgement at all, is not something that can be determined a priori and is not something that has been determined in the Second Analogy" (1973, 122). This is the case because the understanding can provide neither the motives nor the presuppositions required for asking and answering questions of experience.

These two difficulties, which prevent this low-level knowledge from becoming full-fledged science, are connected: all genuine science is the product of freedom. The capacity to demand explanations of experience requires the capacity to go beyond experience, for we cannot investigate the given until we refuse to take it as given. To ask a question about some aspect of experience, we must be able to think the thought that it could have been otherwise. Without this thought, we cannot even formulate the vaguest *why*. This thought is unavailable to understanding, whose whole content is experience. Kant's repeated statements that the categories of the understanding are restricted to experience and have no content apart from sensibility must be taken very literally. These statements have been seen solely as directed to ruling out the possibility of understanding's claims to knowledge of noumena. In order to rule out that possibility, they must, however, be part of a systematic and general view. Understanding not only lacks the tools for achieving knowledge of a noumenal world but of anything other than the present given. Once again, this is not to deny the role that understanding plays in constructing the experience that is given to us. Precisely because that role is so crucial, understanding has no position distinct from experience, from which experience could begin to be questioned. To describe the understanding as restricted to experience is neither to belittle it nor to assimilate it to a more empiricist, Humean notion of principles derived from experience. It is, rather, to define its powers in as exact a way as possible. Kant can be viewed as demanding a purer and more consistent empiricism than the empiricists: when he appeals to experience, he is careful to have isolated its components. His conception of experience is, in this sense, narrower than that of an earlier age, free of the theoretical presuppositions that allowed other writers to claim that the transition from scholastic to modern science was made possible by the abandonment of speculation in favor of pure observation. For Kant, experience means just that which is immediately given—which necessarily includes the categories of the understanding.

It may seem paradoxical that it is the capacity to go beyond experience that yields the capacity to discover empirical, in addition to transcendental, laws. But this is just the result of Kant's view that all possible experience requires some rule-governedness. That is, the experience that is the product of the cooperation of understanding and sensibility is an experience formed by the very general laws of the categories and the forms of intuition. Hence, the advance from minimal to scientific knowledge will be an advance from the general to the particular. Because of Kant's theory of the construction of experience, this advance is equivalent to the idea that we must advance from accepting the given to questioning it in order to construct science.

The fact that the heteronomy of the understanding is connected with its abstractness provides a key to grasping why reason must be introduced; for the abstractness of the laws of the understanding does not by itself explain the need to invoke another faculty in order to obtain empirical laws. The point that the metaphysical generalities of the "Analytic" are not yet science but, at most, part of the foundations for it, is a rather obvious one: the claim that every event has a cause is hardly the goal, but the starting point, of every working scientist's endeavors. One might easily grant this without supposing that a radically different capacity is required to do something that may appear to consist in filling in the details of an already constructed edifice.

We can see why reason alone can do this work if we consider the alternatives available to Kant, given the faculties already introduced. One possibility would be that understanding provided its own specification a priori. In this case particular laws of nature would be deduced directly from the general laws of the understanding. Now Kant denies that empirical laws can be derived from the categories, although they are all subject to them (A127, B165). What are the grounds for this denial? The attempt to deduce empirical laws from transcendental ones would substitute a rationalist conception of science for a genuinely empirical one and must be rejected for the reasons suggested in the discussion of the *Metaphysical Foundations of Natural Science*. But if the laws of natural science cannot be directly deduced from the understanding, it might be asked whether some further reference to the faculty of sensibility would be successful. If what is missing in the transcendental laws of understanding is empirical detail, why can't sensibility provide the observation necessary to supply it?

The answer to this question is that a great deal more is presupposed by observation than sensibility is able to provide. The crude empiricist idea that the observation requisite for natural science is to be obtained by simply looking to the things themselves is vitiated, for Kant, by two considerations. The first is that the wealth and variety of data is so great that a number of theoretical principles must be presupposed in order for research to begin: "It is undoubtedly certain that nothing suitable would ever have been found through mere empirical groping around, without a leading principle according to which one searches; for only the *methodical* reflection upon experience is *observation*" (VIII, 161). Genuine observation, then, is something quite distinct from "mere empirical groping around." The rational determination of concepts and a host of general principles of reason must precede it, for "one finds in experience what one needs only when one knows beforehand what one is to seek" (VIII, 91). Experience will not of itself offer what we require (VIII, 164). We must sort, refine, and discard experience before we can appeal to it; the idea of a science constructed directly from pure observation statements is incoherent. While this point may be a commonplace in contemporary philosophical discussions of science, it was rarely acknowledged in Kant's day; and only recent scholars of Kant's work have attended to his discussions of it. The idea that untestable theoretical principles are presupposed in empirical research is not the least part of Kant's reconciliation of rationalism and empiricism. It may, indeed, be regarded as a higher-level statement of the more commonly discussed instance of that reconciliation, the cooperation of understanding and sensibility in constructing experience.

A second reason why sensibility cannot provide the material needed for the construction of science is that sensibility, even more than understanding, lacks the motive force to do so. Sensibility is purely receptive—a capacity of being affected in a certain manner with representations, adding nothing to the given manifold except the forms of space and time. Like understanding, therefore, it will prove incapable of questioning the given. All sensibility can do is provide it. As in the case of under-standing, the heteronomy of sensibility has its advantages, being just the other side of the certainty we attach to it. The ineradicably passive character of sensibility, though described by Kant as the "source of all the evil things said about it" (VII, 144), is intimately connected with our willingness to take it as a direct source of access to external objects. The fact that data are forced upon us without our choice seems to mark them as proceeding from a world outside ourselves. But although this feature may guarantee the reliability of sensibility as a source of the raw material of observation, it precludes it from containing within itself the impetus to observe or to do more than present every datum. This impetus, we shall see, must come from elsewhere.

The final reason that bars further appeal to sensibility as a way of filling the gaps left by understanding is of a different nature. This is the fact that the principles required to fill those gaps are not instances of knowledge (as anything produced by the proper cooperation of understanding and sensibility would be). Nor, on Kant's account, could they perform their function if they were knowable, as will be argued in section VII. Kant takes the idea that these principles are unknowable for granted, accepting Hume's charge that we cannot know like causes to have like effects. Nor, Kant will add, do we know a variety of other methodological principles, such as Occam's Razor, the Law of Least Action, and others, which are nevertheless needed in successful scientific inquiry. These principles must therefore have their source in some faculty whose purpose and structure is not one of attaining knowledge.

The arguments for Kant's claim that reason must be introduced in order to fill the gap between the minimal knowledge supplied by sensibility and understanding and full-fledged science may now be summarized. This gap must be fulfilled by principles that precede all observation and experiment but that cannot be known to apply to the world. At the same time, the introduction of purpose and motive is required in order to ascend from the simple recording of experience to the explanation of it. Because of Kant's construction of reason, in which theoretical and practical reason form a unity, these requirements are connected: the impetus necessary for observation coincides with the principles involved in it. In other words, the possibility of questioning experience implies that explanations of experience can be given, which in turn, Kant will show, presupposes a number of other assumptions about nature. Reason provides both these requirements in one blow. Its regulative principles provide the motive to structure and systematize experience as they provide the very possibility of structuring it. The fact that reason is the sole autonomous faculty, independent of the confines of experience, enables it to be the faculty whose sphere is the order of ends. Only reason is directed by ends that it sets for itself. Because of this, reason is the only possible candidate for making the transition between low-level knowledge and science.

III. The Ends of Science

Even when it seems clear that understanding and sensibility are, by themselves, inadequate to bridge the gap between lowest-level observation and natural science, Kant's initial statements of the manner in which reason fulfills this function seem unpromising. Reason, he tells us, provides the idea of the Unconditioned, which is required for the study of nature. The Unconditioned and "the totality of all conditions" are equivalent titles for all concepts of reason. This suggests that all other ideas that are designated as products of reason should be understood to be further specifications of the idea of the Unconditioned. But what sense can be made of Kant's claim that the Unconditioned is necessary for the construction of science? While it can never be known, this idea, he tells us, serves as a principle providing the greatest possible extension of the understanding, as well as the means to the systematization of knowledge that understanding obtains. This systematization is what raises ordinary knowledge to the rank of science. The obscurity of Kant's explication of the sense of 'systematization' in question has led most readers to suppose that a rather trivial matter is at issue. Kant's insistence on the importance of reason's systematization was traditionally viewed as a result of a personal attraction to baroque forms of classification, and his use of the term 'Unconditioned,' as an unfortunate relic of traditional metaphysics. Neither our understanding of science nor Kant's own would seem to require the use of a principle enjoining would-be scientists to seek the Unconditioned. So Guyer (1979) concludes:

> On the whole, Kant seemed to believe that reason's idea of systematicity is necessary only to motivate the understanding and to assist it in reaching coherent results in occasional cases of its failure, and not that systematicity is one of the necessary conditions of empirical knowledge. The Transcendental Deduction and the Analytic of Principles are taken to have stated all of the latter, and the idea of systematicity seems to be an afterthought, something to occupy reason once it has been deprived of transcendent metaphysics. (43)[21]

Some of the obscurity of Kant's discussion results from a major flaw in his exposition. His discussion of the Unconditioned begins at the opening of the "Dialectic," that chapter of the "Doctrine of Elements" meant to be devoted to reason's contributions to experience. After a fairly brief exposition of the ideas of reason in general, he moves to long analyses of the classical errors committed by reason, leaving to the curiously titled "Appendix" a description of the correct use of reason in science. Having been introduced to the notion of the Unconditioned, the reader must digest over two hundred pages of polemic against its abuse before being offered an account of its proper function. It is therefore no wonder that many have despaired of finding a positive function of reason at all. Structurally, it may be helpful to view book 2 of the "Dialectic," despite its bulk, as a very long and crucial footnote. This helps to emphasize the conclusion Kant wishes to draw: though the hypostatization of the Unconditioned is a transcendental error that leads to dogmatic metaphysics, the Idea itself is a necessary one. Having understood the illusions to which it can lead, we are better placed to determine its real use.

As in the case of the categories of the understanding, Kant hopes to find a clue to the real use of reason from its relatively unproblematic logical use. His explication of the process of reasoning by means of the structure of logic is probably more illuminating than the analogous attempt with regard to the understanding. We saw that Kant holds logic to consist not of independent principles but of "links in a chain of method" or ways of transforming and relating statements already given. Similarly, he will determine the real use of reason to involve no constitutive principles. Reason "contains knowledge of objects and their conditions just as little as does logic, but only gives a principle for the progression according to empirical laws, through which the investigation of nature becomes possible" (XX, 204−5). Having no direct relation to objects, theoretical reason directs the understanding and orders its statements about objects. This it does, Kant says, through the regulative principle to seek the Unconditioned. Reason's drive to seek the Unconditioned is absolutely necessary; for it is an analytic proposition that once the conditioned is given, a regress in the series of all its conditions is set us as a task (A498/B526). Here again, the connection with logic is important: the assumption that if the conditioned is given, a regress in the series of its conditions is prescribed is "simply the logical requirement that we should have adequate premises for any given conclusion" (A500/B528).[22]

This may be understood as follows. A state of affairs is presented in appearance. Reason is thereupon moved to ask for its conditions, that is, the premises upon which it appears in just this way at just this time. The regress thus prescribed is simply the attempt to explain the ordinary data of experience. A full explanation cannot rest content with the statement of the conditions of the initial state of affairs that demanded it. These conditions, in turn, must be explained, and their conditions, until we reach a point at which no further explanation is conceivable. This point, at which the given would appear as self-explanatory and hence necessary, is the Unconditioned.

Kant holds that human reason can no more reach the Unconditioned than it can fail to seek it. To pretend to state anything about it − that is, to treat any point along the regress as if it were the Unconditioned − is to overstep the boundaries of the sensible, produce the antinomies, and engage in intellectual sloth. Within experience, every condition is again conditioned (A508/B536). Hence, the Unconditioned is only legitimate as a regulative idea prescribing a regress that is to take place in terms that are fully empirical:

> It must always advance from every member of the series, as conditioned, to one still more remote; doing so by means either of our own experience, or of the guiding-thread of history, or of the chain of effects and causes. And as the rule further demands, our sole and constant aim must be the extension of the possible empirical employment of the understanding, this being the only proper task of reason in the application of its principles. (A521/B549)

This rule does not and cannot prescribe any determinate regress; it only requires that the regress proceed from appearance to appearance, refusing to treat any condition as final. Thus, the idea of the Unconditioned serves as a *focus imaginarius*: while it is the goal toward which all the efforts of the understanding are directed, the point at which the routes marked out by all its rules converge, it is illusory to think that the conditions we discover actually proceed from it. This illusion is, however, indispensable if the understanding is to be directed beyond present experience.[23] Elsewhere, Kant compares the idea of the Unconditioned to a horizon, which we can continue to approach but never reach (A650/B686; IX 43, 48). It should be noted that all of Kant's attempts to define the Unconditioned must be metaphorical and hence inadequate; for the Unconditioned is an idea (indeed, the chief idea of reason) and Kant insists on a strict definition of 'idea' as a concept to which no corresponding object can be given within sense experience (A327/B384). No idea, therefore, can ever be *known*; although it belongs to every actual experience, no actual experience is ever adequate to it (A311/B368).[24]

Now it seems clear that the idea of the Unconditioned, thus described, is nothing other than what I have called the second part of the principle of sufficient reason, the idea that the world as a whole is fully intelligible. Were we to grasp the totality of all conditions, we would have reached a point where the world was transparent to human reason, having followed every condition to its final, necessary source. Because Kant holds this vision to be unrealizable, he denies that a constitutive version of this principle is possible. The assertion that the Unconditioned is to be found in an object, that is, the cessation of the search for conditions at any point, declaring the series of conditions for a given conditioned to be either finite or infinite, is the source of the antinomies. As a regulative principle, however, this idea is "a *problem* for the understanding, and therefore for the subject, leading it to undertake and to carry on, in accordance with the completeness prescribed by the idea, the regress in the series of conditions of any given conditioned" (A508/B536). The regulative idea of the Unconditioned, Kant holds, is required for scientific inquiry to begin. Without it, although we would, to be sure, have the first part of the principle of sufficient reason, it would do us no good. For as we have seen, the knowledge that every event has a cause is useless without the idea that human reason is capable of tracing the series of causes to a point at which the events that make up the world become intelligible. It is this second idea that first provides the possibility of a concept of explanation.

This idea, which is a product of reason, must be kept distinct from any claims about the world. The demand that reason have adequate premises before making a conclusion is a logical requirement upon reason's correct use. Adherence to this demand is a need of reason; reason is compelled to attempt to satisfy the conditions of its proper employment. We have no justification, however, for asserting that nature is subject to the requirements that constrain reason: "Such a principle . . . does not justify us in demanding from the objects such uniformity as will minister to the convenience and extension of our understanding; and we may not, therefore, ascribe to the maxim any objective validity" (A306/B363). We cannot ensure that nature's conclusions—the conditioned given of the experienced world—have adequate grounds in a series of conditions that, as a whole, is fully explicable. But reason has a right and a need to assume this to be the case. Reason must view nature as constructed in accordance with its own needs so far as this is necessary to render nature accessible to reason's exploration. Reason must, in short, assume that the world is intelligible; or rather, it is allowed every assumption needed in order to make the world intelligible to itself. Without these assumptions of reason, Kant says simply, understanding could not orient itself in nature (V, 193).[25]

If the Unconditioned is the idea of the complete intelligibility of the world as a whole, it is equally the idea that the world as a whole forms a system according to laws. Kant's use of the idea of the Unconditioned is a response to Hume as well as to Leibniz. As argued in section II, Kant's version of Hume's problem of induction involved the claim that the categories determine only the most general form of objects, saying nothing about their empirical uniformities.[26] The phenomena of appearance is so diverse that we might be unable to discover any uniformities at all, experiencing instead a disjointed, disorderly world where we could not predict, much less explain, that one event followed another. We might, by happy chance, discover connections between events here and there. But each of these connections would be accidental from the point of view of understanding—a system of such connections, even more so. (XX, 210; V, 179–80). In order to qualify as empirical law, however, these connections must be thought as necessary; but this necessity cannot be provided by the understanding. Understanding might, that is, make the connection between the rising of the sun and the ending of the night, having had the good fortune to perceive through the myriad of other phenomena that just this combination of events takes place every twenty-four hours. It cannot record this connection as a law; lacking the notion of experience as a system, it has no concept of empirical law (A653/B681; V, 184–85). At most, it could record the continuing presence of this uniformity.

Rather than expecting nature to guarantee the uniformities which regulate our lives, Kant makes our capacity to regulate the source of the possibility of these uniformities. Both in giving sense to the notion of causality and in giving sense to the notion of particular causal regularities, Kant acknowledges Hume's point from the start: neither of these notions can be derived from our experience of nature, they must be found in ourselves. The concept of causality, placed in the understanding, will be constitutive of the possibility of experience. In treating the question of particular causal regularities, Kant goes a step further. Again, he accepts Hume's point that experience does not present us with anything but accidental regularities. Since for Kant, unlike Hume, the categories of the understanding are a necessary part of experience, he will add that particular regularities are accidental *from the point of view of the understanding*, which can discover no source of necessity for any causal connection it has the fortune to find. But Kant presents another point of view in addition to that of the understanding. Reason's postulation of a systematic order in nature is the claim that the empirical regularities we discover must be thought as necessary, that is, as laws of nature: "These rules . . . must be thought by the understanding as laws (that is, as necessary): for otherwise they would not make up an order of nature; even though it neither knows their necessity nor will ever have insight into it" (V, 184).

The concept of the possibility of particular causal laws is thus a product of our freedom. If it is to be part of our experience we must find it there. Kant's intention is not to license scientists to make up uniformities and call them laws of nature. It is, rather, to say that the number of possible uniformities to be gathered from observation is so great that the ones to be counted as lawlike must be determined by the scientist's creativity. Of course there are constraints on such activity, the accepted canons of scientific method, as will be shown below. But only those uniformities which scientists incorporate into a systematic theory will be regarded as lawlike. It should be emphasized that Kant does not hold the act of picking out some uniformity to confer lawlike status on it. On the contrary, Kant's point is that the scientist's choice of a particular uniformity for investigation presupposes something about nature itself. The scientist assumes that nature is systematic and that the process of science is one of uncovering, not of constructing, nature's systematicity: "Now it is clear that reflective judgement could not, in accordance with its nature, undertake to *classify* all of nature according to its empirical differences without the assumption that nature itself *specifies* its transcendental laws according to some principles" (XX, 215). The assumption that the uniformities determined to be lawlike are nature's own uniformities is necessary to distinguish scientific research from art or fantasy. Kant emphasizes this while insisting that the assumption is not a fact that we can know about nature, "thereby one neither prescribes a law to nature, nor does one learn a law from nature through observation (although this principle can be confirmed through observation)" (V, 186).

Kant's discussion is as subtle and difficult as is the notion of a regulative principle. It is misleading to say that the scientist *assumes* nature to be systematic if this is taken to mean (as it did for Hume) that the scientist holds a hypothesis about the world that can never be confirmed. Rather, Kant writes that "the systematic unity (as a mere idea) is, however, only a *projected* unity, to be regarded not as given in itself, but as a problem only" (A647/B675). By describing the idea of systematic unity as a problem, Kant suggests that the scientist, in being guided by a regulative principle of reason, accepts an injunction to go on with the business of attempting to uncover systematicity. It is misguided to question whether there is good evidence for assuming that nature is systematic, for the evidence is nothing less than the whole of natural science itself. All of that evidence, however, still leaves us without guarantees: this is just Hume's point. Kant's response is to refuse to treat the problem of induction as if it were a matter of extracting a promise from the world to behave in certain ways; put this way, the problem is tainted with anthropomorphism, as well as insoluble: nothing can tell us that the regularities we experience in nature will continue to hold.[27] Stating the problem thus makes clear the impossibility of a solution in terms of an increase of knowledge and allows us to consider other ways of regarding it—as a question about us, rather than about the world or, more exactly, as a question about what is reasonable for us to do in the face of the fact that we cannot obtain the desired guarantee from the world.

It is, in short, a question for the province of reason, not of understanding. No fact about the world—no product of the understanding—can resolve a question that is really one of the rationality of our behavior. To think that the solution to this problem is to prove the necessity of natural laws is to confuse the realms of reason and understanding, to ask for a constitutive principle where only a regulative one will do. Constitutive principles determine what is, regulative principles, what ought to be; so Kant sometimes says that constitutive principles concern the possibility, regulative principles, the perfectability, of experience. It should be clear how this distinction can be applied to scientific as well as moral activity. The idea of the Unconditioned expresses reason's insistence that the world ought to be thoroughly intelligible. Recognizing that this idea is a demand upon, not a fact about, nature allows Kant to relocate the problem of induction so that its solution involves not a further attempt to confirm a hypothesis but a justification of the scientist's activities. That justification will take place within the context of a reconception of reason as a whole. Here, as elsewhere, Kant condemns attempts to gain knowledge of what is in principle unknowable in favor of a resolutely practical focus on what we can, and ought, to do.

And yet, it may be retorted, there is something dizzyingly unpractical and resonantly metaphysical in the notion of the Unconditioned itself. In arguing that the idea of the Unconditioned is implicit in every inquiry into nature, Kant sometimes says that the system of science, as opposed to a mere aggregate of common knowledge, rests on the idea of a whole that must precede its parts (IX, 110). It could be objected that this idea, reminiscent of rationalism, is far too strong. Modern science, satisfied with a more pragmatic—indeed, aggregate—conception of knowledge has long since ceased to hold such an ideal. Hence, Kant's claim that the idea of the Unconditioned plays a crucial role in scientific inquiry is at best obsolete, holding only for those more optimistic centuries whose goal was a systematic intelligibility so comprehensive that it is itself hardly intelligible to us today. This objection fails to appreciate Kant's insistence that the idea of the Unconditioned is a regulative one. The suggestion that the hope of a fully intelligible world must be abandoned as unrealistic would come as no surprise to Kant: his own insistence that this hope is unrealizable marks, perhaps, his greatest break with Leibnizian rationalism. His point is, rather, that this hope, as an idea of reason, is nevertheless presupposed in every scientific investigation. Without the idea that behind every conditioned stands another conditioned, and so on ad infinitum, we would have no reason to question the world as it appears; we could not begin to form the concept of such questioning.

While we can, and ought to, give up the hope that we will achieve an explanation that makes the world fully intelligible, we cannot give up the search for such an explanation if we are to engage in the process of explanation at all. This suggests that Kant urges us to adopt an attitude that is paradoxical, even absurd; but what he means is rather simple. He writes that it is an analytic truth that if the conditioned is given, the regress in the series of its conditioned is *given us as a task*: "for it is involved in the very concept of the conditioned that something is referred to as a condition, and if this condition is again itself conditioned, to a more remote condition, and so through all the members of the series" (A498/B526). In saying that the Unconditioned is a necessary idea of reason, Kant is saying that once we have the idea of finding the conditions for one conditioned, it cannot be limited. Any number of external grounds—lack of resources or time or interest or patience—may bring a given investigation to a halt at any point. But once we have begun to determine the series of conditions for any given conditioned, there is no natural place at which to stop the process until we arrive at a point that is self-explanatory, hence absolutely necessary. It is in this sense that the Unconditioned is presupposed in the concept of the conditioned. We may choose to ignore it, we are certain never to attain it, but it is this idea which is the ground of the very concept of explanation itself. There is no

notion of explanation that is not a notion of complete explanation; partial explanations are simply an arbitrary limitation of an idea that is given as a whole.

Now the thought that we must have the idea of the possibility of explanation before
we can begin to explain anything may be uncontroversial. Kant's insight is that this idea
has a radically different character from the kinds of concepts that can belong to the
understanding. The understanding can have no concept of the Unconditioned; for
understanding "merely represents things *as they are*, without considering whether and
how we can obtain knowledge of them" (A498/B526; see also A326/B383). The idea of
explicability involves the idea that there is something behind given appearances, even
though it be, to begin with, only further appearances. It is therefore an idea that cannot
be supplied by a faculty that "merely represents things *as they are*." The idea of
explicability cannot be derived from experience; for it involves the right to make
demands upon experience, an activity that only reason may perform. This claim in no
way underestimates understanding's part in constructing experience: as we have seen, it
is not despite, but because of, understanding's role in shaping experience that it is
incapable of looking beyond it. Note that the idea that explanation, in seeking the
ground of a particular experience, presupposes something behind given appearances is
as valid of mechanistic, as it is of teleological, explanation, which is why Kant calls
both ideals of explanation products of reason (V, 312). For the law that all events are
caused, though necessary for the possibility of mechanistic explanation, is not, by
itself, sufficient to provide the idea of explanation in general.

Kant's point is directed against a view such as Hume's, according to which the
mind is caused to advance from sense data to science by the combination of ideas
presented to the senses with Hume's three principles of association. Hume describes
the process thus:

> All belief of matter of fact or real existence is derived merely from some object,
> present to the memory or the senses, and a customary conjunction between that and
> some other object. Or in other words; having found, in many instances, that any two
> kinds of objects—flame and heat, snow and cold—have always been conjoined
> together; if flame or snow be presented anew to the senses, the mind is carried by
> custom to expect heat or cold, and to believe that such a quality does exist, and will
> discover itself upon a nearer approach. This belief is the necessary result of placing
> the mind in such circumstances . . . which no reasoning or process of the thought
> and understanding is able either to produce or to prevent. (1975, 46–47)

For Hume, the mind is stimulated to generate beliefs, from which it builds theories,
by the action of objects working upon it. Science is the product of generalizations that
have been provoked by the encounter with the objects themselves; reasoning can
neither produce nor hinder this process. Kant argued, of course, that even the most
low-level generalizations require the operation of the categories whose existence
Hume does not acknowledge. Important for our purposes is the further point that such
generalizations cannot form a foundation for science, for they contain nothing within
them that would provide a stimulus to explanation. Ideas of objects and principles of
association might suffice to provide us with collections of very minimal statements of
fact. Lacking the possibility of conceiving anything beyond those statements, they
cannot suffice to drive them to form something that would constitute experience. For
this, what Kant calls transcendent principles are necessary.

We might try to make this clearer by attempting to imagine a tribe of people who had only the principles that Hume describes.[28] This would give them, according to Kant, something like the capacities of Adam and Eve before the Fall. These would surely include the ability to make and remember such generalizations as "If I put my hand into the fire, it will hurt," which they might sort into higher-level generalizations like "Fire is hot." But a traveller who asked them, "Who do you think made the world?" would not be understood, for his subjects would neither have a notion of 'world' nor of its absence. Thus, these people would lack not only natural science (though they might enjoy a very limited technology) but the rudiments of religion and philosophy as well. To speculate about the nature of creation, we must be able to imagine the possibility that the world we know might not have existed. But counterfactuals are required not merely for speculation about general questions concerning the world as a whole but for those concerning any particular piece of it. The capacity to ask why something is the way that it is presupposes the capacity to imagine that the present state of affairs might be other than it is. Thus, one could say that our fictitious tribe would have no curiosity, but this is not a psychological point: they would lack that which makes curiosity possible. This includes, at least, the capacity to conceive of the world as a (potential) system of connections uniting while transcending the particular objects we experience.

These suggestions are, in a large measure, simply elaborations of Kant's general claim that ends are needed for action, and ends are something that by their nature, go beyond that which is given. The casualness of Kant's statement of the equivalence of ideas and ends may, however, raise the following objection. Grant that the idea of explicability is needed for us to begin to explain anything and that this idea, going behind given experience, is fundamentally different from those of the understanding. This may show the idea of the Unconditioned to be necessary for the purposes of explanation, but it does not show it to be sufficient. How, it may be asked, can the possession of this idea alone be a motive to explanation?

Kant's distinction between regulative and constitutive principles is, among other things, an attempt to remove the temptation of objections such as this one. The positing of an end is equivalent to a demand for its realization, and ideas of reason simply are ends. This is what is meant by Kant's statement that they are not items of knowledge but bearers of guidance (A827/B855). Ideas do not first tell us about the world and then tell us what to do about it. They do not tell us about the world at all but are purely subjective, concerning how we are to behave. So in the third *Critique* reason appears not only as the faculty of ends but the faculty of desire. To ask why the mere possession of the idea of the Unconditioned is sufficient to move us to seek it is to reify the idea of the Unconditioned: that idea, functioning as the title of all concepts of reason, is not the representation of an object but simply the basis of principles whose sole function is to "incite us to tear down all the boundary fences of an entirely new domain." Further examination of how regulative principles provide the structure of science should make this claim a little clearer.[29]

Kant's equation of ideas and ends connects two questions about the construction of science that have been held separate. The first is a question about what moves us to do science. Perhaps because a distinction between the context of discovery and the context of justification would assign such a question to psychology, this issue has received little attention. Still, early empiricist accounts of science are such, Kant would argue, as to permit no tenable answer to the question, and it is not difficult to find modern statements of just the sort of account that Kant opposes.[30] The second question concerns the theoretical presuppositions that pervade those sciences devoted to the observation of experience, a question of great interest to contemporary philosophers.[31] Kant's connection of these questions has a variety of grounds. Those theoretical presuppositions must be the work of reason, though they are not knowledge of observation; and reason is not a contemplative faculty but one that finds its function in practice. Thus, the regulative principles of reason are in a position to provide both the motive and the presuppositions of science.

IV. Systematic Unity

The previous section should have shown that Kant's claim that reason is needed to provide systematization to the truths of the understanding is hardly a trivial matter or an afterthought. In seeking the explanation of experience reason seeks its systematization. The idea of the Unconditioned is the idea of a systematization of the whole aggregate of knowledge provided by the understanding. In functioning as the end of scientific inquiry, the idea of the Unconditioned presents the possibility of a systematization of the very basic observation-statements that understanding produces. Without the assumption that nature as a whole forms a system according to empirical laws, there would be no grounds for science to begin.

This is perhaps the most fundamental sense in which reason provides systematization, yet Kant speaks of several others. The task of the present section is to examine the particular ways in which reason constructs knowledge through its search for systematic unity. If understanding produces merely statements of fact and the general truths of the categories, it contains no principle of organization with which to encompass them. In part, the principles of organization required are logical ones. Reason organizes the statements of understanding into premises and conclusions, grounds and consequences. Kant argues that this logical use of reason is not sufficient; a real use must occur as well. An idea of science as a whole must precede these logical transformations by providing a motive for them to take place, as well as a structure through which they can find meaning (IX, 71–72). The organization of the material provided by understanding requires principles of selection and choice, notions of relevance and appropriateness. None of these can fittingly be called items of knowledge: they are derived neither from experience nor from the conditions of its possibility. Yet it is certain that they are basic to our construction of knowledge. One might think of the faculties of sensibility and understanding as functioning like a movie camera without an editor, blindly recording the passing show, or of understanding as capable of forming sentences but not paragraphs. These metaphors are not wholly satisfactory. Kant, as we saw, gives no description of the experience of a creature lacking reason but not understanding, perhaps because he believed no real description of such experience to be possible. The difficulty of such description only serves to emphasize the depth of the structure that reason's principles give to the products of understanding.

Let us examine the ways in which reason produces systematization. The least important, although the easiest to recognize, is the classification that produces the aesthetic pleasure to be gained from the greatest possible systematic interconnection of our knowledge. Kant describes this pleasure as follows: "The discovery that two or more empirical heterogeneous laws of nature may be combined under one principle comprehending them both is the ground of a very marked pleasure, often even of an admiration, which does not cease, though we may be already quite familiar with it" (V, 187). Kant's frequent mention of this gratification has led to the suggestion that he had converted his peculiar taste for contemplating Linnean classifications (an example he often cites with approval) into the highest form of intellectual activity; his recurrent interest in apparently superfluous details of the architectonic of his own philosophical work has seemed to confirm this suggestion. Actually, the systematic comprehension that Kant more likely has in mind here is Newton's achievement, whose spectacularity was largely seen to consist in the provision of a unified explanation for apparently diverse phenomena.[32] Thus, he writes:

> [Reason] seeks for the unity of this knowledge in accordance with ideas which go far beyond all possible experience. . . . Thus, for instance, if at first our imperfect experience leads us to regard the orbits of the planets as circular, and if we subsequently detect deviations therefrom, we trace the deviations to that which can change the circle, in accordance with a fixed law, through all the infinite intermediate degrees, into one of those divergent orbits. . . . Thus, under the guidance of these principles, we discover a unity in the generic form of the orbits, and thereby a unity in the cause of all the laws of planetary motion, namely, gravitation. (A662/B690)

As this quotation shows, the attainment of systematic unity on Newton's scale is not merely an aesthetic byproduct of Newton's achievement but is central to that achievement itself; in this case, the discovery of unity becomes explanatory. As wonderful as Kant took even this systematization to be, however, it is clearly secondary to the other kinds of systematization that reason is to perform.

A second function of systematization is that intended in Kant's statements that reason secures the greatest possible extension of the understanding (A645/B673, A680/B708). Reason's capacity to surpass the confines of experience allows theory to be extended to the realm of the unobservable. In this way, it both constructs and anticipates entities that could not otherwise be incorporated into science. In the passage just quoted, gravitation is one such construction of reason; magnetic force and absolute space are others. Kant uses the following example to describe the function of theoretical constructs in science:

> By general admission, *pure earth, pure water, pure air*, etc. are not to be found. We require, however, the concepts of them (though insofar as their complete purity is concerned, they have their origin solely in reason) in order properly to determine the share which each of these natural causes has in producing appearances. Thus in order to explain the chemical interactions of bodies in accordance with the idea of a mechanism, every kind of matter is reduced to earths (*qua* mere weight), to salts and inflammable substances (*qua* force), and to water and air as vehicles (machines, as it were, by which the first two produce their effects). The modes of expression usually employed are, indeed, somewhat different; but the influence of reason on the classifications of the natural scientist is still easily detected. (A646/B674)

In this example, theoretical constructs that cannot be given in experience are needed in order to determine the causal principles of events in experience. Because the notions of pure earth, and so on no longer play a role in chemistry, this example may appear "bewildering" (Kemp Smith 1962, 551); but Kant's use of regulative principles of reason to resolve the debate between atomistic and dynamic conceptions of matter will be more convincing to modern readers.[33] A somewhat different way in which reason extends the scope of the understanding is to be found in Kant's suggestion, confined to a footnote in the third *Critique*, that some version of an evolutionary hypothesis may be true. He calls such a hypothesis a daring venture of reason, neither suggested nor confirmed by any experience yet capable of playing a role in the explanation of phenomena: "Certain water animals transform themselves gradually into marsh animals and from these, after some generations, into land animals. A priori, in the judgment of reason alone, there is no contradiction. Only experience gives no example of it; according to experience, all generation that we know is *generatio homonyma*" (V, 419). Because reason may speculate unconstrained by experience, it is able to introduce concepts to which no experience is adequate. This introduction takes place on several levels. In the example of gravitation, reason constructs entities that serve as the ground of a variety of phenomena. In the case of pure earth, or ideal motion, reason creates ideas that will never be given in experience but that provide the paradigms in terms of which existing objects will be explained. In the evolutionary example, reason is able to propose hypotheses that explain phenomena in terms never yet experienced. These constructs serve functions as diverse as their status. Some are objects of possible experience, even if our particular position in time and space precludes such experience; some are not.[34] Still, all these concepts must play a certain role with respect to experience before they can be used as part of an explanation of it. But reason's introduction of theoretical constructs is not the result of empirical generalization but is prior to any experiential grounding: "These concepts of reason are not derived from nature; on the contrary, we interrogate nature in accordance with these ideas, and consider our knowledge as defective so long as it is not adequate to them" (A645/B673).

Why does Kant call reason's introduction of theoretical concepts part of a search for systematic unity? Such concepts are surely needed for constructing any knowledge we might regard as systematic; but in some instances, at least, Kant has something more direct in mind:

> We may illustrate this by an instance of the employment of reason. Among the various kinds of unity which conform to the concepts of the understanding is that of causality of a substance, which is called power. The various appearances of one and the same substance show at first sight so great a diversity that at the start we have to assume just as many powers as there are different effects. . . . Now there is a logical maxim which requires that we reduce, so far as possible, this seeming diversity, by comparing these with one another and detecting their hidden identity. . . . Though logic is not capable of deciding whether a *fundamental power* actually exists, the idea of such a power is the problem involved in a systematic representation of powers. (A649/B677)

Here reason's postulation of a power – one cause behind the multiplicity of effects – leads to a search that understanding could not begin. Kant calls this a search for unity;

it is clear that the attempt to find one power underlying the various manifestations of power is at the same time the search for anything that could count as explanation.

Reason's systematization encompasses not only the postulation of unobservable entities but an even more fundamental aspect of theory construction. Reason is responsible for distinguishing the genuine observation of nature from "mere empirical groping around." It forms the hypotheses and sets the experiments that yield the data from which explanations are formed; it provides methodological principles that guide scientific inquiry. Reason's ability to do this stems from characteristics we have already noted: its role as an autonomous power gives it the capacity to select the elements of experience that are to be considered as well as, more generally, the capacity to formulate hypotheses that are not simply abstractions of statements derived from experience. The importance of these abilities is emphasized by Kant in a crucial passage added to the second edition:

> When Galileo caused balls, the weights of which he had himself previously determined, to roll down an inclined plane; when Torricelli made the air carry a weight which he had calculated beforehand to be equal to that of a definite volume of water; or, in more recent times, when Stahl changed metals into oxides and oxides back into metals, by withdrawing something and then restoring it, a light broke upon all students of nature. They learned that reason has insight only into that which it produces after a plan of its own, that it must not allow itself to be kept, as it were, on nature's leading-strings but must itself show the way with principles of judgement based on fixed laws, constraining nature to give answer to questions of reason's own determining. Accidental observations, made in obedience to no previously thought-out plan, can never be made to yield a necessary law, which alone reason is concerned to discover. Reason, holding in one hand its principles, according to which alone concordant appearances can be admitted as laws, and in the other hand the experiment which it has devised in conformity with these principles, must approach nature in order to be taught by it. It must not, however, do so in the character of a pupil who listens to everything the teacher chooses to say, but of an appointed judge who compels the witness to answer questions which he himself has formulated . . . It is thus that the study of nature has entered on the secure path of a science, after having for so many centuries been nothing but a process of merely random groping. (B xii)

In this quotation, reason is responsible for a variety of tasks. Most obviously, reason devises the experiments upon which progress in natural science is based. Observations that are merely accidental, passively made of whatever phenomena nature happens to present, can yield no laws of nature. In constructing these experiments, reason relies on principles of judgment that, embodying expectations about the general tendencies in nature, provide directions as to how the inquiry is to proceed. Even more importantly, only reason's principles determine whether lawlike appearances are admitted as laws. I quote this passage at length in order to stress the degree to which Kant's view is opposed to the prevailing scientific ideology of his day. For other writers — rationalists, as well as empiricists — the scientific revolutions of the sixteenth and seventeenth centuries were thought to have been effected by the advance from unconstrained speculation to the patient observation of natural phenomena. Those features of theories and theorizing that did not derive from observation, crudely understood, were left unremarked by philosophers of science, as well as scientists themselves.

The revolutionary nature of Kant's claims can be seen most dramatically when contrasted with Bacon's *New Organon*. Although a quotation from the latter serves as motto to the first *Critique* and the paragraph before the passage just quoted credits Bacon with a leading role in the revolution of natural science, Kant's explanation of progress in science is diametrically opposed to that of Bacon. Here is one of Bacon's attacks on Aristotle, who is charged with sophistry despite the fact that his works include "frequent dealing with experiments":

> He did not consult experience, as he should have done, for the purpose of framing his decisions and axioms, but having first determined his questions according to his will, he then resorts to experience, and bending her into conformity with his placets, leads her about like a captive in a procession. So that even on this count he is more guilty than his modern followers, the schoolmen, who have abandoned experience altogether. (Bacon, 1960, 1. 63)

Kant, we have just seen, attributes the revolutions in natural science to exactly the sort of process that Bacon condemns. Only by "constraining nature to give answer to questions of reason's own determining," as a judge compels a witness, could physics be placed on the sure path of a science. Kant's remarks point to the beginning of a sophisticated account of the elements involved in theory construction, next to which Bacon's discussion appears quaint and rhetorical. Nor should it be thought that the years between Bacon and Kant, which saw such advances in natural science itself, brought significantly more developed views of the role of theoretical principles in empirical observation.[35] Newton, for example, claimed to have achieved his results by following Baconian dicta of pure reliance on observation.[36] To be sure, even Bacon himself sometimes acknowledges that blind experience "merely gropes in the dark," that progress in science requires experiment to proceed in some regular order (Bacon, 1960, 1. 79, 100) But his account of the way in which science is to develop from what he calls obedience to experience is both crude and metaphorical, leaving open all questions about how the experimental order is to be constructed. Hence, the prevailing conclusion of the *New Organon* is that one need only remove dogmatic prejudices and lead scientists to the phenomena themselves in order for science to flourish.

Kant is well aware of the danger of reading our own preconceptions into observation but insists that this abuse cannot undermine the validity of the claim that principles of reason must precede and guide observation and experiment (VIII, 161). Note that Kant does not merely maintain that these principles are *permitted* to play a role in scientific inquiry that transgresses Baconian strictures; it is, he holds, precisely the recognition that reason must take an active role in guiding and judging experience that is responsible for the spectacular discoveries of seventeenth-century science. In particular, reason's capacity not only to extend beyond, but even to contradict, the testimony provided by the senses is the source of scientific progress. Thus, Kant writes:

> The fundamental laws of the motions of heavenly bodies gave established certainty to what Copernicus had at first assumed only as an hypothesis, and at the same time yielded proof of the invisible force (the Newtonian attraction) which holds the universe together. The latter would have remained forever undiscovered if Copernicus had not dared, in a manner contradictory of the senses but yet true, to seek the observed movements, not in heavenly bodies, but in the spectator. (Bxxi)

Kant's suggestion that the revolutions in scientific thought turned not on the direct observation of nature but on a theoretically constructed conception of nature that was directly opposed to immediate experience and common sense is confirmed by many contemporary philosophers and historians of science.[37] We may indeed suppose that just because Copernican and Newtonian assumptions have long been part of our own observational equipment, Kant was far more aware than we can be of the degree to which these assumptions have their source in a capacity to transcend, even resist, direct sensory experience, despite the fact that this source, for reasons that would surely be interesting to explore, was obscured by the scientific ideology of his time.

Important as are the functions fulfilled by all these aspects of reason's search for systematic unity, a final sense has been suggested that is even more fundamental.[38] This sense is implicit in the discussion in section III, where reason's regulative principle that nature forms a system according to law is the basis for every attempt at explanation, but it specifies reason's contribution to science at a further, more determinate level. This is the suggestion that systematic unity is a criterion of empirical truth itself. If transcendental idealism denies us access to a noumenal realm of truths independent of all human cognitive capacities, the necessity of empirical truths can no longer be grounded in alleged insight into the nature of things in themselves. Kant proposes, instead, a version of what is known today as a coherence theory of truth.[39] Reason's search for systematic unity is the search for this coherence. While isolated observation-sentences may be confirmed by sense experience, any statement of empirical law can only be regarded as such in virtue of its incorporation in a system of beliefs as a whole. Butts describes this contrast succinctly: "The test of the truth of attempts to understand is the correspondence of concept to empirical instance; the test of truth of attempts to be rational is coherence of isolated bits of what we truly understand" (1984, 247).

This test places reason at the end as well as the beginning of the scientific endeavor. We saw that the highest principle of reason, the idea of the Unconditioned, was required to provide the possibility of, and the desire for, explanation required to question the world as it is given to us. The idea that explanation is possible and the idea that nature is systematizable are virtually equivalent, so that the idea of the Unconditioned is an injunction to proceed with the discovery of systematic unity in nature. That process requires the use of reason in more determinate ways, as a faculty free to set hypotheses and research programs, to postulate the unobservable factors needed for testing them, and to determine which aspects of data are relevant to test. At the end of all these activities, it is reason's search for system that again proves to be crucial: only those generalizations that can be integrated into a body of explanation will be counted as empirical laws.

V. The Means to Science

If Kant's claim that reason's search for systematic unity is necessary for the possibility of science is understood to encompass such aspects of theory construction as those just described, then the charge that his notion of systematization could prove superfluous is ungrounded. Far from being dependent upon an obsolete idealist goal of total intelligibility, Kant's notion of systematization contains elements that no contemporary philosopher would deny to be essential to scientific inquiry. To be sure, the Baconian picture of science as founded on straightforward ascent from observation to generalizations derived from experience has not lacked modern defenders.[40] But even those philosophers who hoped to reduce all scientific theory to observation-sentences would not assert that science could actually be constructed from low-level empirical generalizations without the systematic elements that Kant describes. Reason is required in order to connect previously unrelated phenomena like the moon and the tides; to postulate unobserved or unobservable entities like atoms and gravity; to provide paradigms, like pure earth and ideal motion, which are used in explaining actual experience; to posit hypotheses, like that of evolution, which experience cannot confirm directly; to provide methodological principles, such as Occam's Razor, which direct scientific inquiry; to organize data based on principles of selection and relevance; and finally, to reformulate the problem of induction so as to provide grounds for assuming that we can discover natural laws at all. Thus, Kant's conception of reason's search for systematic unity may seem in danger not of proving unnecessary but of being so obvious as to appear merely trivial.

This very obviousness is, however, precisely the strength of Kant's view, given his most general aims. For in constructing a conception of reason, Kant is not primarily concerned to develop new insights into the history and theory of sciences, although he actually did so.[41] His discussion of the role of reason in science *should* issue in a description of scientists' need for theoretical elements that no serious thinker would dispute. By giving an account of science that everyone will grant, which is made on the basis of a reconstructed notion of reason, Kant provides the foundations for a model of reason that should come to seem equally obvious. His goal is to demonstrate the unity of reason, that is, to provide a conception of reason that functions comparably in science, religion, morality, and philosophy. If his insistence upon the need for reason in constructing science can be shown to be thoroughly uncontroversial, then the suggestion that reason, functioning similarly, is equally necessary in other areas, acquires considerable plausibility. For the argument for the need for reason in science was not an argument for any undetermined model of reason but reason construed in such a way as to be appropriate to these other realms as well. Kant's demonstration that regulative principles of reason are fundamental to the foundations of Newtonian science is the key to his defense of a regulative conception of reason.

Having shown some sort of systematic activity on reason's part to be necessary, it remains to examine Kant's directions as to how this activity is to take place. Kant says that reason provides a number of principles that guide inquiry into nature, offering some criteria for applying the general regulative principle to seek nature's systematic unity. He gives several lists of such principles, which he variously describes as well-known maxims, currently fashionable formulas, and aphorisms of metaphysical wisdom. One such list runs "Nature takes the shortest way; yet it makes no leaps, either in the sequence of its changes, or in the juxtaposition of specifically different forms; its vast variety in empirical laws is, for all that, unity under a few principles, and so forth" (V, 182). The status of such principles is difficult to determine. This is partly because Kant often lists them in order to argue that regulative principles of reason are, in fact, presupposed in working natural science. Although philosophers have not hitherto acknowledged it, Kant writes, their formulation of such maxims indicate that they, too, hold scientific procedures to depend upon the regulative principles he has stated (A651/B679). The demonstration of a principle's implicit use by rational inquirers is, then, meant to function as part of an argument that a principle is a principle of reason. But it is important to emphasize the difference between Kant's use of these principles and those of other thinkers. Leibniz's reliance, for example, on the same principles takes place without a trace of the self-consciousness about their status that is to be found in Kant. For Leibniz, Occam's Razor is of just the same order as an empirical law of nature. Rather than arguing that certain presuppositions are necessary in order for science to proceed, Leibniz argues that certain metaphysical propositions, which play a role in scientific investigations, must be necessarily true.

Kant's discussion may suggest that the maxims he lists are only common versions of the regulative principle to seek the Unconditioned. This is misleading: the maxims are further specifications of that principle and thus provide some guidance in following it. Although part of the argument used to justify these maxims depends upon their being simply special cases of the general principle, Kant also tries to provide individual arguments for their use.

The argument likely to seem most convincing is that given for the use of Occam's Razor, a maxim Kant includes in each of his lists of methodological canons. Here is one statement:

> That such unity is to be found in nature, is presupposed by philosophers in the well-known scholastic maxim, that rudiments or principles must not be unnecessarily multiplied. This maxim declares that things by their very nature supply material for the unity of reason, and that the seemingly infinite variety need not hinder us from assuming that behind this variety there is a unity of fundamental properties – properties from which the diversity can be derived through repeated determination. (A652/B680)

Kant's point here is simply that in using the maxim that entities are not to be multiplied beyond necessity, scientists must make the assumption that nature is constructed so as to be appropriate to such a maxim. But in prescribing Occam's Razor, scientists do not merely acknowledge the need for some regulative principle of reason to direct their inquiry. The idea that there is some unity behind the infinite diversity of nature does not require the idea that nature contain the smallest possible number of basic entities. This latter idea is a further claim, intended as a prescription for seeking nature's unity. To understand just how it is meant to work, we must consider another principle introduced in the first *Critique* discussion, the opposite of Occam's Razor. If Occam's Razor is to be formulated as the principle that entities are not to be unnecessarily multiplied, the principle that Kant calls the law of specification is the claim that entities are not to be unnecessarily diminished. These principles must be used together, each balancing the other. Occam's Razor directs us to seek the Unconditioned by finding as much unity in nature as possible. On the other hand, Kant points out, knowledge is determinate, achieved in part by the continued specification of our concepts (A656/B684). The law of specification is required because an explanation that did not incorporate nature's diversity would be neither empirical nor interesting. A good explanation balances the claims of unity and diversity, showing how fundamental underlying principles manifest themselves as the differences of the natural world.

Two kinds of explanations may be mentioned here in order to illustrate the temptations against which Kant invokes the two principles just described. One is the scholastic explanation by reference to powers or virtues of entities, which makes no attempt to discover an underlying structure of the behavior of the *explicandum*. We have learned nothing when we have learned that opium produces sleep because of its dormative virtue, for we have thereby done nothing to go beyond the given phenomena. This explanation provides no principle that we could use in connection with the rest of the body of our knowledge; it merely redescribes the question raised. Consider, on the other hand, Thales's supposed discovery that all is water. Here, indeed, is an assertion of the underlying unity of nature; but it is no more useful than the preservation of diversity that vitiated scholastic attempts at natural explanation. Each kind of explanation fails to be genuinely explanatory because neither provides principles that could be incorporated into a systematic treatment of nature embracing both the unity and the diversity to be found in it. Kant holds that each of these kinds of explanation is the outcome of a natural tendency of human reason. Neither tendency is derived from nature, although each may find its own confirmation there:

> If it rested on empirical grounds it would come later than the systems, whereas it has in fact itself given rise to all that is systematic in nature. The formulation of these laws is not due to any secret design of making an experiment, by putting them forth as merely tentative suggestions. Such anticipations, when confirmed, yield strong evidence in support of the view that the hypothetically conceived unity is well grounded; and such evidence has therefore in this respect a certain utility. (A660/ B689; see also A657/B685)

Human reason's task is to balance these tendencies and, by the manipulation of each, to produce an explanation that succumbs to neither.

It may be tempting to view these principles as having more of an abstract status than they do. In this case, Occam's Razor could be equivalent to the injunction to seek the Unconditioned, while the law of specification would forbid us to find it in nature. But this would be mistaken. Reason is forbidden to posit either complete unity or complete specification as given in the natural world, just in virtue of the fact that its principles are regulative; no further constraints are necessary. Nor is the Unconditioned to be initially conceived as anything more ontologically determinate than a complete explanation of the world as a whole. The specificity and unity we are enjoined to seek are simply necessary components of such an explanation. The principles that Kant gives are, therefore, alternating steps in the search for the Unconditioned. Kant illustrates the ordinary character of these maxims by describing each as a mode of thought that often predominates in different thinkers. Some temperaments are more attached to unity, some, more to manifoldness. Similarly, he writes, greater reliance upon one or the other of these maxims will lead to different kinds of discovery.

Kant attempts to derive another principle, the principle of the continuity of forms, from these two. This third principle, also stated as the claim that nature makes no leaps, embodies the idea that nature is composed of a continuous scale of created beings, in which each species is related to others by gradual degrees of difference. This idea guided most of the scientific research of Kant's day;[42] its abuse is criticized by him in the first *Critique*:

> Observation and insight in the constitution of nature could never justify us in the objective assertion of the law. The steps of this ladder, as they are presented to us in nature, stand much too far apart; and what may seem to us small differences are usually in nature itself wide gaps, so that from any such observations we can come to no decision in regard to nature's design — especially if we bear in mind that in so great a multiplicity of things there can never be much difficulty in finding similarities and approximations. (A668/B696)

The constitutive version of this principle, then, is thoroughly unjustified. Experience does not confirm it, nor is the progress of science furthered by the assertion that the distance between natural species is infinitely small. There is, however, a more plausible, regulative version of the principle, which is the result of the combination of the two principles already discussed. Kant's idea is that the completeness of systematic explanation requires both an ascent to the higher genera (a discovery of principles of unity) and a descent to the lower species (a complete specification of phenomena). If both of these processes were to occur, it would be seen that all the manifold genera are simply divisions of a single universal genus (A659/B687). This, I think, is simply to reiterate what was just stated: a genuine explanation must account for diversity as the product of an underlying unity. From this, Kant says, it is a direct step to the claim that all differences of species border on one another or that there are no gaps in nature. He summarizes the relationship between the three principles thus:

> The first law keeps us from resting satisfied with an excessive number of different original genera, and bids us pay due regard to homogeneity; the second, in turn, imposes a check upon this tendency toward unity, and insists that before we proceed to apply a universal concept to individuals we distinguish subspecies within it. The third law combines these two laws by prescribing that even among the utmost manifoldness we observe homogeneity in the gradual transition from one species to another, and thus recognize a relationship of the different branches, as all springing from the same stem. (A660/B688)

Kant's wording is important, for it indicates that the principles state not facts about the world but suggestions about how we are to approach it. The law of the continuity of forms bids us direct our inquiry in a particular way, proceeding from each species to every other by a gradual increase of diversity. It is this character that prevents Kant from engaging in the excess that this principle allowed to Leibniz, excesses that Kant himself details in the penultimate passage quoted.[43]

The regulative principle of the Unconditioned contains a twofold idea: we must seek systematic unity in nature, and it must be possible to find it. All three principles discussed are specifications of this general principle. They provide rules for obtaining systematic unity; or rather, they embody the rules that scientists have used in obtaining it. Kant sketches arguments for the validity of these rules and takes Maupertuis to have justified another one, the Law of Least Action. But Kant does not seem to hold these or any other particular principles to be necessary. They are, rather, the most reliable canons of scientific method available. His lists of them vary, although there is much overlap, and they are deliberately open-ended. This suggests that Kant intended to leave specifications of the methods of inquiry rather fluid, so that new rules could be added and old ones discarded as need required. Nevertheless, it is clear that they are rules and not psychological descriptions; they do not tell us how judgments have been made but how judgments should be made. Thus, they are in no sense empirical but are principles of reason (V, 182).

Now this entails that the application of the idea of the Unconditioned is indeterminate. Kant gives no sure guidelines for the systematization of nature. Indeed, he explicitly states that the law of continuity, while not a "mere methodological device," gives us only very general instruction: it "yields no criterion whatsoever as to how far, and in what manner, we are to prosecute the search" (A661/B689). This is surely the case for the other methodological principles on Kant's lists. The guidelines that he offers for controlling reason's postulation of unobservable entities or untestable hypotheses (roughly, that such acceptance is contingent on the real, not merely logical, possibility of such entities; that it must contribute to an explanation of observable aspects of experience; and that it must cohere systematically with the rest of our theories) might easily be extended to apply to reason's methodological principles.[44] These criteria, however, may put constraints on the acceptance of particular principles, as on the acceptance of entities or hypotheses, but they will determine the former no more than the latter.

Does this suggest that the regulative idea is lacking in content? Such a suggestion may be furthered by the fact that Kant's attempt to provide criteria for its application leads to principles that are the opposite of one another. The maxim urging us to seek the greatest possible unity and the maxim enjoining us to seek the greatest possible diversity seem to cancel each other out. Kant tells us, however, that only constitutive statements lead to real conflict. Depending on our line of inquiry at a particular time, we may choose to follow one regulative maxim and ignore the other. A fuller discussion of the nature of the content of regulative principles will be given in section VIII. Let it be emphasized here that the application of an idea of reason cannot be automatic: choice and awareness are required to determine how reason's principles are to be employed. Were the rules of scientific method determinate, they would imply a constitutive claim about the natural world. And this, of course, would involve us in an attempt at an a priori construction of natural science. It should be noted that the lack of determinacy of methodological guidelines is not a feature peculiar to Kant's account of science. No philosopher of science has been particularly successful in providing specific rules to guarantee a maximum of scientific truth, although attempts to construct a "logic of inquiry" have been made often enough.[45] Kant's distinction between regulative and constitutive principles shows why this failure is natural, and equally, undetrimental to the continued pursuit of scientific truth. What is most crucial about the methodological rules Kant lists is that they prescribe a regress from the given conditioned to the totality of all conditions, while requiring that the regress advance only from appearances to appearances. The fact that they embody ways that have fruitfully guided the search for systematicity in the past is not unimportant, but Kant is not committed to these particular guidelines. Other general principles that performed the same function could replace them.

VI. The Teleological Account

The third *Critique* treats at length a suggestion that was briefly made in the first: although explanations of nature must be given in mechanistic terms, we must assume the universe as a whole to be purposive, the product of a wise and omnipotent author. This assumption, he tells us, is a need of reason, which cannot be fully satisfied with a merely mechanistic account of nature. Kant thus introduces as necessary for the practice of science an idea that seemed to be an impediment to its progress. As we saw in chapter 1, the use of final causes was already anachronistic in Leibniz's day; and Kant himself insists that the argument using evidence of design in nature to demonstrate the existence of a supreme designer had been finally and decisively undermined by Hume's *Dialogues*. To be sure, Kant subjects reason's use of teleological concepts to severe strictures: they cannot form part of a proof of God's existence, nor can they be used in actual explanations of nature. Yet Kant's invocation of these strictures has seemed unconvincing. The absence of sustained discussion of the way in which the appeal to teleology is meant to further the construction of science has left many readers bewildered or embarassed by a discussion that seems to be nothing but a weakened and covert version of the argument from design. What was Kant's intention in reasserting the necessity of final causes?

It is sometimes suggested that Kant's interest in teleology was the result of his thought about biology. Since no biology in Kant's day was equipped to come close to an explanation of living phenomena in mechanistic terms, Kant was forced to appeal to purposive explanation. Kant does discuss the inadequacy of mechanistic explanation for biological processes in several portions of the third *Critique*. But this discussion concerns the explanations of living things considered as individuals, not of nature as a whole. To argue from the inadequacy of mechanistic explanation for some natural beings to the inadequacy of such explanation for the natural world as a whole would be fully unwarranted. Kant discusses biological phenomena, rather, because such phenomena "first accord objective reality to the concept of a purpose of nature," introducing the notion of teleology into the science of nature (V, 376). Rather than supposing Kant to have concluded that nature as a whole required teleological explanation solely on the basis of reflections about biology, Buchdahl has proposed that Kant was influenced by Maupertuis's discovery of the Law of Least Action, which, he argues, "provided a clinching paradigm" for the purposive organization of nature as a whole (1969, 521). If the Law of Least Action is viewed primarily as a specification of the assumptions of the systematicity and simplicity of nature, this suggestion is a great deal nearer the truth than the references to biology. But it is misleading to view Maupertuis's discovery as having provided the impetus to Kant's assertion of the necessity of teleology by providing evidence for it. To search for the motives of Kant's appeal to teleology in this way is to fail to appreciate the exact content of that appeal as well as its regulative status. The question whether the organization of nature is possible only on the supposition of a system of final causes is a question for metaphysics, not physics. (VIII, 179). Though his discussion makes use of examples from the natural sciences, Kant states that any attempt of natural science to determine the matter on the basis of the evidence of its own labors would be meddling in others' business (V, 382). To understand the meaning of Kant's appeal to teleology, we must look past any particular problems or discoveries of natural science.

I will argue that the injunction to assume that nature is purposive while permitting only mechanistic explanations in science is simply a further specification of the injunction to seek the Unconditioned but to refuse to find it in the natural world. The whole content of the appeal to teleology is the idea that natural science requires the assumption that there is order and systematicity in nature; we must be able to think nature accessible to reason before we can begin to make it intelligible to ourselves. Kant's connection of teleology and intelligibility should seem less surprising in light of chapter 1, where I argued that the notion of final causes is central to Leibniz's construal of the principle of sufficient reason. As he asserts against Spinoza, only a world that is the product of an intelligent author's free choice is a world we could hope to understand. In section III, I claimed that Kant's idea of the Unconditioned is equivalent to the second part of the principle of sufficient reason. It follows that Kant's use of teleology can be viewed as a radical transformation of Leibniz's attempt to determine the conditions that allow us to make the world intelligible.

This transformation is dependent on the notion of a regulative principle. Kant claims that the only way in which we can conceive nature to be systematic is by conceiving it to have been created by an intelligent author acting according to ends. But this claim is entered as a claim about our abilities: it is not necessary in itself, and it certainly tells us nothing about the world. For example, he writes:

> It is one thing to say, "The production of certain things of nature or of nature as a whole is only possible through a cause which determines itself to action according to design" and quite another to say, "I can, *according to the peculiar constitution of my cognitive faculties*, judge concerning the possibility of those things and their production in no other way than by conceiving for this a cause working according to design, i.e., a Being which is productive in a way analogous to the causality of an intelligence." In the former case I wish to establish something concerning the object and am bound to establish the objective reality of an assumed concept; in the latter, reason only determines the use of my cognitive faculties, appropriately to their peculiarities, and to the essential conditions of their range and limits. (V, 397–98)

The point of Kant's appeal to teleology can only be understood if his insistence that it does not give us knowledge of the world is fully appreciated. In this passage, as in many others, Kant contrasts his assertion of purposiveness with previous, constitutive versions. All possible objective positions concerning the purposiveness of nature have, he says, been tried and found wanting; the only remaining possibility is a critical solution, that is, one whose capacity to direct the use of reason is grounded solely on an investigation of our faculties of knowledge. Kant's assertion of teleology will not determine any objects in the world but only our relation to them. This means that the assertion, like the assertion of other regulative principles, is not a statement in an ordinary sense. Its real content is a directive for our behavior. What looks like a cognitive claim (that God created the world according to ends) is simply a model that we can use in giving life and body to the directive to seek systematic unity. We neither need to use, nor are justified in using, that model for other than illustrative purposes. Kant often uses the word 'analogy' in explaining his appeal to teleology; we can only understand nature as a product created after the analogy of our own creation of objects. Analogy is, for Kant, no means to knowledge but an aid for the imagination: the directive for our behavior is all we are entitled to assert.

That this directive is simply the injunction to seek the Unconditioned is casually mentioned in the first *Critique* (A616/B644). Kant's arguments for the two claims make this clear. We saw that the need for the regulative idea of the Unconditioned depends on the fact that the existence of transcendental laws does not entail the existence of empirical laws. We cannot know of any connection between our capacities for knowledge and the composition of the natural world. Hence the possibility of discovery of any laws of nature seems utterly fortuitous. Here, Kant places this contingency in the constitution of our faculties of knowledge. It is a peculiarity (*Zufälligkeit*) of our understanding that it is discursive, that is, it consists of universal categories that do not determine the particular. It must therefore be contingent for the understanding "what and how various the particular may be, which is given to it in nature, and which can be brought under its concepts" (V, 406). Perhaps we can imagine an intuitive understanding for which knowledge did not proceed from the general to the particular but was so constructed as to know the general and the particular immediately, as a whole. For such an understanding, the question of the agreement between its faculties of knowledge and the natural world would not arise. For us, however, if empirical knowledge is to take place, the particular must be subsumed under universal laws. That the particulars of nature should be so constituted as to be amenable to the requirements of our capacities for knowledge is a state of affairs so unnecessary in itself that we can only imagine it to have taken place by design. In order to grasp such a possibility, we imagine an accord between our understanding and the universe to have been determined by an intelligence that created both. The harmony that is preestablished between nature and our capacities for knowing it can only be comprehended if we suppose that it was intentionally arranged.

Yovel notes that Kant's lifelong preoccupation with teleology was inspired not by medieval or Aristotelian sources but by his interest in the geographical and anthropological discoveries of his own day. He was repeatedly fascinated by the variety of ways in which human beings adapted themselves to the most different kinds of conditions—"an adaptation that presupposes not only man's faculties but a certain responsiveness or even cooperation of nature itself" (Yovel 1980, 128). The human capacity to adapt our faculties to allow us to flourish in diverse environments seemed to Kant so miraculous as to require the design and cooperation of nature; and thinking about this miracle seems to have led him to think about an even greater one. Yovel's suggestion is particularly compelling because the move from this manifestation of teleology to the most general assertion of purposiveness that Kant wants to make is a natural one, and Kant's arguments for the two are similar. The first question asks how it is possible that human beings are so constructed that their faculties can adjust to be in accord with changing conditions of nature. The second question asks how human faculties can accord with nature at all. Kant holds that both questions can only be answered by assuming the existence of a designer who arranged this agreement. In assuming this, however, we are simply assuming, in the only way available to us, that nature is systematizable. Kant summarizes the argument:

In order now to be able at least to think the possibility of such an accordance of the things of nature with our judgment (which we represent as contingent and consequently as only possible by means of a purpose directed thereto), we must at the same time think another understanding, by reference to which and above all to the purpose ascribed to it we may represent as necessary that accordance of natural laws with our judgment, which is only thinkable for our understanding by means of purposes. (V, 407)

Nature must be regarded as if an understanding had created it for the benefit of our faculties of knowledge in order to make possible a system of experience according to natural laws. Thus, the appeal to teleology plays the same role as the appeal to the Unconditioned. This is further confirmed by Kant's arguments that the established canons of scientific method, the maxims discussed in section V, are all instances of the use of teleology at the metaphysical level (V, 184; XX, 210). Maxims such as "Nature takes the shortest way" (the constitutive version of Occam's Razor) or "Nature takes no leaps" (the principle of the continuity of forms) express assumptions of the purposiveness of nature. Adherence to the regulative character of the teleological principle ensures that it serves the same function as its earlier counterpart. While, as will be shown, the teleological formulation asserts a further claim about us, it makes no further statements about the world.

Asserting the functional equivalence of the appeal to teleology and the idea of the Unconditioned may seem to reduce Kant's claim to a currently acceptable but colorless statement, suggesting that Kant did not take teleology seriously but viewed it as a merely pragmatic device. I think, on the contrary, that Kant's attitude to the problem of teleology is extremely complex. Privately, he seems inclined to a belief in the purposiveness of nature that is as simple and resolute as that of any Leibnizian. Some of the most lyrical passages in his writing suggest the depth of this belief:

No one can have such a high opinion of his insight as to wish to assert definitely that, for example, the most admirable preservation of the species in the plant and animal kingdoms — whereby each new generation produces, every spring, its original, new and undiminished, with all the inner perfection of mechanism and (as in the plant kingdom) even with their delicate beauty of color, without the otherwise so destructive forces of inorganic nature in the bad weather of autumn and winter being able to harm their seed at all in this respect — no one, I say, will assert that this is the mere result of natural laws, rather than that an immediate influence of the Creator is required every year. (VI, 89)

The argument from design is the only proof of God's existence that Kant designates as deserving of respect before proceeding to demolish it and the only argument that he describes as equally appealing to the intelligence of the man in the street and to that of the most subtle thinker (V, 481). This is unique and highest praise. Yet the relationship between these sorts of observations and the assertion of the need for teleology remains at most suggestive. Kant is tireless in denying that natural investigations provide decisive evidence for the existence of a creator acting according to ends; it is possible, he says, that all of the appearance of design that we encounter was produced by natural necessity without intention or wisdom. Nor, on the other hand, can the regulative idea of teleology provide us with insight into particular natural phenomena: the statement that a supreme architect created the forms of nature gives us no clue to the principles and ideas according to which they were built (V, 410). Thus, the principle that we must represent nature as a whole as purposive leaves undetermined whether individual objects of nature are to be judged according to principles of purposiveness. All concrete investigation of nature must therefore proceed by searching for the mechanical causes of phenomena; the injunction to assume the existence of final causes operates at the transcendental level.

Kant's unwillingness to allow the assertion of teleology to play any constitutive role is surely founded in part, on a knowledge of the abuses that resulted from earlier employment of teleological principles. Attempts to explain the natural world in teleological terms resulted in accounts that were as presumptuous as they were ultimately empty. We may, Kant says, observe that certain cold countries are provided with snow as well as easily tamable reindeer and wood floated in from warmer regions, but to assert that all these things are so ordered as to ease human intercourse by means of sleighs brings us not one step further in understanding either nature or its first cause. Thus, while we may admire the apparent concurrence of many natural phenomena to a single purpose, "to say that vapor falls from the sky in the form of snow, the sea has its currents which float down wood grown in warmer lands, and large sea animals filled with oil are there because the Cause which creates all natural products has the idea of an advantage for certain poor creatures would be a very presumptuous and arbitrary judgment" (V, 369). We have no ground to assert that nature was created in order to satisfy any of our own needs *excepting our need for knowledge*. Even this is not quite an accurate rendering of Kant's statement of teleology: that statement allows us only to assert that nature and our faculties of knowledge were so created as to be in accordance with one another. Kant's refusal to ground this assertion in any facts about the world is not only the result of his dismissal of teleological accounts that may now appear ridiculous or of obedience to the systematic demands of his own theory of knowledge but of an awareness of the depth at which such belief operates. That is, if the assumption of teleology is equivalent to the idea of the Unconditioned, it is teleology that provides the possibility of an end of scientific inquiry. This end cannot, by definition, be given in nature; we can only represent the Unconditioned negatively, as the absence of all conditions. The appeal to teleology involves a concession to our capacities of imagination, permitting us to represent nature's systematicity by analogy with that of our own artifacts. But although this representation may seem to have the form of a weakened claim about the world, it could not serve its purpose if it were that. As section VII will show, the constitutive version of the principle of teleology would be self-defeating. Far from weakening Kant's original intention, the equivalence of the functions of the principle of teleology and the idea of the Unconditioned shows the importance of his use of teleology in a way that has been unappreciated. The assertion that nature is purposive is, for Kant, not merely an article of faith but an assertion that is deeply embedded in his views about our knowledge of the world: "What the category is in regard to every particular experience, is the purposiveness or appropriateness of nature (also in regard to its particular laws) to our faculty of judgment" (XX, 204).

While the teleological formulation asserts no further claim about the world than does the earlier account, it does assert something further about us. Kant makes no further claim about another need of reason but describes the form that our satisfaction of the original need will take. Hence, it is unsurprising that the third *Critique* offers little in the way of argument for the necessity of the principle of teleology; the argument for science's need of some regulative principle of reason is primarily provided in the first *Critique* discussion of the Unconditioned. In the third *Critique* Kant states that the only way in which we can follow the injunction to seek the Unconditioned is through the assumption that the world has an intelligent creator. In other words, the claim that we must think nature to be systematic is tied, though contingently, to the claim that we must think nature to be purposive; the latter is the only way for us to realize the former. This connection is contingent because it is based on the conditions of human experience, not those valid for all rational beings as such, who may be able to do without the principle of teleology. That principle is subjectively but inseparably attached to the human race (V, 400–401). It may seem as though Kant records this as an accidental fact about us: it just turns out that we can only conceive of nature's systematicity in terms of purposiveness, as it just turns out that we have five, not six, senses. In fact, Kant offers an explanation of this constraint upon our possibilities of imagination.

Buchdahl, attempting to justify Kant's "accidental-seeming" connection of systematic unity and purposiveness, argues that the teleological explanation has often held a preferential status because it seemed to provide an internal bond between events and thus to be genuinely explanatory in a way that mechanistic explanations were not. This is correct; it should further be pointed out that the achievement of the "Critique of Teleological Judgment" is to explain why such explanations have seemed genuinely explanatory, satisfying in a way that no mechanistic explanations can be.

Kant's explanation of this fact occurs most clearly in the attack upon Spinozism that takes place in the third *Critique*. Spinoza, Kant says, "thought to find contentment for reason" by substituting pantheism for reason's demand for the unity of nature. Thus, he

> introduced the idealism of final causes by changing the unity (so difficult to explain) of a number of purposively combined substances from being the unity of causal dependence *on one* substance to be the unity of inherence *in one*. . . . This system does not so much resolve as explain away into nothing the question of the first ground of the purposiveness of nature, because this latter concept, bereft of all reality, must be taken for a mere misinterpretation of a universal ontological concept of a thing in general. (V, 439)

Spinozism is here viewed as an unsatisfactory attempt to answer the same problem for which the regulative idea of teleology is invoked. The Spinozist recognizes reason's need to seek the Unconditioned, to derive the ground of the whole of the world from a unified, single principle. Spinozism attempts to satisfy that need by making the world the manifestation of a single substance, rather than the product of a purposive author. Thereby, it derives nature from a single principle, as reason's needs dictate. Kant, however, holds this to be a rejection of reason's question, not an answer to it. Spinoza's mistake is to provide an ontological answer to a problem of reason. In so doing, Kant charges, he did not simply make metaphysical claims he could not justify. More important, he failed to answer the issues to which that account was really addressed (V, 421).

Reason, which has insight only into what is produced after a plan of its own, cannot be satisfied with an account that banishes its own essential characteristic from nature. The faculty of ends can only be satisfied by an explanation that appeals to ends. This is the kind of condition that it can understand as unconditional. Spinozism fails to recognize this and thinks that the Unconditioned can be given without any reference to notions of purpose, thus assimilating reason to nature and denying reason's claims. In so doing, of course, the Spinozist gets into a great deal of more orthodox trouble. But with this Kant is not explicitly concerned. Kant acknowledges Spinoza's deep appreciation of reason's need to seek the Unconditioned. His charge is that it cannot be satisfied with an ontological solution that does not incorporate the notion of purpose.[46]

Kant's criticism of Spinozism is thus a reformulation of Leibniz's insistence that only a world that incorporates the familiar notion of purpose is one we can find ultimately intelligible. The changes that took place between Leibniz's work and Kant's make the problems to which this critique was addressed more acute even as they make its resolution easier. Here, we need only consider the crisis to common understanding caused by the advances of mechanistic science that seemed increasingly to underline the fundamental disjunction of human beings and the natural world, making their possible connection seem increasingly contingent and inexplicable.[47] Kant's own work is a philosophical expression of this disjunction: the distinction between regulative and constitutive principles is the acknowledgement of an unhealable rift between reason and nature. If reason is independent of nature, it is also, very clearly, cut adrift from it. Reason may create its own laws; nature's cooperation with such laws is utterly fortuitous. Yet just as Kant's distinction makes the need more demanding, it also points to its fulfillment. The idea of the Unconditioned was the idea of a world that was thoroughly intelligible. Kant's regulative principle of teleology adds the information that our reason can only find intelligible a world that is structured according to its own principles. The anthropomorphism implied in this assumption, which was just below the surface in Leibniz, is wholly explicit in Kant. Thus, he writes,

> In thinking the cause of the world we are justified in representing it in our idea in terms of a certain subtle anthropomorphism (without which we could not think anything in regard to it) . . . for the regulative law of systematic unity prescribes that we should study nature as if systematic and purposive unity, combined with the greatest possible manifoldness, were everywhere to be met with *in infinitum*. (A700/B728).

The idea of the purposiveness of nature is based solely on our own experience: "We perceive in ourselves a capacity to connect according to purposes (*nexus finalis*)" (XX, 294). This capacity provides the only instance in our experience of the determination of an object according to an idea—that is, of purposiveness—and thus the only means by which we can represent the production of the purposiveness we perceive in nature.

> A fundamental power through which an organization would be effected must be thought as a cause which acts according to ends, and indeed in such a way that these ends must be the ground of the possibility of the effect. But we know of such powers through experience only *in ourselves*, namely, in our understanding and will, as a

cause of the possibility of certain end products which are completely established according to ends, namely, works of art. (VIII, 181)

Our own production of artworks and artifacts is, Kant claims, the only model we have available for conceiving the creation of a systematic, organized whole. Teleological explanations seem more genuinely explanatory than others because they explain systematicity in terms most comprehensible to us, by analogy with our own experience of free causation. We can understand the universe to be systematically unified if we can understand it to be the product of a reason that, like our own, acts according to ends that it sets for itself. Reason, which Kant defines as the capacity to act according to purposes, must seek its own reflection in nature (V, 370). Kant does not shrink from the most extreme consequences of this view:

> One cannot blame the ancients too much when they . . . represented all their gods, including the supreme one, as limited in human ways. For when they observed the arrangement and the course of things in nature they found reason enough to assume a more than mechanical cause, and to suspect intentions of certain higher causes behind the machinery of this world which they could not think as other than superhuman. . . . Their judgment of the highest cause of the world could hardly be otherwise so long as they proceeded consistently according to the maxims of the mere theoretical use of reason. (V, 439)

It is practical reason that provides considerations that limit the temptation to a fully anthropomorphic picture of the world. Were we guided solely by theoretical reason, we would be fully consistent in projecting all of our characteristics onto the cause of nature.

Kant's forthrightness in acknowledging the anthropomorphism that underlies our predisposition to teleological explanation is the result of the regulative character of his use of teleology. By insisting that nature makes its own demands, which are unaffected by reason's claims, Kant is left free to acknowledge the character of those claims in a manner more radical than earlier thinkers allowed themselves to do. For Leibniz, the question of a gap between the needs of reason and the demands of nature did not arise. Sensing a need of reason for purposive explanation, he had no choice but to argue that the universe *is* the best product of a purposive author. Yet under pressure of the Cartesian critique of final causes, Leibniz was unable to make the nature of this need explicit. We found many hints, but no full statements of the idea that the only unconditionally satisfactory explanations are those given in terms that we understand by analogy with our own behavior. Kant's situation is different: in claiming that the faculty of ends can only find repose in an explanation that is structured in its own terms, he is doing no more and no less than giving credence to the needs of reason. Thus, his insistence upon the necessity of final causes coexists with, and even incorporates, the attacks to which they have been subject. Kant would, for example, have no quarrel with Bacon's statement that "final causes have relation clearly to the nature of man rather than to the nature of the universe" (Bacon, 1960, 1. 48). Kant simply refuses to sacrifice the needs of either humanity or the universe to the other. The notion of a regulative principle is an attempt to hold each in balance:

> But what does the most complete teleology prove in the end? Does it prove that there is such an intelligent Being? No; it proves *nothing* further than that according to the

constitution of our faculties of knowledge, in connection of experience with the highest principles of reason, we can make absolutely no concept of the possibility of such a world save by thinking a supreme cause acting intentionally. (V, 399)

Such a passage displays the unique character of Kant's position. For critics of the use of final causes, the statement that the best teleology proves nothing about the world but only something about our capacities for understanding it would serve as a reason for dismissing teleology. Without the notion of a regulative principle, those critics had no place for a legitimate reference to the needs of reason. Hence, any indulgence of those needs had to be attacked as the covert projection of human demands onto the natural world. For Kant, by contrast, this statement is made without a trace of disparagement. The best teleology proves no more than that *we* can only conceive the world as the product of an intelligent author, but this is something that is eminently worthy of proof.

Is this a theodicy or the rejection of the very possibility of theodicy? Kant thought it was the latter. This is not, I believe, merely the result of his own epistemological convictions that speculative proofs of the world's purposiveness are unattainable. Not the harmony of structure between reason and nature but its absence is the dominant tone of Kant's work. The question of theodicy will be treated at greater length in chapter 4 through an examination of Kant's discussion of the highest good. For in ethics as in science, the Unconditioned is not a given but a demand. In both cases Kant offers us no more — but no less — than hope and the notions we require to sustain it. His use of the principles of teleology is one such notion. If the world as a whole *can be thought as* the product of purpose, our efforts to find it intelligible may be successful. Thus, regulative principles connect human beings with the world while insisting on acknowledgment of their separateness. They function by providing an ideal whereby this separation is overcome, maintaining all the while that this ideal is not to be found in the world that we know. They assert "the harmony of nature with our faculties" *as a possibility*, urging and sustaining our efforts to achieve this harmony, condemning every doctrine that would treat it as given (V, 185).

VII. The Impossibility of Knowledge

We are now in a position to state certain general claims about the nature of a regulative principle. Seen at work in natural science, regulative principles serve to determine our own behavior rather than any facts about the world. The way in which they do this is by functioning as ends; this makes them simultaneously ideas of, and motives for the realization of, a certain possibility. Thus, we can understand Kant's claims that the use of reason is directed to the determination of a subject rather than an object (B167) and his description of a subjective judgment as one that is not cognitive (*kein Erkenntnisurteil*) (XX, 221). Statements like these begin to undermine the picture of regulative principles as attempts to second-guess the supersensible. Regulative principles are not hypotheses because their concern is not with objective reality but with subjective determination — not with what is but with what ought to be. Constitutive principles tell us what the world is like; they must, therefore, be grounded in an object. Regulative principles concern our needs and capacities and are grounded in the same. This not only allows them to forego the standards of proof and demonstration we use in accepting cognitive statements; it also frees them from many of the connotations normally entailed by designating them as ideas. Thus, the notion of design in the third *Critique* becomes almost a technical one: a design that we can never know to be a design lacks some of the content of its determinate counterpart (V, 381–82).

Yet it is just these features that have made the notion of a regulative principle seem suspect. Kant's repeated statements that we cannot know the Unconditioned or the purposiveness of nature may support the claim that reason's task is not one of obtaining knowledge, but only, it may seem, because the ideas he attributes to reason have been widely discredited as false. Kant's insistence that knowledge of the regulative ideas would transgress the limits of experience is likely to seem dogmatic to those not already convinced of the validity of transcendental idealism. Indeed, it is just the insistence on these strictures, understood in the wrong way, that is likely to make Kant's teaching as a whole appear dogmatic. Responses to the supposed arbitrariness of Kant's restrictions have taken different directions. Absolute Idealists tried to demonstrate that reason can have knowledge of the supersensible, while empiricists tend to view Kant's limitations of knowledge as an attempt to mystify obsolete nonentities. Both sorts of responses assume that Kant has no internal reasons for denying us knowledge of the ideas of reason. Thus, regulative principles come to be viewed as failed constitutive principles. Kant's own examples do little to undermine this view. For example, he contrasts the constitutive version of the principle of teleology—"Some production of material things is not possible on mere mechanical laws" (V, 387)—with its regulative counterpart: "Some products of material nature cannot be estimated as possible on mere mechanical laws (that is, for estimating them a quite different law of causality is required, namely, that of final causes)" (V, 387). The difficulty is to find a reason for the shift from the first to the second formulation that does not rest on the fact that Kant failed to prove the first. It is not easy, initially, to discover other force in the difference between the two versions of the maxim. The difference between 'is' and 'must be estimated as' seems only to be a difference between asserting with confidence and hedging one's bets.

Properly understood, a regulative principle should show itself to be necessarily regulative. It should, that is, show that the functions it performs are ones that no constitutive principle—no item of knowledge—could fulfill. If it could be shown that there were internal reasons for Kant's denial of knowledge of the regulative principles, the notion of an idea to which we have no cognitive relation would become far more acceptable. Such reasons cannot be found in Kant's appeals to the constraints of his own systematic metaphysics.[48] While these are given the most frequently, they give us no clue to understanding why regulative principles must remain unknowable in order to perform their tasks.

More suggestive passages condemn the attempt to treat regulative principles as constitutive ones as an act of laziness:

> If instead of looking for causes in the universal laws of material mechanism, we appeal directly to the unsearchable decree of supreme wisdom, all those ends which are exhibited in nature, together with the many ends which are only ascribed by us to nature, we make our investigations of the causes a very easy task, and so enable us to

regard the labor of reason as completed, when in fact we have only dispensed with its employment. (A691/B719)

Use of a constitutive version of a teleological principle would, Kant says, cut off science where it ought to begin. The appeal to God's purposes in the business of giving explanations of nature is the resort of those whose reluctance to do the work involved in science would cut off all progress in it. The sterility of scholastic science was the result of the constitutive use of teleology, allowing investigations to rest content with vague ascriptions of the final causes of phenomena rather than exploring their causes and functions within a system of nature. Put thus, Kant greatly understates his own case. Our knowledge of a principle of teleology would simply preclude the possibility of scientific inquiry, for it is the fact that the Unconditioned is a thing beyond experience, a pure possibility, that allows it to function as end. A state of affairs that was given in experience could not function as the object of an effort to realize it. Kant, who called himself an inquirer prone by nature to "feel the consuming thirst for knowledge, the eager unrest to advance even further" could not have been uninfluenced by the romance of eighteenth-century science most famously expressed by Lessing:

> If God were holding all the truth that exists in his right hand, and in his left just the one ever-active urge to find the truth, even if attached to it were the condition that I should always and forever be going astray, and said to me "Choose!," I should humbly fall upon his left hand and say "Father, give! Pure truth is for thee alone." (1959, vol. 12, p. 24)

As usual, Kant does not simply echo, but provides the metaphysical grounding for, the thought of his time. An Unconditioned that was given would render much of human inquiry impossible, precluding the important aspects of science. Not the fear that the joys of scientific searching would come to a halt but the recognition that they could never begin leads to Kant's insistence upon the regulative character of the Unconditioned. We have seen that an end must be something that is yet unattained. In order for science to have an end, therefore, the principle of teleology must remain regulative, unknowable. Kant's denial of our knowledge of the Unconditioned results from his careful appreciation of the role of ends in human activity, theoretical as well as practical.

The idea that knowledge of the Unconditioned would deny us the most important part of human inquiry is virtually equivalent, for Kant, to the idea that whatever inquiry was left to us would lack autonomy. I have argued that the work of recording performed by the understanding is, compared to the work of reason, characterized by passivity. Reason operates according to laws that it gives to itself. The laws of the understanding are not derived from a source external to the understanding, but they are restricted to experience and applied automatically, leaving no room for the exercise of choice and judgment involved in the application of a regulative principle. This makes the principles of the understanding second-rate. The capacity to act freely according to chosen ends confers value not only upon all human activity but, Kant suggests, upon the world as a whole. (V, 434). A science that dispensed with reason's use, substituting constitutive for regulative principles, would be the work of automata, bereft of the value that belongs to our pursuit of natural science.

Is such a science imaginable at all? Can we conceive of an activity performed by a race of beings to whom the Unconditioned was known that consisted in recording observations and making inferences in accordance with an already known plan, without understanding its interest or contributing ideas of their own? It is just this fantasy that inhabits Leibniz's discussions of the universal calculus. As was seen in the previous chapter, the science that Leibniz wished to ground would proceed so mechanically that some thought must be given to tending the amour propre of future scientists, since so little would be left to motivate them to discovery. Such a fantasy may be ultimately incoherent, but it is indeed the fantasy most consistent with Leibniz's construal of the principle of sufficient reason. Against this fantasy Kant would place Lessing's vision. To deny that reason can unceasingly seek the Unconditioned, he would argue, is to deny reason satisfaction. It is human reason's peculiar fate to find satisfaction in what might seem to be perpetual dissatisfaction, forever exercising its freedom in seeking an end that it cannot obtain. It will seem surprising to accuse the greatest of rationalists with the failure to give reason satisfaction, but herein lies the power of Kant's reconception of reason. Kant's charge is not merely that rationalism, in considering reason to have knowledge of the Unconditioned, gave reason an overweening role that could not be supported. More immediately, rationalism did not give reason what it needs most, a field in which to exercise its real powers. Reason itself is unhappy with rationalism: dogmatism is not merely false, that is, inattentive to the claims of nature, but inattentive to the claims of reason.[49]

A constitutive version of the idea of the Unconditioned would lead to a political quietism that Kant is committed to avoid. The assertion that the world is ordered according to divine purposes would result in an acquiescence to the present state of reality and a limitation of human freedom, most cogently expressed by Leibniz: "If we could sufficiently understand the order of the universe, we should find that it is impossible to make it better than it is" (ML 652). While this consideration clearly plays a role in Kant's refusal to give constitutive status to the ideas of reason, it is not my present concern. Here it is mentioned to underline, by analogy, the similar concern at work in questions internal to the practice of natural science. A constitutive version of the principles would lead to the loss of the freedom that Kant is most concerned to guard, but prior to that would be the loss of science itself. Reason's need is for activity, the continual attempt to force nature to be adequate to its ideas. The regulative version of the principle of teleology does not tell us that the world is divinely ordered for the best, transparent to the needs of reason, but only that the evidence of purposiveness we find in the world must be thought as the product of an intelligent creator. In so doing it serves as a challenge to reason to continue its explorations, making demands on nature until it meets reason's needs. The autonomy of the principles of reason permits them to function as a standard by which experience can be judged: by providing a vision of intelligibility that the given world does not meet, they urge us to continue our labors until this ideal is attained. The constitutive version of the principle of teleology, by contrast, bids us to be content with the intelligibility with that the world presents us.

Kant's second internal ground for the denial of the possibility of knowledge of the Unconditioned is that such knowledge would make the unity of nature accidental. He initially discusses the idea in the first *Critique*, writing:

The regulative principle prescribes that systematic unity as a *unity in nature*, which is not known merely empirically but is presupposed a priori (although in an undeterminate manner), be presupposed absolutely and consequently as following from the essence of things. If, however, I begin with a supreme purposive being as the ground of all things, the unity of nature is really surrendered, as being quite foreign and accidental to the nature of things, and as not being capable of being known from its own universal laws. (A693/B721)

The purpose of the regulative principle is to help us discover the unity that is present in nature. To this end, we are permitted to think an intelligent creator as the source of that unity. Were this idea to be used constitutively as part of the explanation of nature, it would defeat the purpose it was meant to serve; for it would make the unity of nature something external and contingent to nature itself. The argument continues, "We were not justified in assuming above nature a being with those qualities, but only in adopting the idea of such a being in order to view the appearances as *systematically connected with one another* in accordance with the principle of a causal determination" (A700/B728; my italics). Kant is responding here to the fantasy of obtaining God's promise that, say, Newton's first law of motion is true and will continue to hold—otherwise known, perhaps, as a proof of preestablished harmony. Kant argues that such a fantasy is incoherent: in gaining God's guarantee that observed regularities were indeed laws of nature, we would lose the character that made them lawlike. If we knew nature to be the product of an intelligent author, its laws would have no internal necessity but would be simply the expressions of that being's will. Such views were held by some philosophers, perhaps most notably by Berkeley, who wrote, "There is nothing necessary or essential in the case, but it depends entirely on the will of the governing spirit, who causes certain bodies to cleave together or tend toward each other according to various laws, whilst he keeps others at a fixed distance; and to some he gives a quite contrary tendency to fly asunder just as he sees convenient" (1940, 106). This sort of view would be intolerable to Kant, for whom our own experience of constant conjunction is merely chance custom, unable to yield the connection necessary to constitute causality. God's similarly conjoining things would make particular causal regularities no less arbitrary. Without an understanding of how things are connected *with one another*, we lack real knowledge that this connection is grounded. The point is not simply that we may have no guarantee that God's decrees will not change or will require natural changes which would undo our scientific laws. Not the uncertainty but the lack of grounding in the nature of things would undermine the scientific character of laws that were held to be laws merely by divine guarantee. One way to understand this thought is by way of the idea of intelligibility. Science's task is to make the world intelligible to us, although it will never succeed in doing so completely. To accept a law on God's guarantee would be to give up this idea of intelligibility, for it would admit a fundamentally arbitrary feature into our explanation of the nature of things. We cannot appeal to something outside the world as any part of an explanation whose purpose is to make the world intelligible on its own terms. In constructing science we seek to discover laws that express something about the essential nature of objects in the world, not decrees that happen to govern their behavior.

A satisfactory account of the way in which laws might be grounded in the nature of things is not easy to find. We saw Leibniz struggle with it in his critique of Descartes's views on God's creation of the eternal truths. Leibniz held that eternal truths would be arbitrary unless true independently of God's will; his attempt to determine the source of their necessity led to a neo-Platonic view fraught with problems. Now many of these problems simply do not arise for Kant, for whom knowledge of things in themselves is excluded. But the problem posed by attempting to delineate a notion of the internal necessity of natural laws is a similar one. Kant does not, I think, devote sufficient attention to it; his assertion that we must think empirical laws to be necessary without, however, sacrificing their empirical character is not wholly satisfactory.[50] If Kant fails, however, to provide an account of this internal necessity, his distinction between natural and supernatural laws shows what would exclude it. Explanations of nature that appeal to supernatural causes would lose their very capacity to explain anything about nature as such: "A theological physics would be a nonentity [*Unding*], for it would propose no laws of nature, but ordinances of a highest will" (V, 485). The problem would arise not only if we knew which purposes a given law was meant to serve. Simply by knowing the general truth that nature's laws were the product of a divine purposiveness, we would sacrifice the internal necessity of those laws.

As Kant points out at the close of the third *Critique*, just the same problem arises with the regulative principles of practical faith. As will be seen in chapter 4, morality requires the regulative use of the postulates of practical faith; but knowledge of those postulates would thoroughly undermine morality. Similarly, the pursuit of science requires the regulative use of the idea of the Unconditioned, later expanded to include the principle of teleology. Knowledge of the ideas, however, would render incoherent the scientific enterprise of discovering the fundamental principles underlying natural phenomena. Rather than urging us to continue to seek the principles by which the world is to be made intelligible, they would lead us to rest content with the illusion that intelligibility has been achieved. The constitutive version of the principle of teleology would quite simply wreck science. It would no longer be free inquiry, nor would it any longer be natural inquiry but merely an inventory of the arbitrary decisions of a being external to nature.

VIII. Justification

In the first *Critique*, Kant says the regulative principles are synthetic a priori propositions with objective but indeterminate validity, for which no transcendental deduction is possible (A664/B692). A few pages later he writes that no a priori concept can be employed with certainty unless a transcendental deduction of it has been given. He therefore proposes to "complete the critical work of pure reason" by giving a transcendental deduction of the regulative ideas, although allowing that this deduction will be different from that given for the categories of the understanding (A670/B698). These different kinds of statements are likely to leave the reader bewildered as to what sort of justification of the regulative ideas Kant believed to be possible.

I think that Kant's vacillations on this point are a result of several factors. The first has to do with the meaning of 'deduction.' Most often, Kant uses the term to refer to a conclusive proof: a deduction shows a principle to be absolutely necessary. In the more limited case, a transcendental deduction shows some principle to be necessary for the possibility of experience, a state that we cannot choose to accept or reject. This is the most common and most rigorous sense of 'deduction,' but Kant also uses the word, on occasion, to mean simply "justification." Kant slides between these two uses without warning, allowing him to consistently say that the regulative ideas permit of no deduction (in the rigorous sense) while proposing, later, to give a deduction, that is, a justification, of them. This deduction cannot show the necessity of the principles it justifies for the possibility of experience. Kant believes that self-reference (though probably little else) could take place in a world whose appearances were too chaotic to admit of the discovery of natural laws. But there is another kind of justification that, though not absolute justification, is perfectly legitimate. Its form is the argument that some principle is necessary, given some end. All of the work of this kind of justification consists in showing the necessity of a principle *given* a prior end, leaving the adoption of that end a matter of choice. This is the kind of deduction that Kant gives for the regulative principles of reason, though his unclarity about the narrow and broader senses of 'deduction' prevents him from specifying just what form of justification is provided.

A second factor produces unclarity about the kind of justification involved in the regulative principles. This is the fact that our choice to accept or reject the end that requires the use of regulative principles is a rather nominal one. Kant says that the regulative ideas are required for the perfection, not the possibility, of experience; but his notion of perfection in this case is very minimal. Experience without the use of regulative principles would be so impoverished that it is tempting to deem it impossible. Kant seems occasionally to be moved by this temptation but never quite succumbs to it. An experience in which science in the broadest sense was impossible would be severely limited, but this is no argument against its possibility.

Despite the confusion produced by these factors we can, then, discover a perfectly legitimate form of argument that is given for the regulative principles. That form is simply this: If science is to take place, the regulative principle of the Unconditioned is necessary. This is clear and above-board. The sense that something is illegitimate about Kant's procedure may, however, remain. For even if the form of that procedure is admitted, there remains a question about how well he has satisfied that form. Kant's argument for the necessity of the regulative ideas has seemed elusive, at best, to many scholars. Thus, one complains: "[Kant] admits that the deduction to be offered will be very different from that which is available in the case of the categories. In fact it turns out not to be a deduction at all, but simply a redescription of the role of ideas already sketched, along with a series of references to individual ideas" (Walsh 1975, 245). In fact, this description of the role of ideas is all Kant has to offer by way of a deduction, but it is far from clear that this is insufficient. What has to be shown is, first, that there is a certain gap left by the experience that would exist without the introduction of the regulative ideas, and, second, that only a particular kind of thing can fill that gap. If the arguments I have made in this chapter are correct, Kant has shown both of these things. In detailing a variety of functions that the principles of the understanding leave unperformed and in showing that no other kind of principle could perform them, Kant has demonstrated the need for regulative principles of reason. While this kind of argument can well be called a redescription of the role of those principles, it is difficult to imagine what other kind of justification could be given for them, once it is seen that they cannot be deduced to be principles of the possibility of experience. Kant states this clearly:

> No objective deduction, such as we have been able to give of the categories, is, strictly speaking, possible in the case of these transcendental ideas. Just because they are only ideas, they have, in fact, no relation to any object that could be given as coinciding with them. We can, indeed, undertake a subjective determination of them from the nature of our reason, and this has been provided in the present chapter. (A336/B393)

Kant is explicit about the Platonic origin of the notion of an idea of reason. He shares with Plato the notion of the idea as archetype, "something that not only can never be borrowed from the senses but far surpasses even the concepts of understanding, inasmuch as in experience, nothing is every to be met with that is coincident with it" (A313/B370). Plato's mistake, Kant tells us, was the hypostatization of these ideas, the attempt to reify as otherworldly entities what are in fact products of reason alone. But the conception of ideas as something that cannot be instantiated in experience remains firm. This means that undemonstrability is a feature of their very nature: defined as notions to which no experience can be adequate, their function as standards and ends places them beyond the reach of objective justification appropriate to knowledge.

Yet it is just this deliberate renunciation of the possibility of objective justification that has made regulative principles seem, to many writers, deeply illicit. The arguments that Kant gives for the necessity of the ideas lack most of the features we normally require in determining whether to accept or reject a statement. Unconstrained by normal standards of justification, our acceptance of the ideas can be at best arational, and at worst fanatical or delusional. Guyer states this objection succinctly: "One must wonder whether merely postulating or presupposing that an object will meet one's needs, rather than obtaining evidence that it does which is independent of one's own wishes, can make it rational to behave as if that object really will meet those needs. A delusion, after all, is no rational basis for action" (1979, 50). Guyer echoes the very natural objection first brought against the notion of a regulative principle in Kant's own day. Kant's response, given most directly in the second *Critique*, will be treated at length in chapter 4. Briefly, we may say that his answer to this kind of objection is divided into three stages. The first is the attempt to distinguish between a genuine need of reason and a wish or desire. The latter cannot ground regulative principles, while the former provides a basis for them. Kant's distinction between needs of reason and those of mere inclination appeals to criteria of universality and general importance. The second part of Kant's answer to this objection involves the claim that the normal canons of justification are insufficient to resolve questions for which a regulative principle is required. To suggest that we should refrain from asserting nature to be systematic until we have better evidence for that assertion is radically to underestimate the kind of systematicity that is at issue. All of natural science is evidence for nature's systematicity, but nothing that science could further do or discover would provide more conclusive evidence of the foundation of science itself. Nothing we know today could prevent the laws of motion from ceasing to hold tomorrow. What is at stake is a question for which, it is agreed, no evidence can be obtained. Regulative principles are valid only where evidence independent of the subject's needs is impossible to obtain, because the questions they are intended to settle are not primarily questions about the world but about the behavior of human beings in the world. Thus, to view them as standing in need of better evidence is to misunderstand the role that Kant believes they must play.

This leads to the final stage of Kant's response to this kind of objection, which emphasizes the uniqueness of regulative principles. Guyer takes the postulation of a regulative principle to be something like the wishful assertion of an untested hypothesis; and if this were the case, it would be reasonable to ask for further evidence before permitting such assertions. I have argued, however, that such a view is misleading. Most important to the denial that regulative principles are untested hypotheses is Kant's insistence that we would not want them to be confirmed: as argued in section VII, knowledge of the regulative principles would render them self-defeating, unable to fulfill the function for which they are required. Kant's point is that reason's needs are not for determining truth—even in science, whose ultimate goal is to obtain truth. Further, Kant shows that the obtaining of truth itself is a far more complicated affair than earlier thinkers had concluded.

Yet even those recent scholars of Kant's philosophy of science whose work has enriched our understanding of this latter point share a version of Guyer's worry. While holding, as Guyer does not, that the regulative principles reason uses to search for systematicity are essential to the construction of science, a number of authors find that this leaves science on rather shaky ground. The fragility felt to be entailed by these foundations is conveyed in the very adjectives 'only' and 'merely,' which habitually precede the word 'regulative,' but it is often made even more explicit. So astute a commentator as Robert Butts writes that the proper employment of the regulative ideas encourages us "to settle for the kind of knowledge that positive science yields" (1986 b, 165)—as if Kant viewed Newton's achievement as something we must *settle for*—and describes the regulative ideas as "concepts that have had their Leibnizian metaphysical content drained away, leaving a merely methodological framework *for which there are no purely rational guarantees*" (1984, 11; my italics).

It is a central claim of this book that Kant is engaged in a redefinition of the rational. If this is the case, of course, then the concern that Kant's regulative ideas are without rational guarantee must be understood in different terms. Correspondence to an object, we have seen, cannot be part of such a guarantee, and logical possibility is merely its necessary condition.

Kant's revised notion of reason will contain an ineradicable tension in its attempts to balance reason's claim to autonomy—that is, its utter independence from objects—and its claim to be binding—that is, its availability to some form of the justification we normally call objective. Without forfeiting its right to legislate how experience ought to be—its very function in making imperatives—reason cannot be tied to experience as claims of knowledge are. In underlining reason's need for autonomy, Kant goes so far as to describe the objective justification involved in knowledge as a kind of compulsion. Knowledge is not, he writes, "intentional or even responsible (because everyone must believe a fact which is confirmed just as much as a mathematical demonstration, whether he will or not)" (VIII, 146). Yet some constraints must be provided in order to show that the regulative ideas are not arbitrary and to prevent one from simply stipulating any principle whose legitimacy is troublesome to be a product of reason. Such constraints cannot be provided by attempts to cite necessary and sufficient conditions of the reasonable; if Kant's reconception is truly radical, its legitimacy cannot be tested for correspondence with another concept of reason. Rather, each regulative idea must be shown to be part of a coherent and consistent notion of reason as a whole. This kind of justification is, of course, consonant with Kant's general ideas about the confirmation of theories. Having rejected the idea that the justification of a theory rests on its correspondence to things in themselves, we should not be troubled by the absence of such a confirmation of Kant's theory of reason itself. Rather, we may seek justification in the coherence and power of the account of reason as a whole. At the core of that account is the criterion of universal communicability (V, 238–39, 279–80). What cannot be expressed publicly – with the openness to argument and revision such expression implies – cannot belong to the rational.

Only in the context of a complete account of reason, then, can Kant provide a justification for the introduction of the regulative principles. That justification has the following form: if science in the broadest sense is to be practiced, something performing the roles fulfilled by the regulative principles is required. In showing their function as ends and presuppositions of science, I hope to have provided such a justification for Kant's insistence on the need for regulative principles in scientific inquiry. Yet even if successful, this shows the regulative character of the principles, rather than anything about their content, to be necessary. It may be asked whether this is sufficient for Kant's purposes. Does he need to prove something more specific than the need for a general regulative principle of reason?

This question may arise from two sorts of concern. The first is that the arguments I have given may support the more abstract formulation of the first *Critique* but not the claim of the third *Critique* that the only form in which we can conceive the Unconditioned is one of a divinely ordered nature. This may well be true, but it does not damage the essential part of Kant's case. Kant insists that the form that our search for the Unconditioned is to take is purely a matter of the peculiarities of our constitution. The fact that reason is only fully content with explanations that appeal to structures like its own is one of the facts about reason that may be open to change. Kant distinguishes between absolutely necessary and relatively necessary needs of reason. As chapter 4 will argue, this seems to allow for the possibility, which Kant does not explicitly state, that reason's needs can change with historical conditions. One such change may be that the idea of teleology is no longer required to think the Unconditioned. Even while appealing to teleology, Kant wrote that "It must be a matter of indifference to us, when we perceive such unity, whether we say that God in his wisdom has willed it to be so, or that nature has wisely arranged it thus" (A699/B727). Reason's need for some form of regulative principles to orient its activity in the realms where it cannot obtain knowledge remains constant; the description of that form is less significant and may need to be provided anew.

The second concern that motivates the question about particular regulative principles is more troublesome. If, as concluded in section V, Kant has no fixed criteria that guide the use of regulative principles in science, something further may seem necessary in order to give content to those demands. Recall that strict criteria for the application of the idea of the Unconditioned would amount to a set of rules for the pursuit of progress in natural science. The failure of earlier philosophers to provide such rules is not accidental: too great a specification of methodological principles would amount to a prioristic anticipation of the natural world, not a method for the investigation of it. But the Kantian suggestion that it is only our freedom and activity that give content to the general regulative ideas leaves many readers concluding these ideas to be empty.

The charge that the ideas are empty is, at bottom, another version of the belief that they are intolerably uncertain. They stem from a particular view about the nature of reality that holds, roughly, that the real is exhausted by the objective. What does not determine an object is not real but fictional. Whether one attempts to develop a theory that stresses the usefulness of fictions or one that restricts them to the province of literature, one who holds this view is profoundly and literally uncritical. For the view ignores the very posing of the problem that Kant listed as primary in the history of philosophy: to determine the status and nature of reality itself. The equation of indeterminacy with emptiness represents an assumption that would preclude rather than examine Kant's central question: What kind of reality do ideas of reason possess?

That something about this question is crucial to Kant's procedure is acknowledged by those recent discussions of Kant's scientific methodology which argue that his position cannot be assimilated to traditional debates between realism and instrumentalism. Because regulative principles are neither substantive claims about nature nor heuristic fictions, Kant offers a new perspective on the disputes about the status of scientific explanation.[51] This perspective, like so much of Kant's work, will be best appreciated when seen in its broadest context. In science as in other areas, Kant presents a view of reason's ideas that insists on their reality while denying their reification.

Historical considerations may have led to Kant's emphasis on the latter task to the detriment of the former. The fact that his primary attention is devoted to attacking Leibnizian excess (in particular, the tendency to ascribe primary reality to supersensible objects of the intellect and to view the senses as sources of confusion) may have led him to underestimate the power of the empiricist response. Could Kant have imagined that his destruction of the foundations of every attempt to provide objects for the ideas of reason (otherwise known as traditional metaphysics) would seem naturally to support the conclusion that if not objective, the ideas must be fictitious? Probably not. Yet at bottom, Kant might say that metaphysics and skepticism are driven by the same illusion: the belief that determining an object is the only guarantee against the arbitrary. The tendency that drove Plato and Leibniz to secure the validity of the ideas by positing supersensible objects is the same tendency that led their skeptical opponents to conclude that the absence of such objects left the ideas devoid of reality.

A tendency so general is likely to be deep-seated and persistent, fueling our inclination to precede the word 'regulative' with the qualification 'merely' and to refer to those concepts whose essence is to be without objects as *only* ideas. Even attention to Kant's splendid invective against the disparagement conveyed in the expression "It is only an idea" cannot wholly dispel this inclination (A328/B385ff.), particularly when Kant himself is often given to similar formulations.[52] I believe that our tendency to disparage the power of ideas without objects is just the tendency that Kant identified as transcendental illusion. If this is the case and if transcendental illusion is one that persists even after it is detected (A297/B354), it is no wonder that Kant often lapses into formulations against which he himself has warned. The problem of determining the status and content of regulative principles is not external to Kant's texts: his description of the process whereby reason continually seeks knowledge that is neither attainable nor desirable fully anticipates the reader's unease. No lacuna in his account, but an inevitable temptation of human reason is the ground, Kant would claim, of our difficulty in accepting the legitimacy of the notion of a regulative principle.

Transcendental illusion is driven by our desire for certainty, the source of our temptation to view constitutive principles as necessary for content where only regulative ones will do. The tension between the desire for certainty and the need for autonomy is basic to Kant's description of the human condition. Neither coming to maturity nor doing critical philosophy can resolve it, though both, I will argue, crucially involve acknowledging it. Kant's systematic goals—the demonstration of the unity of theoretical and practical reason, based on a noncognitive account of the notion of reason—require him to preserve the autonomy of reason by stopping short of a deduction that reason's ideas are necessary. Yet he himself is occasionally troubled by the suggestion that this leaves the ideas without sufficient or certain foundation. The tension thus reflected will reappear at points throughout his philosophy.

Notes

I am indebted to the extensive comments of an anonymous reader for Oxford University Press, which prompted significant revisions in this chapter.

1. See Kant's letter to Marcus Herz on 21 February 1772 (X, 129–30; see also Konhardt (1979, 5–11, 91).

2. Guyer, (1979; 1989a) 7, argues just this. For a full discussion of this problem, see chap. 3.

3. See, e.g., Guyer (1979) Kemp Smith (1962).

4. Gerd Buchdahl's (1969) *Metaphysics and the Philosophy of Science* was pathbreaking in this respect; my account of Kant's views of science draws heavily on his work. See also Butts (1984; 1986a) and Friedman (1991).

5. This is not to deny Kant's interest in specific problems of Newtonian physics or his belief that certain of Newton's concepts needed philosophical grounding. Kant wrote and lectured on a range of subjects extraordinary even for his day, and his interest in Newton was ongoing. See Friedman (1986). My claim is simply that this interest, while present in the *Metaphysical Foundations of Natural Science* and elsewhere, cannot be the driving force behind the theory of knowledge and reality undertaken in the first *Critique*.

6. For some statements of this objection, see Frege (1978, 6), Russell (1971, 145), Kemp Smith (1962, 40–43); and Bennett (1966, 4).

7. For further discussion, see Parsons (1969); Hintikka (1969; 1973); Friedman (1985); and Young (1982).

8. Thompson (1972) argues that only empirical intuition can provide objects for mathematics; see also Friedman (1985). Some passages in the first *Critique* suggest, however, that Kant has pure intuition in mind (A8/B4, A711/B739, A715/B444).

9. See Kitcher (1990–10) and Bencivenga (1987, 78, 117).

10. See Westfall (1977, 66).

11. Here, and in the following discussion, I have used the tripartite division of faculties that Kant signals as primary in the first *Critique*, ignoring the introduction of the faculty of judgment in the third *Critique*. When discussing the latter work, I have followed a number of commentators in taking its "reflective judgment" to be equivalent to the whole faculty of reason in the first two *Critiques* and the later distinction to mirror the earlier one between reason and understanding. (See the writings of Buchdahl, Butts, Friedman, Horstmann, Konhardt, Krausser, and O'Neill.) The decision to do so reflects my primary interest in the systematic reconstruction of Kant's views rather than the historical examination of the changes they underwent during the Critical Period; for in this case, the changes seem to insubstantial that only one scholar has proposed a compelling reason for the switch from 'reason' to 'reflective judgment.' Guyer (1989a; 1990) argues that Kant's desire to restrict autonomy and self-legislation to practical reason accounts for his reassignment of the tasks assigned to theoretical reason in the first *Critique*. I believe this view is fundamentally mistaken, as will be argued in the present and the following chapter. Other reasons, such as further reflections on the nature of creative endeavor, may well have played a role in Kant's introduction of another faculty or power (see Vania 1989). They do not affect the fact that Kant's use of the crucial regulative/constitutive distinction is applied in the same way in all three *Critiques* so that reason and reflective judgment perform the same role with respect to our knowledge.

12. See XX, 260; see also A15/B29.

13. The strongest and most detailed version of this interpretation is provided by Buchdahl. See also the writings of Allison, Beck, Butts, Friedman, Kitcher, Krausser, and Melnick.

14. I am also inclined to agree with Friedman's suggestion that the weaker version is not coherent.

15. But see Butts (1986a) for further discussion of the *Metaphysical Foundations of Natural Science*.

16. A few instances of such statements occur at B165, A158/B198, and A776/B794, and V, 179. See also sec. IV–V.

17. See Duncan (1986) and Friedman (1991; 1992b, 165–210).

18. Kitcher (1984) and Parsons (1984).

19. Friedman (1992a); see also Friedman (1991).

20. Friedman probably expresses this objection most clearly: "Accordingly, there is no guarantee whatever that the requisite empirical concepts and laws will in fact be found; there is only the merely regulative demand that we continue the search without end. How, then, are the categories really constitutive? What does a guarantee of the existence of substances in general amount to if there is no guarantee of the existence of particular kinds of substances? What does a guarantee of the existence of causal connections amount to if there is no guarantee of the existence of particular causal laws?" (1991, 77–78). See also Guyer's recent papers.

21. Of course, the task that Guyer describes as "only motivation" is one that I take to be crucial (see sec. II). Guyer's position has been refined in recent works, but his fundamental conviction that the systematization performed by reason is not essential to the construction of science remains unchanged (see Guyer 1990).

22. Cohen summarizes, "Das Prinzip des Schlusses ist die Idee des Unbedingten" ("The principle of inference is the idea of the Unconditioned") (1910, 79).

23. On the importance of the *focus imaginarius* metaphor, see Butts (1984, 216); 1986b, 191–92).

24. In the letter to Garve of 7 August 1783, Kant says that the absolutely Unconditioned appears among things-in-themselves (X, 315–322).

25. Saner's description of the nature of reason's principles is a good summary of their most important and problematic features: "Everything depends on knowing how to use principles. Principles are not imposed on nature by the intellect; they are inserted into nature for the purpose of observing it. They are . . . means of orientation, not definitions of being; premises of our ability to see, not things we see. They have a touch of the fictitious, but without the moment of randomness, and they have a touch of the necessary, without the moment of objectivity. They are . . . means to make the phenomenality of nature, which is unintelligible in itself, appear so that man can understand it – in other words, means to make it appears as the product of an intellect." (1973, 181)

26. For further discussion of Kant's views on induction, see Buchdahl (1969); Butts (1986a), Kitcher (1986).

27. Section VII will argue that even the fulfillment of the anthropomorphic fantasy could not satisfy us; a promise that nature will remain uniform would be self-defeating.

28. This example was suggested by John Rawls.

29. Yovel writes: "In saying that reason is 'practical' Kant means, among other things, that it is endowed with sufficient motivational power to realize its own prescriptions, regardless of any other interests. Since it is fundamentally an *interest*, reason can spontaneously generate the motivating principle needed for its actualization" (1980, 15). Because of this, Yovel continues, Kant's conception of reason may be described as having a erotic nature – hence the reference to reason's "needs," "satisfactions," "strivings," "affection," and so on. See also Yovel's contrast of reason and intelligence, which he ascribes to the understanding and hold to consist of an instrumental capacity whose ends are dictated by sources external to it (190). Beiser argues that the view that reason alone is sufficiently motivational is a fundamental one uniting diverse members of the German Enlightenment (1992, 5).

30. Moritz Schlick's description of the construction of science from protocol sentences is a particularly explicit example: "From them would gradually arise the rest of the statements of science, by means of the process called 'induction', which consists in nothing else than that *I am stimulated or induced by the protocol sentences* to establish tentative generalizations (hypotheses) from which those first sentences, but also an endless number of others, follow logically. . . . Thus in the schema of the building up of knowledge that I have described, the part played by observation sentences is first that of *standing temporally at the beginning of the whole process, stimulating it and getting it going*: (1959, 220–21; my italics).

31. Buchdahl mentions Duhem and Kuhn as holding Kantian views about the construction of science (1969, 510–11). It might be added that every critique of logical positivism has stressed the importance for scientific inquiry of principles that are not derived from the observation of nature.

32. The passage cited goes on to say that the division of nature into genera and species has become too familiar to evoke this sort of pleasure. On unity of explanation as the distinguishing feature of Newton's achievement, see Koyre (1965, 15); on Enlightenment responses to Newton, see Gay (1969, chap. 4); on Newton as providing Kant's paradigm for the notion of systematic unity, see Buchdahl (1969, 484–85).

33. This is found in the *Metaphysical Foundations of Natural Science*. See Okruhlik (1986, 314).

34. Okruhlik's excellent article "Kant on Realism and Methodology" (1986) discusses in detail the difference between several kinds of theoretical entity used by Kant.

35. See Buchdahl (1969, 497).

36. See Koyre (1965). Duncan (1986) has an interesting discussion of what he terms Newton's methodological conservatism as a reaction to the metaphysical excesses of scholastic science.

37. Westfall, for instance, in discussing just the experiments that Kant mentions at Bxii, writes: "Does not the principle of inertia merely express the observed facts of motion? The suggestion embodies our conviction that modern science rests on the solid foundation of empirical fact, that it was born when men turned from the empty sophistries of medieval Scholasticism to the direct observation of nature. Galileo, alas, is difficult to fit into such a picture, and the concept of inertia even more so. Throughout the *Dialogues* it is Simplicius, Galileo's own creation to expound the viewpoint of Aristotelianism, who asserts the sanctity of observation. Salviati, who speaks for Galileo, has ever to deny the claims of sense in favor of reason's superior right. 'Nor can I ever sufficiently admire the outstanding acumen of those who have taken hold of this opinion [Copernicanism] and accept it as true; they have through sheer force of intellect done such violence to their own senses as to prefer what reason told them over that which sensible experience plainly showed them to the contrary.' Not the least of what sensible experience showed men — or perhaps seemed to show them before Galileo instructed them to interpret experience otherwise — was that force is necessary to keep a body in motion. Indeed, where is the experience of inertial motion? It is nowhere. Inertial motion is an idealized conception incapable of being realized in fact. If we start from experience, we are apt to end with Aristotle's mechanics, a highly sophisticated analysis of experience" (1977, 21). See also Toulmin (1961), Koyre (1965), and Arendt (1977).

38. For further discussion, see Kitcher (1986), Okruhlik (1986), and Butts (1984).

39. See Kemp Smith (1962, 36–37).

40. Hans Reichenbach, for example, elaborates such a picture with the "logical device" of a diary containing reports of every observation made by someone who does not know the difference between dreaming and waking. Reichenbach's description is worth quoting in full: "A perfect diary of this kind, which collects reports of all our observations, but does so without criticism and abstains from inferences going beyond what is actually experienced, may be regarded as the logical basis of human knowledge. To study the build-up of knowledge, the philosopher has to consider the inferences which lead from this basis to statements about physical objects, dreams, and all kinds of scientific constructions, such as electricity or galaxies or a guilt complex. Let us therefore imagine a man who tries to construct a system of knowledge from the report sentences which he finds in his perfect diary. He would try to construct an order into these sentences by arranging them in groups and formulating general laws holding for them. For instance, he would discover the law: whenever there is a sentence reporting that the sun shines, there is a later sentence reporting that it gets warmer, which result he then formulates as a relation between things: whenever the sun shines it gets warmer" (1973, 260).

41. Compare Kant's claim in the *Groundwork* that he has interest in attempting to propose not a new moral principle but, rather, a way of grounding and describing a moral principle that is, in fact, already a part of our moral consciousness.

42. Lovejoy's (1936) *Great Chain of Being* is the best-known account of the influence of the notion of a continuous scale of created beings upon scientific thought.

43. For further discussion of these three principles and their relationship to one another, see Butts (1986b).

44. For discussion of such constraints, see Buchdahl (1986) and Butts (1984).

45. The indeterminacy of Descartes's *Rules* prompted Leibniz to remark that Descartes's guidelines were like the rules of some chemist: take what you need and do what you should and you will get what you want. But neither Leibniz nor anyone who followed him seemed successful in obtaining more specific rules.

46. There is good evidence for the idea that the importance of distinguishing his view from Spinoza's was a major cause of the emphasis on teleology in Kant's later work. Kant had been accused of Spinozism during the pantheism controversy and was concerned to refute the

accusation; and a major part of the attack on Spinoza included an attack on the latter's denial of final causation (see *Hauptschriften* 1916, 236, 245, 276, 315). Only one reference to Spinoza occurs in Kant's earlier writings (Vorländer 1924, 331). Hence, the attack on Spinoza's purposeless conception of the Unconditioned in the third *Critique* is likely to be significant, providing Kant with an internal way of distinguishing his view from rationalism and fatalism.

47. For good discussion of these matters, see Arendt (1977), Böhme and Böhme (1983), and Yovel (1980). Böhme and Böhme point out that the loss of a "natural" connection to nature took place at the same time as the Enlightenment's destruction of a religious worldview: "It is as if one took away the ground under our feet and the roof over our heads at the same time" (1983, 70). The fear and alienation caused by this double loss, they argue, is the source of the tremendous effort to prove the goodness and intelligibility of nature that pervaded seventeenth- and eighteenth-century epistemology, theology, and economics.

48. For some instances of such appeals, see A482/B510; A514/B542; A698/B726; V, 185, 193; XX, 216.

49. Kant expressed this most clearly in a passage of the essay "The End of All Things," which compares Spinozism and Eastern religions, concluding with a scathing dismissal of both: "[Pantheism] is merely concerned that people may finally enjoy eternal rest, which is supposed to make up their blessed end of all things—really a notion whereby human beings lose their understanding and all thinking itself comes to an end" (VIII, 335–36).

50. For a discussion of related questions, see Friedman (1991; 1992b).

51. See, e.g. Kitcher (1984a; 1986), Buchdahl (1969; 1986), Butts (1986b), and Okruhlik (1986).

52. But Cohen claims that there is irony in the expression 'only an idea': "The object that is given in experience congruent to the concept is *only* an object. By contrast, however, the world is an idea" (1910, 88).

3

The Primacy of the Practical

The clearest example of a regulative principle of reason is given to us as the categorical imperative. "Act as if the maxim of your action were to become through your will a universal law of nature" is the principle by which our actions, insofar as they are moral ones, are guided. It cannot be known in any ordinary sense, nor does it give us access to knowledge: we are commanded to obey it but can never know whether we are successful in doing so. It functions as a directive for ordering our experience without determining that experience directly, linking us to the world without being derived from it. Though it is derived from the notion of a rational subject, it is not psychological but binding for all rational beings as such.

While no single principle exhibits these features of Kant's reconception of reason so purely, the categorical imperative has seldom been examined with reference to this context. This chapter will attempt to fill that gap. Its goal is not, of course, to provide a general account of Kant's ethics but to examine certain features of them in light of the claims I have made about Kant's notion of reason. This task is central to demonstrating the unity of theoretical and practical reason and giving content to the most crucial features of Kant's notion of reason itself. It will also, I hope, shed light on certain aspects of Kant's practical philosophy that have seemed problematic.

Structurally, this chapter follows many of the lines of the previous one. Section I examines Kant's attack on empiricism in ethics and show why empirical practical reason is as inadequate a basis for morality as sensibility proved to be a basis for science. Section II discusses the ways in which pure practical reason seeks the Unconditioned by setting particular ends for human action and addresses the so-called content problem (the charge, made famous by Hegel, that the categorical imperative is unable to determine specific moral principles) in light of the discussion of the notion of a regulative principle. Section III examines the differences between theoretical and practical reason, with attention to Kant's claim that reason is constitutive in the practical realm. Section IV explores Kant's denial of knowledge in morality, while section V treats his justification of the moral law.

I. The Role of Moral Theory

The *Groundwork of the Metaphysics of Morals* begins with an attack on a traditional conception of reason that is, in its way, as scathing as any in the first *Critique*. As theoretical reason mistakenly believes its object to be knowledge, practical reason holds its own to be happiness. Yet practical reason is as inadequate as a vehicle for the satisfaction of needs as theoretical reason proved to be as an instrument for obtaining knowledge. Rather than providing certain answers to the object of our inquiries, theoretical reason's search for knowledge merely produces endless and irresolvable speculation. Similarly, when practical reason views its goal as one of satisfying desire, it succeeds only in inventing new sources of dissatisfaction. Echoing Rousseau's brilliant critique of the way in which civilization drives us perpetually to produce new needs, leading to permanent discontent, Kant concludes that instinct would be far better suited for obtaining happiness than is reason.[1] The realization that reason is more successful at multiplying desires than at fulfilling them can easily lead, Kant warns, to a hatred of reason and a tendency to envy those who seem to use it as little as possible.

Kant, of course, has as little intention of joining these misologists in the practical realm as he did in the theoretical. The fruitlessness of reason's efforts to obtain knowledge or happiness is the ground not for a rejection of reason but for a reconception of it. The teleological language of the *Groundwork* passage may distract modern readers, but Kant's point can be made without reference to concepts like nature's purposes. If reason has proved markedly unsuccessful in obtaining its alleged ends, it makes good sense to ask whether its task has been misconstrued. So Kant sets the stage for a new conception of practical reason: only when understood as the means to producing a good will, rather than satisfying natural desires, can reason find "its own peculiar kind of contentment" (IV, 396).

It is important to ask why Kant goes to the trouble to repeat, in his ethical writings, the kinds of move familiar from the critique of theoretical reason. Why must practical reason be examined as well? The first *Critique*, if successful, has demonstrated the uselessness of reason as an instrument of knowledge. Its "Canon of Pure Reason," the only chapter explicitly devoted to reason's correct employment, tells us that reason's sole legitimate use is practical, its only genuine interests moral ones. The "Canon" concludes with a sharp and stirring passage insisting that in these matters, philosophy can advance no further than the common understanding.

Such a passage might easily be used in service of the misology that the *Groundwork* condemns; Jacobi was quick to cite it in his attempt to place Kant in his own antiintellectualist "party of faith." It is easy enough to read the first *Critique* as a condemnation not merely of speculative metaphysics but of philosophy in general, urging us to turn our attentions from useless intellectual efforts to the practical business of determining what we ought to do. Yet this latter task, Kant repeats, can be completed just as well, and often better, by the most ordinary intelligence as by that of the philosopher. The questions become acute when Kant tells us that he has no intention of introducing a new principle of morality (V, 8) and that "there is no need of science and philosophy for knowing what man has to do in order to be honest and good, and indeed to be wise and virtuous" (IV, 404). Moral philosophy is not needed to teach us our duties; for these, Kant says, we already know. The reader who has taken seriously Kant's claim that the point of all reason's efforts is a practical one might well ask why Kant needs a moral philosophy at all. Kant's own answer, as it stands, is not wholly satisfying. Practical philosophy is required not to instruct us in our obligations but to determine their source. What *practical* matters depend on this determination? Is Kant's concern with the foundations of morality an instance of precisely the sort of fruitless metaphysical meandering he condemned on epistemological and moral grounds?

The practical point of Kant's moral philosophy can only be understood by looking at its targets. It has been noted that Kant is not concerned to refute the thoroughgoing moral skeptic, whose demand for an answer to the question "Why be moral?" cannot be met in Kantian terms.[2] Contemporary readers may find in his work a response to, if not a refutation of, moral skepticism and relativism, but they are not the positions he holds to be significant. The real danger, he says, is the empiricism of practical reason, which bases the concepts of good and evil on the search for happiness (V, 71). Kant's claim that empiricism thereby undermines the purity of morality has fostered an image of his ethics as promoting a dour stoicism; his insistence on showing that pure practical reason alone can give us a true principle of morality may seem a quirky metaphysical point. For in an individual context, what does it matter whether I serve my friend out of duty or inclination? Schiller may have been crude, but he was hardly mistaken, to suggest that individual actions done from inclination—love, affection, and concern for another's welfare—are often preferable to those undertaken out of principle.[3]

Kant's remarks assume a different caste when we move from questions of individual ethics to those concerning political choices. Perhaps the clearest statement of his concerns can be found in the late essay "On the Old Saw: That May Be Right in Theory but It Won't Work in Practice." There he argues that a government founded on the principle of benevolence would be "the worst conceivable despotism" (VIII, 291). A paternalistic government, dedicated to maximizing its citizens' happiness, would deprive them of the most fundamental human rights. These remarks suggest that it is not riotous individual hedonism but deliberate, organized despotism, which is the outcome Kant most fears from theories that try to derive right from inclination.

This suggestion is confirmed by Beiser's recent work, which shows the extent to which German conservatives explicitly depended on the claim that the purpose of the state is to promote its subjects' welfare. The fact that the leading journal of reactionary opinion in late eighteenth-century Germany was entitled *Eudämonia* underlines the degree to which paternalistic despotism and the pursuit of civil happiness were linked in the minds of Kant's contemporaries (Beiser 1992, chap. 12). Yet long before, and often since, the Enlightenment, political theorists and politicians have sought to defend elite institutions of government by appealing to the welfare of the common citizen. These appeals are most noteworthy not in the claims that upsetting the status quo can cause turmoil and bloodshed but in the everyday sort of conviction that the common person is not ready for, or desirous of, the freedom and activity implied in full participatory citizenship. They yearn, rather, for the benevolent care and control exercised by a competent father; and their needs are best satisfied by the government that most resembles him.

Kant is rarely so striking as when he agrees with this claim. He does not accuse those rulers appealing to it of hypocrisy; indeed, some of his more difficult political discussions rest on the dubious assumption that the despot's claim to be acting on behalf of his people's welfare is genuine. Kant states that the benevolent despot normally not only truly intends to serve his people's happiness, but in fact, often succeeds in doing so; for people "always prefer that passive state to the perilous position of seeking a better one. . . . One is content with the constitution one lives under. Hence, from the viewpoint of *the people's welfare*, no theory properly applies at all; instead, everything rests on a practice submissive to experience" (VIII, 306). In "What Is Enlightenment?," Kant names laziness and cowardice as sources of the preference most people show for that self-incurred immaturity that is the opposite of enlightenment: "It is so convenient to be immature! If I have a book to have understanding in place of me, a spiritual advisor to have a conscience for me, a doctor to judge my diet for me, and so on, I need not make any efforts at all. I need not think, so long as I can pay; others will soon enough take the tiresome job over for me" (VIII, 35).

Attentive readers will hear gentler echoes of Rousseau's dictum that men must be forced to be free. *As they are now*, most people are happiest in a paternalistic state that furthers their passivity. Hence, if inclination is made the basis of morality, the best of all governments is an enlightened despotism. Kant is not concerned with the abuses that often lead to institutions' falling far short of that option. Even were despotism always and in fact the guarantor of the greatest possible happiness, it would undermine that freedom which is the essential quality of humanity. If promoting that freedom leads to a decrease in happiness, so much the worse for happiness.[4]

The *Groundwork* tells us that autonomy is the ground of the dignity of human nature, the *Critique of Practical Reason*, that freedom is the keystone of the whole architectonic of reason. The idea of human nature, as defined by its (potential) freedom, is the point on which Kant's philosophy rests.[5] This fact means that Kant's view of human life is one that contains a perpetual struggle or balance between two realms. Those realms are not helpfully viewed as ontological ones, containing two sorts of selves.[6] Rather, human nature is perpetually torn between its knowledge of the way the world is and its vision of the way the world ought to be—between the actual and the possible, the natural and the reasonable. That these standpoints guarantee a perpetual struggle is clear not only from his repeated insistence that the concept 'ought' has no meaning in nature but also from his occasional suggestion that it arises in opposition to nature.[7]

Kant's moral philosophy—and indeed, his philosophy as a whole—may be viewed as an attempt to legitimize this struggle. By ridiculing the very notion of a possible world that is not derived from the actual one, the empiricist would undercut this struggle from the start. While the empiricist's appeal to questions of practicality and the lessons of history is cast as simple common sense, Kant shows it to be foul play; the appeal to experience is often an appeal to conditions caused precisely in order to make particular political institutions appear necessary. In no case may the validity of moral ideas be judged by the very experience they call into question; for if the ideals had been realized—and this is always possible—that experience would have been very different (A317/B373).

Kant's reconception of reason is an attempt to undercut the metaphysics that make the appeal to experience in moral and political questions seem a natural one. Reason's role is to provide laws that tell us what ought to happen, even if it never does, not laws of nature, which tell us what does happen. The rightfulness of reason's laws is not to be determined by experience; rather, the worth of experience is to be judged by its ability to meet the ideals of reason. Kant knows that the views to which this leads are commonly ridiculed as visionary; his aim is to show that ridicule to be philosophically illegitimate. The empiricist assumes, without argument, that experience is the proper standard by which ideals are to be evaluated. Kant constructs an entire philosophical system showing that it is, on the contrary, reason's function to set ends and ideals for experience. Those who deride such ideals as unrealistic have begged Kant's questions about the nature of reality. No one knows better than he does that ideas of reason are not things in the world. His attack on rationalism and his exposure of transcendental illusion depend on the recognition that reason's ideas are not objects of experience. Having demonstrated this claim with an analysis of what it means to be an object of experience, Kant is able to complete his task by showing how ideas of reason, though not things in the world, nevertheless play a crucial role in it. The examination of the peculiar sort of reality that is proper to accord to ideas of reason begins, of course, with his analysis of the task of reason in science. By showing that regulative ideas that can never be known are necessary for the construction of anything we could call knowledge, Kant prepares the way for validating their legitimacy in the construction of human society.

The attempt to dismiss demands for radical social change by appealing to the sorry facts of past experience is as familiar as the claim that these demands run counter to general welfare and inclination, with which it is intimately connected. Conservative attempts to uphold present states of affairs by means of what Kant holds to be a metaphysical error are easy to find in every historical period. It will be useful, however, to examine this move by looking briefly at the writing of Edmund Burke, who embodies precisely the sort of empiricism in morality that Kant aims to undermine.

Burke's *Reflections on the Revolution in France* is an attack on the very idea of revolutionary change. The demand for such change, he writes, is the result of "dissolute," "extravagant," and "presumptuous" speculation, which "despises experience" in favor of rights of man that admit of no compromise (1969, 124, 148, 154). The revolution suffers from a mistaken "political metaphysics," which judges the legitimacy of a government by its conformity to abstract theories of right, rather than its success in increasing human welfare (1969, 149). Part of Burke's defense of the monarchy consists in an inventory of its tangible contributions to general happiness: the wealth and magnificence of the cities, industry, and arts of the ancien régime are admiringly put forth as standards by which to judge whether a government should remain (233–34). The revolutionaries would abandon the interests of the public, proven to have been served in the past by particular institutions, "to the mercy of untried speculations [that have] nothing in experience to prove their tendency beneficial" (277). What is philosophically interesting in Burke is not his passionate decryal of those who "act as if they could begin everything anew" nor his staunch determination to follow, by contrast, the example of his ancestors (375). This sort of rhetoric might—and usually does—form part of any conservative polemic. But his description of revolution as "unnatural" and the revolutionaries as people "at war with nature" expresses the implications of the metaphysics developed by Hume (138). Political institutions should conform to nature's "unerring and powerful instincts," rather than "the fallible and feeble contrivances of our reason" (121). In adjuring a good legislator to study "human nature and habits" rather than "metaphysics," Burke does not, of

course, consider that his own position depends on a particular and powerful metaphysics with its own conception of human nature (299). Like many other political
commentators, he finds it sufficient to deride those who propose different ones as,
alternately, bumbling, incompetent "professors", and "desperate," "intoxicated"
"adventurers" (155, 349, 360).

Few people would so cheerfully accept Burke's description of those who "expect
heaven and earth to bend to grand theories" (323) as Immanuel Kant. It was Kant,
after all, who wrote that "even the Holy One of the Gospel must first be compared
with our ideal of moral perfection before we can recognize him to be such" (IV, 408).
It has been argued that "On the Old Saw" was written in response to Burke's
Reflections. Though Kant refrained from saying so explicitly to avoid arousing the
Prussian censors, no contemporary reader would have missed the allusion to Burke's
text, which had appeared the previous year.[8] Even if the *Reflections* is not Kant's
explicit target, "On the Old Saw," written during one of the more difficult phases of
the French Revolution, forms a powerful answer to the kinds of foundational arguments used against radical change by conservative thinkers, if seldom as clearly
formulated as in Burke's work.

Kant's essay attempts to match and undermine Burkean rhetoric. Those who
believe that the ideas of reason must be judged by experience have the conceit to
believe that one can "see farther and more clearly with the eyes of a mole, fixed upon
experience, than with the eyes of a being that was made to stand erect and to behold
the heavens" (VIII, 277). The empiricist's "tone of lofty disdain" is often more
powerful than his arguments; Kant attempts to counter it by appealing to a vision of
the purity of the ideas of reason and the glory of a being who can create and obey
them. Kant believes that people are moved by ideals of reason the more purely and
nobly they are represented; yet we may wonder whether such depiction is enough to
counter the derisive rhetoric that dismisses every such portrait as merely and imprac-
ticably visionary. Embedded in Kant's text are, however, arguments that the empiricist cannot match.

The essay opens with a foundational reference. Anyone who disdained systematic
theory in natural science in favor of "fumbling with experiments and experiences"
would be exposed as an ignoramus (VIII, 275–76). Where theory in science does not
work well in practice, the good scientist supposes the fault to lie in there not being
enough theory and proceeds to try to discover a more correct or extensive one. Here
Kant relies on such texts as the preface to the B edition of the first *Critique*, in which
the revolutions of natural science were described as the result of the use of principles
of reason, which interrogated experience. If we would "laugh at" one who rejected
theory in favor of practice in these cases, why should we accept the "philosophically
scandalous pretense" that this maxim is sound in matters of morality?

Most of the essay is concerned to show that the moral law is not an "empty
ideality" but can establish specific standards by which just constitutions and governments can be constructed. The principle of happiness, by contrast, leads both to
despotism and to blind rebellion. Describing the particular political ends to which the
categorical imperative leads is important for establishing Kant's claim that what is
needed to bring practice in line with theory is more theory, not its absence; those ends
will be examined in section II. Before closing the essay Kant returns to the metaphysi-

cal point. The empiricist's reference to experience can only be a reference to past and particular experience, whose use as a standard would be illegitimate, indeed laughable, in cases of natural science. As long as the impossibility and futility of an effort is not absolutely certain, we cannot abandon the future by reference to the past:

> Empirical arguments against the success of those resolves which rest on hope, are insufficient here. The argument that what has not succeeded so far will therefore never succeed, does not even justify the abandonment of a pragmatic or technological intention (as that of air travel by aerostatic balloons, for instance) much less the abandonment of a moral intention that becomes a duty unless its accomplishment is demonstrably impossible. (VIII, 309–10)

Contemporary voices who would counter this argument with the familiar lament that experience has shown humankind to be far more proficient in technological, rather than political, progress may not be wrong, but they have ignored Kant's metaphysical point.

There are many good reasons to describe Kant as the philosopher of the French Revolution.[9] Eighteenth-century despotism found its ideological base in the demonstrations of the existence of God, providence, and immortality that Kant's epistemology destroyed.[10] And nowhere were the ideas of freedom and equality that became the Revolution's watchwords so clearly defended as in Kant's moral philosophy. Yet without Kant's initial insistence that the possible is not to be derived from the actual, none of these claims hold weight. Every revolutionary proposal is vulnerable to those critics who claim that freedom and equality may be very nice in theory but are invalidated by the "hard facts" of experience. The greatest achievement of Kant's moral theory is the metaphysical foundation of moral theory itself. His aim is to turn the tables on the empiricist critics. That moral theory contradicts experience is no surprise: it is precisely reason's role to deny nature's claim to be definitive and to assert its authority by providing laws to which experience *ought* to conform.

This claim is a metaphysical one. I believe it is only by emphasizing it that we begin to understand Kant's conviction that his lifework was in the service of the rights of man or Heine's description of Robespierre as tame and moderate in comparison to Kant.[11] "On the Old Saw" contains, in miniature, the structure of argument that I have tried to lay out in Kant's texts as a whole. Reason's ideas, which are not derived from experience but structure and guide our relation to experience, are indispensable to science. Once we discover and acknowledge their peculiar reality there, we are able to recognize it in the practical realm where it is most disputed. That this claim was enduring and fundamental can be seen by turning back from "On the Old Saw" to the "Transcendental Dialectic" that opens with a discussion of Plato's *Republic*, the only extended discussion of a moral issue in the first *Critique*: "The *Republic* of Plato has become proverbial as a striking example of a supposedly visionary perfection, such as can exist only in the brain of the idle thinker" (A316/B373). Yet the ridicule this work has provoked does not arise from attention to unavoidable facts of human nature but conditions which are quite remediable, namely, "the neglect of the pure ideas in the making of the laws." Were those ideas applied to experience, the features of Plato's state that seem most visionary—the absence of punishment, a constitution allowing the greatest possible human freedom—could come into being:

> Nothing, indeed, can be more injurious or more unworthy of the philosopher, than the vulgar appeal to so-called experience. Such experience would never have existed at all, if at the proper time, those institutions had been established in accordance with ideas, and if ideas had not been displaced by crude conceptions which, just because they have been derived from experience, have nullified all good intentions. . . . This perfect state may never, indeed, come into being; nonetheless, this does not affect the rightfulness of the idea, which in order to bring the legal organization of humankind ever nearer to its greatest possible perfection advances this maximum as an archetype. For what the highest degree may be at which humankind may have come to a stand, and how great a gulf may still have to be left between the idea and its realization, are questions which no one can, or ought to, answer. For the issue depends on freedom; and it is in the power of freedom to pass beyond any and every specified limit. (A317/B374)

In the meantime, Kant concludes, nothing is more reprehensible than subjecting the limits of what ought to be done to those which circumscribe what is done. The placing of this discussion, in Kant's introductory explication of reason entitled "The Ideas of Reason in General," gives some indication of his views as to its centrality. More telling, perhaps, is its conclusion: "But though the following out of these considerations is what gives to philosophy its peculiar dignity, we must meantime occupy ourselves with a less resplendent but still meritorious task, namely, to level the ground, and to render it sufficiently secure for moral edifices of these majestic dimensions" (A319/B376).

This is, Kant frankly acknowledges, an idealism—in the popular sense of the word—as striking as any to be found in Plato. Plato's mistake, Kant holds, was merely to give the ideas the wrong sort of ontological status. Yet even after attending to the function of the regulative ideas within science, many readers will want to ask precisely what sort of ontological status Kant gives them. This question becomes particularly acute in the face of Vaihinger's interpretation, which has remained influential. Vaihinger sought to show that regulative ideas were fictions and to demonstrate the usefulness of such fictions in many fields of endeavor. Yet the most well-meaning defense of the utility of fictions will not serve to undercut the empiricist who is Kant's target. The possibility of radical social change depends upon showing that ideas of freedom and equality, of a state without punishment and a world without war, are *not* fictions, subject to debate as to their utility but bereft of the reality that is the empiricist's touchstone of legitimacy. Though Vaihinger may have seen himself as defending and expanding Kant's work, his description of ideas as heuristic fictions plays directly into the hands of those who depict revolutionary social institutions as visions "such as can exist only in the brain of the idle thinker." For reason, Kant warns, "cannot command one to pursue an end which is recognized to be nothing but a fiction" (V, 472); and it is just our pursuit of certain ends that he is concerned to secure.

Hence, Kant is explicit in insisting that the ideas are not "mere fictions" or "figments of the brain" (A314/B371 A569/B597). The first *Critique* distinguishes between ideals of reason and products of the imagination and warns against trying to realize the latter through the former. The attempt to depict the character of the perfectly wise man in a novel, for example, can be positively destructive (A570/

B598). Since the unnaturalness of such a person will be clear in any depiction, the reader may conclude that the good itself is a mere fiction. An idea of reason, Kant writes, gives a rule and an archetype. Fictions, by contrast, are products of imagination and sensibility; as concrete sets of particular qualities, they are not determinable by rules.

There are, however, even more important differences between fictions and ideas. Like ideas, fictions are representations that have no object in experience; yet unlike ideas, fictions have no essential relationship to experience at all. The question whether a fiction should be realized or realizable in experience is not a meaningful one; aesthetic considerations alone determine the distance from experience that we prefer our fictions to have. Debates about realism within literature take place in terms internal to the fictional structure itself. The depiction of a fictional character has no fundamental consequences for experience at all.

Ideas of reason, by contrast, make demands on experience. This is part of the meaning of Kant's statement that 'ought' implies 'can': every idea of reason posits a state of affairs that experience could and should fulfill. As the idea of the Unconditioned presents a vision of intelligibility that is a challenge to the unexplained and unsystematic mass of experience in which we find ourselves, so the moral law makes an immediate claim on our behavior. The assimilation of the disjunction ought/is to that of the disjunction fiction/reality leaves no room for the questions that Kant is most concerned to explore, namely, whether there may be different ways in which things can be real. If implicit in the moral law there is not only the idea that something could happen but that it ought to happen, its practical power *in shaping reality* may be far more significant than any particular piece of given reality. Kant's regulative ideas contain a notion of responsibility to experience, but it is not that of the empiricist: an idea of reason is linked to reality by its claim that it ought to be realized in the future.

Vaihinger's claim that we are acting irrationally in following the moral law betrays his lack of awareness of the complexity of Kant's conception of reason, as his assimilation of ideas to fictions fails to attend to the heart of Kant's discussion of reality (Vaihinger 1892, 306). Yet there may remain something disturbing in the claim that in following the moral law, I am commanded to act on an assumption that is not true. The maxim of my action is *not* a universal law of nature. The demand to specify the elusive nature of the ideas' reality becomes most difficult where its need seems greatest: Just what is the sense of the command to act upon a statement that I know to be false?

A fuller answer to this question will be given in section III, when discussing Kant's claim that reason is constitutive in the practical realm. Because we can determine our wills, if not the course of nature, the categorical imperative contains within itself a capacity for realization that no other idea of reason contains. Kant's point, I think, is not only that a moral idea, in making a demand upon the world, always presupposes that its realization is possible, but further, that only by acting in accordance with it can we realize it. That we cannot know whether the idea will be realized is clear from the start: we have to do here with reason, not a matter of knowledge. We can, however, be certain that if we do not act accordingly, the idea will never be realized. If we have a moral interest in the realization of this idea, we therefore have a duty to act as if it were true. Such action has nothing to do with the wishful thinking of a utopian dreamer, for it is only by acting in such a manner that a moral idea can be made to be true.[12]

I would like to explore this thought further by examining what is perhaps the most difficult, and certainly the most central, of Kant's ideas in the practical realm. This is the idea of autonomy, considered as a political, not a metaphysical, problem.[13] Kant's clearest reply to the common empiricist objection to this demand occurs in a footnote to *Religion within the Limits of Reason Alone*.

> I grant that I cannot really reconcile myself to the following expressions, used by even clever men: "A certain people (engaged in a struggle for civil freedom) is not yet ripe for freedom." . . . For according to such a presupposition, freedom will never arrive, since we cannot *ripen* to this freedom if we are not first of all placed therein (we must first be free in order to make purposive use of our powers in freedom). The first attempts will indeed be crude and usually will be attended by a more painful and more dangerous state than that in which we are still under the orders and also the care of others; yet we can never ripen with respect to reason except through *our own* efforts (which we can only make when we are free). (VI, 188)

This passage (published, as Beiser notes, just one month after the execution of Louis XVI) is both strengthened and complicated by the claims of Kant's earlier essay "What Is Enlightenment?" There he writes that the problem is not only that the people, as they are now, are unable to think for themselves but that the rulers have a definite interest in preventing them from doing so. A particularly striking passage in the *Conflict of the Faculties* stresses the ways in which politicians ensure that their subjects remain unfit for citizenry while justifying repression with the spurious appeal to experience they themselves have created:

> One must take men as they are, [our politicians] tell us, and not as the world's uninformed pedants or good-natured dreamers fancy that they ought to be. But "as they are" ought to read "as we have *made them* by unjust coercion, by treacherous designs which the government is in a good position to carry out." For that is why they are intransigent and inclined to rebellion and why regrettable consequences ensue if discipline is relaxed in the slightest. In this way, the prophecy of the supposedly clever statesmen is fulfilled. (VII, 134)

It is not hard to view this problem, which Rousseau formulated but did not resolve, as the central one of modern political philosophy and practice. If rulers have no interest in cultivating genuine autonomy but use every means—from Rousseau's "garlands of flowers" to binding us with false needs to blunt censorship—in order to suppress it, how can those citizens who will form a true republic, rather than a mob democracy, ever be created? *The Social Contract* and *Emile* may be viewed as alternative ways of approaching the problem. The first, taking "men as they are and laws as they should be," shows us what kind of state might encourage the development of autonomous citizens. The second shows how, without changing current forms of social organization, a "man as he should be" might come to maturity. Rousseau never tells us how the gap between the two might be bridged—how people living in gilded chains could come to form a state that would further their autonomy or how a state with an interest in preventing genuine freedom could allow for the education of more than one isolated Emile. Kant seems to suggest a solution in a sort of gradualist bootstrapping: "There will always be a few who think for themselves, even among those appointed as guardians of the common mass. Such guardians, once they have themselves thrown off the yoke of immaturity, will disseminate the spirit of rational respect for personal value and for the men to think for themselves" (VIII, 41).

Is the picture of a people led by a few enlightened rulers who gradually come to be able to think, and then act, freely — so that they could in time be members of a state that fulfills the regulative idea of a social contract — Kant's last word on the subject? It should never be forgotten that all of Kant's texts were written with an eye toward the considerable powers of the Prussian censors and that his popular essays, in particular, are concerned to further the best alternatives possible within tightly circumscribed structures.[14] "What Is Enlightenment?" underlines the difficulty of the problem while shying away from a solution appropriate to it. In the passage quoted from the *Religion*, Kant seems readier to bite the bullet. Though a people may not in fact be ripe for freedom, the only way to make them so is to allow them freedom, that is, *to act as if they were free*. The dangers to which this allowance may lead are now clearly seen to be greater than the pains that attend the process of learning to walk, Kant's analogy in "What Is Enlightenment?" Nevertheless, Kant suggests, the only way to realize this ideal of reason is to act as if it were already true. The conditions for political autonomy are not something we can wait for; they cannot be given but only created. Only by acting freely can we become free. The only alternative to perpetual servitude is the decision to allow people *as they are now* to use their own reason; if they are permitted to do so, Kant holds, they will become a people worthy of freedom.[15] Kant's enthusiasm for *Emile* was surely a result of the way in which it sustains the hope that such a process can succeed. Hope is not a promise; Kant can only show that the alternative course of action rests on, and leads to, sheer hopelessness.

Kant's commitment to acting upon the ideas of reason coexists with a full awareness of the worst features of experience. The book that ends with a call for the freedom to develop the worthiness for freedom begins with a description of our experience of the human propensity to corruption that is as dark as anything our own century has produced (VI, 33). Nothing could be further from a much-caricatured Enlightenment belief in the goodness of human nature than Kant's stunning description of the manifest and hidden barbarities to be found both in the state of nature and in advanced civilization.[16] His opposition to empiricism does not rest on a different description of the facts of experience but on his *denial that those facts are authoritative* for moral practice. It is just his insistence on clear delimitation of the bounds of experience and the claims of reason that makes his idealism mature. Reason is not constitutive: it cannot attempt to derive what is from what ought to be. But it cannot abdicate its right to determine what ought to be by trying to derive morality from experience. Only by understanding the differences between the way things are and the way they should be — between actual experience and the ideas of reason — do we gain the possibility of making those ideas actual.

II. The Politics of Autonomy

If practical reason is an unsuitable means for obtaining happiness, and happiness, an unsuitable basis for virtue, practical reason must, Kant concludes, have another purpose than hitherto supposed. Readers of the first *Critique* will not be surprised to find practical reason's most general goal described as similar to that of theoretical reason: both freely produce ideas that are used to judge and order experience, though they do not determine it. Further similarities are found in Kant's more detailed descriptions of practical reason's structure. Like theoretical reason, practical reason does not provide knowledge but determines ends. This is a matter of motivation and guidance; reason does not tell us what the world is like but how to act upon it.[17] In practice as in theory, reason provides orientation by presenting us with the idea of an Unconditioned, an end whose the positing is sufficient in itself, a point that demands no further justification because its desirability is self-explanatory. For practical reason, the Unconditioned is the good will; every other good is contingent upon it, as the only thing that is absolutely good in itself, independent of all conditions.[18] Practical reason's search for the Unconditioned, like that of its theoretical counter-part, is presented as a task: we can never know whether we have attained it, but the attempt to do so is presupposed in every action that is genuinely moral. So Kant describes the goal of practical reason in terms familiar from the first *Critique*'s discussion of the search for complete intelligibility: "Virtue is always in *progress* and yet always beginning *from the beginning*. It is always in progress because, considered *objectively*, it is an ideal which is unattainable, while yet our duty is constantly to approximate to it" (VI, 409). Finally, this attempt creates a shared order according to law. The search for happiness leaves us at the mercy of private and subjective ends that lead, by themselves, to disharmony and chaos. If our actions are guided by the search for the Unconditioned, they are, by contrast, directed by principle and aim at a common end. Hence, in theory and in practice, reason imposes systematic unity by seeking it. As theoretical reason can only construct science by proceeding as if nature were constructed according to empirical law, so practical reason must proceed as if its maxims were the basis of universal laws of behavior. Though the principles on which they proceed are not objective, they are the only possible means for construct-ing public, intersubjective order for free subjects.

It has often been charged that Kant's moral law is purely formal: the ends that practical reason sets are too general to determine particular courses of action. A number of answers have been made to this charge.[19] Here I wish to argue that considered from the point of political rather than individual ethics, it is striking how much content the categorical imperative actually contains. The suggestion that the broadest goal of Kant's philosophy is political is not a new one,[20] yet I believe it has received insufficient attention in discussions of solutions to the content problem. Kant's own examples have been taken to suggest that his primary concerns were prosaic and individual ones, such as ruling out cheating greengrocers and dishonest trustees. Yet those who work under governments controlled by state censors become skilled in writing—and decoding—texts designed to elude them. The individual character of Kant's examples did not distract Kant's contemporaries from their broader social implications.[21] Kant's warning against deriving morality from exam-ples just before introducing the four famous examples of the *Groundwork* may even be meant to underscore his most general aims.[22]

It should be remembered that under the benevolent despotism that recognized one, and only one, person's will as law, the very form of the categorical imperative makes a radical, republican demand. It has rightly been pointed out that even the formal aspects of Kant's procedures contain political implications. Arendt argues that Kant was the only person in the history of philosophy besides Socrates to emphasize the public, communal nature of thought. The idea that the criteria of the reasonable have to do with general communicability—"the test of free and open examination," rather than truths dependent on isolated and elite authority—is itself a commitment to the most fundamental political egalitarianism (Arendt 1982, 38–40). And Saner emphasizes the antiauthoritarian form of Kant's use of the method of polemics, underlining his description of philosophy itself as a permanent party of opposition, devoted to setting forth all rational objections to existing doctrines (1973, 102, 197).

I have suggested that Kant did not differ with the early definition of the human being as the rational animal; he rather redefined the meaning of rationality. These considerations suggest that the concept of the person and of reason—which is the foundation of Kant's philosophy as a whole—itself embodies a political demand. The connection of reason and autonomy, and hence of freedom as the essential quality of humanity, may seem too obvious to require emphasis, but its consequences gain force when it is contrasted with the two most common competing conceptions.[23]

Those conceptions can be attributed, at least embryonically, to Leibniz and Hume. For a Leibnizian, moral philosophy requires what Rawls refers to as a sparse conception of the person, the idea of the person as knower. This is because moral principles are given independently of all rational beings, so that moral action depends upon knowing the appropriate truths. Rawls has explained why Kant must reject such a conception as heteronomous:

> Kant's idea of autonomy requires that there exist no such order of given objects determining the first principles of right and justice among free and equal moral persons. . . . Heteronomy obtains not only when first principles are fixed by the special psychological constitution of human nature, as in Hume, but also when they are fixed by an order of universals or concepts grasped by rational intuition, as in Plato's realm of forms or in Leibniz's hierarchy of perfections. (1980, 559)

We must add that the heteronomy described by Rawls has direct political consequences. The conception of the person as knower is both private and hierarchical, supporting fanaticism and elites. If knowing is held to be the fundamental human act, those claiming superior knowledge will find it easy to defend a right to make fundamental political decisions for others. Here, Kant's distinction between knowing and thinking becomes crucial. In repeating that enlightenment is not a matter of knowledge but of resolution and courage, he underlines his commitment to a deeply egalitarian view. Anyone can think for himself, and anyone can fail. Shifting the focus from our capacity for knowledge to our capacity to reason allows Kant to sustain a commitment to the importance of increasing enlightenment while undercutting the claims to political authority that depend on superior knowledge.[24] Kant's concern to deny such claims forms the basis of his rejection of the other dominant conception of the person as a container of desires. As we saw in section I, this Humean conception leads to heteronomy not only in the Stoic sense of individual enslavement to a series of sensual desires. Even more threatening is the fact that the concept of the person as, fundamentally, a bundle of desires leads inevitably to the

conclusion that the best form of government is that which most nearly satisfies them—
which is, Kant argues, paternalistic despotism.

In section I, we saw Kant's argument against the metaphysical error of deriving
conclusions about the way society ought to be structured from a particular, and fixed,
empirical conception of human nature. In fact, any conception of human nature is a
constructed one. The vision of human nature with which Kant opposes both the idea
of the person as knower and the idea of the person as a bundle of desires is no
exception. Stemming from Rousseau, Kant's conception of persons as, most fundamentally, free and equal moral persons is no more fact than vision and contains a
normative element. This is especially clear in light of Kant's statements that most of
us are not yet free but must learn to become so. These represent at least a tacit
acknowledgment that Kant's conception of humanity is itself a regulative ideal. In at
least one passage, this acknowledgement becomes explicit:

> We must appraise this power [to fulfill the law] on the basis of our rational knowledge
> of what men should be in keeping with the idea of humanity, not on the basis of an
> empirical knowledge of men as they are. . . . Our high esteem for the ideal of
> humanity in its moral perfection can lose nothing of its practical reality by examples
> to the contrary, drawn from what man now is, has become, or is likely to become in
> the future. (VI, 403–4)

The moral autonomy that we potentially possess is a demand for freedom in (at least) two
senses: the freedom from the authority of anything but our own reason to determine our
wills—whether in moral questions or those concerning our happiness—and freedom to
choose and change the given world in which we find ourselves.[25] And the equality that
Kant insists we all possess is, similarly, a demand to realize a state of affairs that reflects
his claim that in these matters of practical reason far more fundamental than any matters
of knowledge, none of us has a privileged position.

Embedded in Kant's conception of the person, then, are the demands to realize the
first two ideals of the French Revolution. The texts that Kant devoted to political
theory make clear which institutions are ruled out by the moral demand for liberty
and equality. The *Metaphysical Elements of Justice* provides arguments, based on the
moral law, against every form of slavery, serfdom, and imperialism; against a
hereditary nobility and the protection of inherited landed estates; against censorship,
which sets limits to the public use of reason; and against taxation or military
conscription without consent. The *Elements* also provide arguments for the idea that a
republican government is the best one, based on the form of the moral law. *Eternal
Peace* strengthens the claims given there by arguing that only a republican government can secure the enduring peace that we have a duty to promote.

It has often been claimed that the form of the categorical imperative was inspired
by Rousseau's social contract. What seems certain is that Kant's own use of the social
contract is the political expression of the categorical imperative. As every individual
is obliged to test the maxims of his actions by asking if they could become the basis of
a universal law, so every lawmaker is obliged to frame his laws so that they might have
come about as the result of a social contract (VIII, 297). In denying that the social
contract is a historical act, Kant becomes the first modern political theorist to present
a moral argument for the necessity of community. Hobbes and Locke had given

utilitarian arguments for the need to leave a state of nature, in which human life, or at least the enjoyment of property, was perpetually threatened. Rousseau's uncertainty whether the transition from a state of nature to civil society could be given a moral foundation permeates and confuses much of his work. Kant, by contrast, speculated that happiness might be more easily and satisfactorily attained in a state of nature (VI, 318). Hence, his social contract becomes not a historical reality but a moral ideal. We have an obligation to leave the state of nature and enter civil society because only such society can promote our moral development. The goal of a state, therefore, is not to secure its citizens' private interests but to further their development to autonomy. With this argument Kant gives us a version of the third of the Jacobin slogans. Although *fraternité*, as a mere feeling, is not something Kant will make the basis of duty, his claim that we have a moral obligation to enter into community replaces it and puts him at considerable distance from the individualistic social contract theorists with whom he has been compared. For unlike those thinkers, Kant holds community to be required for the development of moral personality — that which distinguishes us from the beasts. If this is not quite the claim that the concept of the person is incoherent without a notion of community, it is the claim that everything valuable in the former depends on the latter.[26]

In providing arguments for the foundations of the three political demands of the French Revolution, Kant ensures that the categorical imperative is more than a method for ruling out (a small set of) individual transgressions, but prescribes a concrete and positive vision of how human society ought to be shaped. The contours of such a society are defined by the three juridical attributes Kant holds every citizen to possess by nature:

> first, the lawful freedom to obey no other law than one to which he has given his consent; second, the civil equality of having among the people no superior over him except another person whom he has just as much of a moral capacity to bind juridically as the other has to bind him; third, the attribute of civil independence that requires that he owe his existence and support, not to the arbitrary will of another person in the society, but rather to his own rights and powers as a member of the commonwealth (hence his own civil personality may not be represented by another person in matters involving justice and rights.) (VI, 314)

Precisely what political institutions are required in order to guarantee these rights may remain a matter of debate, although Kant is clear about which institutions (such as hereditary aristocracy) must by nature preclude them.[27] It should be noted that Kant's disinterest in specifying many details of political organization was characteristic of political debate of his time (see Beiser 1992, 16–17). Of primary importance was clarification about the goals and limits of state and society; questions about the form of government were regarded as secondary. In part, this reflects the view that the best form of government could not be determined a priori but only by looking at the history of particular cultures. Many liberals argued that in England, for example, a mixed constitution had promoted, and would best continue to promote, the autonomy of its citizens, while other solutions might be required for German states with a long absolutist tradition. Such an attitude well reflects a Kantian balance. Once the proper ends of the state are determined, the question of how to attain them must be settled empirically. This means, crucially, that the proper form of political institution cannot be decided for all times and peoples. What can be determined are questions of human rights, and the government's role toward its citizens. The *Metaphysical Elements* states that all innate rights are contained in the principle of innate freedom, the only original right that belongs to everyone in virtue of his humanity (VI, 237); that is, all specific political demands are derivable from the conception of the human as free being that is the basis of Kant's moral philosophy.

If the ideas of the French Revolution seem formal, it may be due to the fact that they have been formally interpreted and never materially realized. It is all too easy to view the political program that follows from the categorical imperative as something that was progressive for a time characterized by state-imposed censorship and hereditary aristocracy but that makes few demands upon, or gives little guidance in shaping, the present structure of reality. But attention to Kant's discussions of the conditions of active citizenship and his description of the ways in which governments have an interest in preventing their citizens from thinking for themselves lend weight to Horkheimer's claim that the Enlightenment that Kant had in mind has not yet been realized anywhere. The principles of Enlightenment on which the French Revolution were based have become so familiar as to seem insipid; but a glance at the political reality of even those Western democracies that claim to be built upon them should convince us that there is a great deal of work to be done before the conditions of civic freedom, equality, and community obtain.

Even for those for whom the demands of the French Revolution are not trivial platitudes, there may remain a question about Kant's own relationship to them. This is the result of his conflicting statements about the Revolution itself, which must be discussed briefly. The *Conflict of the Faculties* designates the French Revolution as the sign that gives us evidence that the human race is progressing toward a better state, while accounts of Kant's contemporaries repeatedly attest to his enthusiastic and public support of the Jacobins. Kant's use of the social contract and his account of the moral basis of political authority seem to entail that when a government fails to further (much less, actively inhibits) the development to autonomy that is its justification, citizens have not only the right but the duty to overthrow it. Yet readers have been baffled by his explicit and repeated denial that there can ever be a right to revolution, which flatly conflicts not only these suggestions but basic tenets of his moral philosophy as a whole. Most explanations of these blatant contradictions appeal to strategic questions and emphasize the threat of censorship under which Kant increasingly stood. Kant certainly feared that open support of the revolution would serve the censors as a justification to further curtail the freedom of the public use of reason on which, he believed, all hopes for change depended.[28] While this would explain Kant's witholding of printed support for the Jacobins, it can hardly explain his outright denial of a right to revolution, given the importance that truth telling plays in his moral views.[29] Recently, Beiser has offered the most original and compelling version of these explanations. By looking in detail at the political conditions engendered by the accession of Friedrich Wilhelm II and his minister of state Wöllner, he argues, we can tie Kant's vacillations on the question of the right to revolution to demands created by the crises of Prussian politics in the early 1790s. Beiser concludes that "Kant sacrificed philosophical consistency for a higher political ideal, freedom of the press, 'the last treasure remaining to us amid all civil burdens'.

Given the primacy of politics in Kant's philosophy, such a sacrifice should not surprise us" (1992, 53). This provides us with a plausible view of Kant's denial of the right to revolution which allows us to avoid both the conclusion that it was egregiously foolish or craven and the assumption that it should be given significant philosophical weight.[30] Even though formulated by Kant, if the reasons for that denial are focused on particular conditions of Prussian politics, we need not unduly heed them. For our interest is less in the texts he wrote for publication in eighteenth-century Prussia than in the question of the most compelling implications of his views.

There are two ways of bringing consistency to a theory that both describes a republican society guaranteeing freedom and equality to each of its citizens as a goal demanded by practical reason, and at the same time, appears to deny us the means of achieving it. The first way would focus on Kant's denial of the right to revolution and hope for whatever gradual change might be brought about by rather limited public criticism and the vagaries of providence. The second would reject his condemnation of active resistance to unjust forms of government as incompatible with the rest of his views.

I believe the latter path is the correct one. Rejecting Kant's denial of the right to revolution is made easier by the fact that his arguments for that denial involve a serious error. He most often argues that a supposed right to revolution would be self-contradictory; for in entering into a social contract, the peole have voluntarily abandoned arbitrary individual coercion for the rule of law. Having given up the right to be judges of their own cause, they cannot retain a right to judge whether a sovereign fulfills the conditions of the social contract. This argument depends on the very confusion between the social contract as an idea of reason and the social contract as an historical fact against which Kant warns. Only the latter conception could provide a foundation (and that not a particularly secure one) for the claim that a people had abdicated their sovereignty for all time. If, as Kant insists to the contrary, the social contract is not a historical occurrence but a criterion by which every law should be tested, it cannot follow that its use would involve a contradiction.[31] It seems rather to oblige us to ask of every law whether it could have been the product of a general law and to leave perfectly open what course of action should be taken when a law, or system of law, fails to meet the ideal. One might even suppose that we are obligated to change such a situation by any means not worse than the existing conditions.

The latter clause highlights Kant's greatest concern in denying a right to revolution. This is the fear of anarchy, a Hobbesian war of all against all through a sundering of civil society. Now the tone of this concern seems at odds with his statements that the state of nature may be a better guarantor of the people's welfare than civil society; but Kant's argument appeals to the need to preserve not happiness but the rule of law. So he claims that an alleged right to revolution would involve another contradiction. If everyone resisted an unjust sovereign, the conditions of justice themselves would be undermined. This claim is hardly as straightforward as Kant thinks. It rests on two empirical assumptions, both of which are false. The first, that every form of government, because involving a rule of law, is preferable to anarchy, is clearly disproved by the existence of fascism. The second, in assuming that every form of resistance leads straight to anarchy, ignores the possibility of civil disobedience, that most Kantian of forms of political action. Those who, by publicly affirming the idea of the rule of law while protesting the law's failure to live up to a standard of justice can hardly be accused of attempting to seek justice while undermining its conditions.

The question of determining when a particular society has reached the point at which commitment to the moral law involves violating a civil one will be a question of judgment; but so, according to Kant, is every moral decision. I believe we should conclude, with van der Linden, that Kant's absolute denial of the right to revolution deserves the same fate as his denial of a right to lie.[32] Kant's arguments for these denials are parallel: as telling the truth is a precondition for a viable human community, obeying the law is a precondition for any civil society. Yet if the very conditions of morality are violated, it may be a duty to commit acts that are otherwise forbidden. Kant's unwillingness to draw this conclusion surely stems from his awareness of the ease with which it may be abused; yet no one knows better than he that freedom involves risk. His denial of the right to revolution seems even more problematic than his infamous denial of the right to lie to a murderer. For the categorical imperative must lead us to conclude that if a government systematically subverts the conditions of autonomy and equality that are fundamental to the idea of humanity, it is our positive duty to change them. Kant's suggestions to the contrary may rest, finally, on his assumptions concerning the fundamental benevolence of the sovereign. Occasionally, he writes as if that assumption might approach the status of a regulative idea; but fortunately, he never quite asserts this. In order to preserve the very notion of the regulative idea as a force by which experience is to be challenged and transformed, rather than a vehicle for wishful thinking, we must reject Kant's condemnation of the right to revolution. Whether Kant's inability to do so was the result of political pressure or personal inability to accept the implications of his own views may remain an open question. The fact that his theory provides the philosophical underpinning for the goals of the French Revolution is not undermined by his unclarity as to what means are permissible to reach those goals.

I have argued, then, that the categorical imperative and the concept of the person that is its basis give us very specific principles for the organization of political society. Though first demanded by the leaders of the French Revolution, the juridical freedom, equality, and independence that Kant holds every citizen to possess have yet to be realized. If the *Groundwork*'s injunction to act so as always to treat humanity as an end in itself seems vague, Kant's political writings make clear what such treatment must entail. Viewed in the first instance as a political demand, the categorical imperative provides much clearer guidelines for action than has been supposed.

It does not, however, provide rules for determining correct action in every situation, and this seems to be demanded by many who have raised the charge that Kant's ethics are empty of content. That he could not have intended them to do so is clear from the range of moral questions he describes in the *Doctrine of Virtue* to be subjects for casuistry, the open discussion and examination of particular moral problems. There he writes that all ethical duties are of wide obligation: "for if the law can prescribe only the maxim of actions, not actions themselves, this indicates that it leaves a play-room (latitudo) for free choice in following (observing) the law, i.e., that the law cannot specify precisely what and how much one's actions should do toward the obligatory end" (VI, 389). Only law, Kant holds, can prescribe specific actions. Ethics, however, concerns the adoption of ends, which must be freely chosen. The "play-room" that Kant thus maintains to be necessary in observing the moral law extends not only to an open-endedness in the very examples that the *Groundwork* may have seemed to determine categorically, such as lying and suicide (VI, 422–23, 429–31). Further, those very circumstances on which nearly every ethical decision turns are described by Kant as empirical and hence not a part of ethics proper, which must be a priori. But these circumstances include: "How should one behave, for example, to men who are morally pure or depraved? . . . How should men be treated by virtue of their differences in rank, age, sex, health, prosperity or poverty, and so forth?" (VI, 468). In describing these questions as involving "so many different *ways of applying* the one principle of virtue" (VI, 468), Kant shows us how much room must be left in the application of the categorical imperative.

Much recent work in Kant's ethics has stressed the importance of this open-endedness for a doctrine in which ethical constraints are constructed (hence autonomous), rather than given.[33] As discussed in the previous chapter, the complaint that the regulative principles are empty or indeterminate also arises in theoretical inquiry, fueling the tendency to regard their import as negligible. I have argued that this complaint arises from a picture of content as exclusively cognitive content, which fails to recognize that if the principles are to fulfill their function as principles of orientation, they cannot be fully determinate. Were the methodological maxims required for science more specific than Kant leaves them, they would become an a priori anticipation of the content of discovery, not a set of guidelines for making further discoveries.[34] If the freedom implicit in the open-endedness of the principles—the fact that their use requires choice and judgment—is necessary in science, how much more crucial must it be in moral matters! This freedom is partly, but not only, itself a moral demand. Guidelines for human action must apply to infinite possibilities in an infinitely changing world. What could possibly serve as a rule that would determine the proper course of action in all of them? As O'Neill points out, a principle that was fully determinate could never cover more than a single case; hence, it could not function as a guide to action (1975, 11). Precisely in order to ensure that regulative principles provide guidance, Kant eschews the useless attempt to fix determinate actions in favor of describing the end of moral action in general, providing some constraints on its realization and perhaps most importantly, showing its possibility.

For similar reasons, Rawls argues that Kant "takes for granted that the application of [the categorical imperative] presupposes a certain moral sensibility that is part of our common humanity" (1989, 82). Something like this must follow from Kant's general claim that determining whether or not something falls under a given rule is a matter of judgment. The attempt to specify how a rule is to apply to every situation must lead to an infinite regress, demanding rules for applying rules for applying rules. Hence, Kant concludes, judgment cannot be taught but only practiced (A133/B172). O'Neill explicates this thought by arguing that reason is not algorithmic; we cannot expect it to generate a series of answers automatically. She believes that the claim that reason is not algorithmic is implicit in Kant's image of reason as a tribunal:

> To have a tribunal is not to have an algorithm that the tribunal follows. If that were what tribunals did, they would be redundant. Tribunals deliberate and reach verdicts; there are moves that they may not and had better not make as they move toward a verdict, but their charters and procedures do not fully determine every move. Theirs

is the genuinely practical task of judging; hence the tribunal provides an appropriate image for a critique or judging of reason. If Kant depicts the authority of reason as a tribunal that judges and deliberates, then presumably he thinks that reason too does not consist of algorithms for thinking or acting, which can be formulated as abstract rules. (O'Neill 1989, 18)

It is surprising that Kant's frequent use of the court or tribunal metaphor has not been more often invoked in discussions of the charge that the categorical imperative is purely formal.[35] For the moral law, like any other, must be applied, and its application will depend on matters of context. The meaning of the law must be interpreted with every application of it, and interpretation involves decision. We do not reject the First Amendment as empty because a series of courts may be required to decide, for example, whether a particular instance of free speech is protected under it or whether an instance of speech, in calling for violence, may undermine the conditions of freedom itself; or because even a final decision is just that, a decision whose correctness may be debated.

Recent work on the categorical imperative has emphasized that it is not intended to rule out formal inconsistences.[36] This is unsurprising in view of the fact that Kant's notion of reason is not a purely formal one; even in theoretical inquiry, the logical use of reason gives us but minimal constraints on rationality. Logic may provide grounds for rejecting some statements, but it cannot determine our acceptance of them; only the real use of reason can do that. We cannot expect the categorical imperative to do for practical reason what logic could not do for theoretical reason, to provide a mechanical test for the rejection and confirmation of every statement. Embedded in the use of reason in both spheres are notions requiring choice. The *Groundwork* examples display two sorts of contradictions meant to be excluded by the application of the categorical imperative, but neither of them is formal. The first is illustrated by the case of false promising.[37] We will look in vain for a logical contradiction in my willing that everyone but myself should keep promises. Rather, in requiring me to take up the perspective of the universal legislator in addition to my own, the categorical imperative embodies a demand regarding the moral equality of persons. My decision to accept that demand can only be a matter of choice.

Choice is even more apparent in the second kind of contradiction rejected by the categorical imperative, illustrated by the maxim of benevolence. Kant admits that there is no inconsistency in a universal law ordering that no one should ever help others; humankind could exist perfectly well in such a world. Yet it is not a world that we would choose to inhabit. Kant writes:

Thus people ask: If one belonged to such an order of things that anyone . . . looked with complete indifference on the need of others, would he assent, of his own will to being a member of such an order of things? Now everyone knows very well that if he secretly permits himself to deceive, it does not follow that everyone else will do so, or that if, unnoticed by others, he is lacking in compassion, it does not mean that everyone else will immediately take the same attitude toward him. This comparison of the maxim of his actions with a universal natural law, therefore, *is not the determining ground of his will. But such a law is still a type for the estimation of maxims according to moral principles. If the maxim of action is not so constituted as to stand the test of being made the form of a natural law in general, it is morally impossible (though it may still be possible in nature).* (V, 69–70; my italics; see also VI, 5–6)

In denying that the categorical imperative is the determining ground of our will, Kant emphasizes that it is, as he says in the passage following the one just quoted, a law of freedom. Since it requires us to consider what sort of world we as free beings would choose to inhabit, it cannot generate automatic results.

It is important to recall Kant's repeated statement that the categorical imperative merely formulates the rule by which everyone does in fact decide whether actions are right or wrong (V, 69), as well as his assertion that no one in fact wills that the maxim of his wrong action should become a universal law (IV, 424). What we will, in such situations, is just the opposite: everyone but ourselves should act according to the law that we would like, at the moment, to transgress. Kant's insistence that he is concerned to clarify the intuitions of ordinary moral consciousness suggests that the categorical imperative is not to provide us with new information but to remind us of what we already know. The central problem of ordinary morality is not knowing what is right but doing it; though conflicts of duties that require adjudication will arise, the more common conflict is between duty and inclination—finding the moral strength to act on the principles we know to be the right ones.[38] This suggests that the tendency to view the main problem with the categorical imperative as an intellectual one may be an instance of the conflict that Kant describes thus:

> Man feels in himself a powerful counterweight to all the commands of duty presented to him by reason as so worthy of esteem—the counterweight of his needs and inclinations, whose total satisfaction he grasps under the name of "happiness." . . . From this there arises a *natural dialectic*—that is, a disposition to quibble with these strict laws of duty, to throw doubt on their validity or at least on their purity and strictness. (IV, 405)

Practical reason, like theoretical reason, has a natural tendency to illusion, which leads to its misuse in subtle and spurious exercises that we today call rationalizations. The inclination to act as if our primary moral problem were the complex *intellectual* demands presented by morality, calling for the determination of conflicting obligations in examples of increasing difficulty, may be one of these. Moral philosophy, both popular and academic, is no more privileged than speculative metaphysics in leading us to seek knowledge where (more) knowledge is not what is needed.

As will be shown, the fact that the goodness of the will is what is at issue in morality proves crucial here; for here, as in theoretical philosophy, we are deeply constrained by our lack of knowledge. Not only can we not know the consequences of our actions, but we cannot even know the motives on which the goodness of our action depends. What is needed here is not knowledge but commitment to action from the perspective we know to be the moral one.[39] The categorical imperative reminds us of that perspective and its constraints.

III. The Objects of Practical Reason

Our discussion up to this point has focused on the similarities between theoretical and practical reason. My intention has been to explicate the unity of theoretical and practical reason that Kant stated to be a requirement of a complete critique of practical reason, "since in the end, there can only be one and the same reason, which must be differentiated solely in its application" (IV, 391). In showing that theoretical and practical reason possess a unified structure and operate according to common principles, I have hoped to provide part of the answer to Kant's question, How can pure reason be practical? If reason as a whole is regulative rather than cognitive, providing ends and standards for activity rather than knowledge, this question becomes less puzzling. For theoretical reason is in this sense already practical, concerned not with contemplation but with directing us to realize its ideas.

Yet Kant also states that there are differences between theoretical and practical reason, both in application and in power. In both, he says, practical reason has primacy. Should there be a conflict between them, theoretical must yield to practical reason as its superior (V, 121). This section aims to understand why Kant insists on the primacy of the practical, in a way that is consistent with his assertion of the fundamental unity of reason.[40] An account of the superiority of practical reason that posits too great a distance from theoretical reason is self-defeating; the greater the differences between theoretical and practical reason, the less plausible is practical reason's claim to be a form of reason at all. Hence, I will argue that the differences between theoretical and practical reason are not to be understood as differences in their essential natures but as differences about the world in which they are applied. This seems to be most in keeping with the *Groundwork* passage just cited as well as the most philosophically plausible route.

This claim is easiest to understand in the question of reason's area of application. Theoretical and practical reason are directed to different tasks: the one guides our investigation of nature, the other tells us how to live morally. One part of Kant's claim that the practical is primary is simply that the latter area is more important. This idea can be found in the autobiographical passage with which this book began, as well as in his statements that the labors of reason would never be undertaken but for practical interest (A797/B825). It has been noted that this evaluation is a reversal of one of the more fundamental tenets of the entire philosophical tradition, which has, since Plato, assigned a higher value to contemplation than to action.[41] The claim that the search for knowledge of the ideas of reason that constituted the history of Western metaphysics was a mistaken distraction from reason's true goal, the duty to realize those ideas in moral activity, is an astonishing reversal of priorities, but we should not look for an argument for it. Kant's attempt to defend this priority by claiming that every interest is ultimately practical seems unhelpful (V, 121). For this claim only makes sense if we understand 'practical' in the somewhat weakened sense that Kant describes in the first *Critique*, as "everything that is possible through freedom." In discussing the use of reason in science, I emphasized the way in which science too must depend on the free use of regulative principles. We might understand the claim that every interest is ultimately practical to be a reference to the regulative, end-positing character of reason as a whole; but in failing to show the differences in reason's areas of activity, this would be useless in explaining Kant's claim that practical reason is primary.

That claim must be understood in light of Kant's assertion that the only unconditioned good is a good will (IV, 393). Part of the meaning of 'unconditioned' is self-explanatory. The Unconditioned is that about which no further questions can be asked, for which no further justification is necessary. Theoretical inquiry is a conditional good while moral action is not. The claim that morality is more important than science is simply rock-bottom, for Kant. While the third *Critique* claims that it is practical reason that gives meaning to the universe as a whole, this is not a claim that can be justified by reference to something other than the foundational belief in the unconditioned goodness of the will.[42] Though it may sometimes seem to have the self-evidence of common sense, Kant's claim that morality is more important than science is a moral one. It can be explicated, though not justified, by appealing to the two moral aspects of persons that Kant holds to be essential. Practical reason exhibits those aspects more strongly than does theoretical reason. It is the more equal power, since the most extraordinary philosopher has no moral superiority over the most common understanding. Even more important, practical reason is the freest power; in creating its own objects, it exhibits, even more sharply than theoretical reason, the freedom we all possess.

The latter characteristic comes to the fore in Kant's second claim about the primacy of the practical. While the first claim concerned the relative importance of the areas of application of theoretical and practical reason, the second concerns their relative power. Practical reason is superior because it is stronger: while theoretical reason is restricted to guiding us in knowing objects, practical reason can make them actual (Bix;V, 89). Indeed, Kant goes so far as to say that reason is constitutive in the practical realm.

It is easy to construe this as a fundamental difference in the structure and nature of the two aspects of reason. Kant's own statements on the subject can lead to a variety of misunderstandings. One is the idea that practical reason can extend our knowledge further than theoretical reason is permitted to do; thus, its superior power is a power of superior cognition.[43] The second *Critique*'s claim that theoretical reason can only show the possibility of freedom, while practical reason demonstrates its reality, seems to support this idea (V, 4−5). But the idea that practical reason has access to a peculiar and superior sort of knowledge is highly problematic. The attempt to delimit a kind of knowledge that is not theoretical knowledge and hence not subject to the powerful strictures Kant himself established in the first *Critique* seems doomed to failure. Understood as a superior sort of knowledge, Kant's notion of practical reason must look like the magic wand that Heine mocked.[44]

Kant's claim that practical reason has the power to realize its objects can also lead to another sort of error, which misconstrues the differences between theoretical and practical reason.[45] Konhardt, for example, writes that practical reason is normative; its interest is not in the knowledge but in the realization of its ideas (1979, 98, 146). The discussion of the previous chapter should have made such a claim seem problematic; for the *correct* use of theoretical reason is not cognitive either, but regulative. The false belief that its task is to provide knowledge is precisely what leads theoretical reason into speculative metaphysics. Kant's alternative, of course, was not to dispense with theoretical reason but to turn its attention from metaphysics to science. By positing the Unconditioned as an ideal of inquiry, rather than attempting to assert something about its content, theoretical reason plays a crucial role in guiding and grounding our intellectual activity. Yet this role must be seen as a normative one: *if functioning properly*, theoretical reason does not provide us with knowledge of its ideas but directs us in the task of realizing them.

If the first mistake is to assimilate practical reason to a (non-Kantian) conception of theoretical reason, the second errs in creating too sharp a distinction between them. In fact, both these ways of understanding practical reason's superior power rest on a mistaken conception of theoretical reason. Both practical and theoretical reason, I have argued, are regulative, not cognitive; they are concerned not with the knowledge but with the realization of their ideas. The difference between them concerns not reason but nature. Theoretical reason's success is crucially dependent on the cooperation of the world. Practical reason, by contrast, can achieve its ends alone.[46] We do not control the forces of nature, but we can determine our wills. If this is the case, it is always possible for practical reason to realize its object. Every time we act according to the dictates of practical reason, we are creating a moral world.[47] So he describes practical reason as a faculty of "determining itself, i.e., its causality to effect such objects (whether the physical power is sufficient to do this or not). For here reason can at least attain so far as to determine the will; and, insofar as it is a question of volition only, reason does always have objective reality" (V, 16).

This allows us to see how Kant holds theoretical and practical reason to be genuinely unified in a common principle, and at the same time, maintains that practical reason has superior power. That power is not based on a different structure or task than that of theoretical reason but on the fact that its task is attainable independent of any facts about the world. Both theoretical and practical reason urge us toward the Unconditioned, providing principles that guide us in the search for systematic unity, the complete intelligibility that is always reason's goal. For theoretical activity, reaching that goal would require a complete knowledge of the world as a whole and its creation. Practical reason, by contrast, can achieve its end by determining a good will. When Kant describes the moral world as an intelligible one, he is not referring to a supersensible sort of reality but to the fact that our free action alone is sufficient, in morality, to reach the Unconditioned. So he states, "The moral law ideally transfers us into a nature in which reason would bring forth the highest good were it accompanied by sufficient physical capacities; and it determines our will to impart to the sensuous world the form of a system of rational beings" (V, 43; see A808/B836).

This gives us the second part of Kant's answer to the question, How can pure reason be practical? If the first part rests on the claim that reason is always active rather than contemplative, the second shows that in morality, reason's activity can always reach its end. And this in turn explains Kant's statement that practical reason demonstrates the reality of that freedom whose possibility theoretical reason provided. This statement should not be understood as a retraction of the argument that we cannot know either of the alternatives of the Third Antinomy. Kant's point is not about knowledge but about creation. Every time we act morally, we *are* free;[48] practical reason has the power not to know freedom but to realize it. While theoretical reason, it was argued, must function free of experience, its aims and results remain dependent on it. Practical reason constructs its own object: the moral world that can be ours every time we act to construct it.

It is important to note that this is not simply true of the good will that is each individual's should he succeed in acting out of pure respect for the moral law. Kant's claim that practical reason has the power to create its own object should not be viewed as a matter of isolated individuals creating their own intelligible worlds through seeking a virtuous character. His examples suggest that not only personal virtue but social institutions can be constructed through the action of practical reason. If we all followed the categorical imperative, the kingdom of ends would be achieved. Note the difference from theoretical reason, which must posit the cooperation of nature in order to continue its search. For practical reason, systematic unity under law just consists in all rational beings' ordering their actions according to the categorical imperative.[49]

Korsgaard (1992) argues that "when we enter into relations of reciprocity, and hold one another responsible, we enter together into the standpoint of practical reason, and create a Kingdom of Ends on earth" (20). The collective decision to enter into this standpoint is all that is required to realize two major ends that Kant names as objects of practical reason: Plato's state without punishment and a world without war. Of course, this requirement can seem overwhelming: the realization of these ideas depends on the decision of (nearly) everyone to take up the standpoint of practical reason. But unlike the objects of theoretical reason, their realization requires neither the cooperation of nature nor the intervention of providence. Practical reason cannot abolish all sources of suffering: an earthquake may destroy an enlightened city, a child may die of incurable disease. Attempts to alleviate what are rightly termed natural disasters soon run up against the limits of knowledge. While these are continually expanded, the structure of experience ensures that they will never be fully overcome. Mortality, in particular, is final.

Practical reason's objects, by contrast, are breathtakingly simple to realize. For human nature is *our* nature; the barriers to realizing the ideas of practical reason are internal ones. The fact that the good will of all rational beings is all that would be needed to establish peace on earth tomorrow is the fact to which Kant points in proclaiming the primacy of practical reason. The distinction between theoretical and practical reason is meant to underline how much lies in our hands alone.

Kant well knows that such claims will be derided as utopian. But those who urge the unlikeliness of all rational beings' deciding to will such an object would do well to remember Kant's warning to counteract our natural concern for the virtue of others and our own happiness by concentrating on their opposites. Could each of us succeed in doing so, the ideas of practical reason would become actual (VI, 384).

IV. Moral Certainty

The incompatibility of certainty and autonomy is a theme that reappears throughout Kant's discussions of reason. The idea that the limitation of knowledge is crucial for human freedom is stated most clearly in regard to the postulates of rational faith: a proof of God's existence would undermine morality, for it would prevent us from freely obeying the moral law for the sake of duty alone. Similar concerns appear, if less dramatically, with regard to theoretical reason as well: knowledge of the Unconditioned would render science impossible. Here I wish to explore Kant's denial of certainty in the moral realm.

As might be expected, many of the claims Kant makes here are parallel to those found in the theoretical sphere. Knowledge of the Unconditioned in the moral realm—the good will of ourselves or anyone else—is as impossible as knowledge of its theoretical counterpart. Indeed, Kant holds that it is impossible to know whether a single moral action has ever been undertaken (IV, 407). Our actions give some key to the disposition which underlies them. The *Religion* even describes actions as the appearances of the moral disposition that, as something supersensible, cannot be known (VI, 70 – 71). These statements occur in the context of Kant's warning against the temptation to "let a previously recognized disposition take the place of action" (VI, 77); Kant is concerned to ensure that his emphasis on the good will as the sole criterion of moral worth does not lead us to allow passive good intentions to take the place of moral engagement. Yet if we can abstract from someone's actions to conclusions about his character, we cannot abstract very far. The shopkeeper who refrains from cheating because the reputation thereby gained is good for his business looks just the same as the shopkeeper who does so out of respect for the moral law; and even the closest acquaintance may not enable us to tell the difference between them. In pointing out such facts, Kant is merely appealing to common moral experience: nowhere do the distinctions between appearance and reality threaten to grow so great as in ordinary cases of morality. The fact that morally, things are often not what they seem is the stock in trade of moralists, writers, and ordinary observers of human behavior. Kant's awareness of our inability to penetrate to the inner character on which the goodness of an action depends is most striking not in regard to our knowledge of others but to our knowledge of ourselves: "Not even does a man's inner experience with regard to himself enable him so to fathom the depths of his own heart as to obtain, through self-observation, quite certain knowledge of the basis of the maxims which he professes, or of their purity and stability" (VI, 63). The claim that we can never be certain of our own character, or even of the real motive of a single one of our actions, is repeated throughout Kant's ethical writings. It follows, of course, from the general anti-Cartesian position of the first *Critique*: we have no privileged access to the inner workings of our souls. The ethical writings disclose the moral thrust of this epistemological point: self-deception regarding the goodness of one's own will is an ever-present possibility:

> Very often [the agent] mistakes his own weakness, which counsels him against the venture of a misdeed, for virtue (which is the notion of strength); and how many people who have lived long and guiltless lives may not be merely *fortunate* in having escaped so many temptations? It remains hidden from the agent himself how much pure moral content there has been in the motive of each action. (VI, 392)

Kant's denial of knowledge of the morality of our actions has an immediate plausibility that his denial of knowledge in other realms may not. We are painfully aware of our tendency to ascribe moral motivations to actions that are guided by various forms of self-love; we are deeply uncertain about our capacities to resist future temptations. These phenomena incline us to accept Kant's denial of the possibility of moral certainty as simple fact: the metaphysical considerations that lead to a limitation of knowledge are buttressed here by our own experience. Yet here as elsewhere, Kant's denial of knowledge is not a matter of brute fact but plays a systematic role as well. We are, after all, enjoined to self-examination as a moral task: the *Doctrine of Virtue* names moral self-scrutiny as the first of all duties to oneself (VI, 440). Kant might have presented us with a viewpoint in which this scrutiny could lead to certain knowledge of our own characters at least. What purposes are served by denying us knowledge of our own morality?

As in the case of theoretical reason, we may try to answer this question by imagining a world in which we could know the Unconditioned of practical reason. This would mean that we could know that we, at least, had a good will: our actions will always not only be in accord with duty but undertaken from a motive of duty. What kind of knowledge could this be? If conceivable at all, it is the knowledge an observer has of events of nature, the ability to predict that certain reactions will occur given certain circumstances. Such knowledge is incompatible with human freedom, for if someone's behavior were in this sense predictable, it would be fully determined. Kant's point, I think, goes even further: it is impossible for us to regard our own behavior in this way. Though we may, with care, be able to assess our past actions from something close to the viewpoint of an impartial observer, we cannot be our own spectators regarding the present or the future.[50] We cannot coherently regard ourselves as both agents and objects of knowledge, for the ability to choose entails an unavoidable element of uncertainty. So O'Neill concludes that "these limits to human self-knowledge constitute the fundamental context of human action" (1989, 85). Here the connection between the limitations of knowledge and the preservation of autonomy is even more straightforward than it was in the case of theoretical reason. For what could it mean to know, of yourself, that you will always act morally? Kant holds such a perspective on ourselves to be impossible, for it would require viewing ourselves as determinate natural objects. But behind the metaphysical incoherence that Kant ascribes to such a stance lies a moral concern.

That concern becomes clear in Kant's question as to whether we might gain knowledge of "that good and pure disposition of which we are conscious." He concludes that certainty with regard to it is not only impossible but detrimental to morality (VI, 71). Earlier, he stated that assurance about our own virtue is "very dangerous" (V, 33). Here Kant points to a fact that may seem paradoxical: certain virtue is not only not virtue, it is terrifying. We know that Kant's concern with religious fanaticism remained deep and constant. Here Kant points to an often connected but more troubling phenomenon, the problem of *moral* fanaticism. He writes, "If fanaticism in its most general sense is a deliberate overstepping of the limits of human reason, moral fanaticism is this overstepping of limits which practical pure reason sets to mankind" (V, 85). It is not only the overzealous inquisitor, certain of his own virtue and contemptuous of that of others, who oversteps these limits. They are also transgressed by such moralists as the Stoics, whom Kant otherwise describes as "heroic" and "noble" (V, 86). For the Stoics, Kant writes, "indulge in fancies of moral perfections"; exaggerating the moral capacity of human beings, "they made their sage like a god in the consciousness of the excellence of his person" (V, 127). Here, as elsewhere, Kant's criticism of Stoicism reveals an attention to human needs that belies the charge of rigorism commonly applied to him. For Kant, human virtue requires a stance that is demanding and complex: we must guide our actions by an idea of reason, yet any purported assurance that we have attained this ideal would be self-defeating.

Kant's insistence on this stance reflects a deep awareness of the place of humility in human virtue. Both the *Doctrine of Virtue* and the *Lectures on Ethics* devote considerable reflection to the nature of humility. Importantly, humility is classified as a duty to oneself. The *Lectures on Ethics* describe humility and "true, noble pride" as the elements of self-respect, while self-respect is the foundation of all other duties; for "only if our worth as human beings is intact can we perform our other duties" (121, 126). The juxtaposition of humility and noble pride is crucial; Kant has nothing but scorn for that servility which is sometimes cast as humility. The *Religion* is explicit in attacking Christianity's "misconceived humility"; where conviction of one's moral insufficiency is genuine, it may be devastating, destroying the courage needed to persevere in the attempt to live morally (VI, 68; *Lectures*, 128). More often, Kant tells us, professions of such insufficiency are insincere and are in fact a form of false pride. False humility is thus the opposite of virtue on several counts; it is not only hypocritical but also a form of ambition. Attempting to "acquire a borrowed worth" by trying to surpass others in waiving any claim to moral worth is a peculiar but persistent way of contradicting one's duty to oneself and others (VI, 436).

Yet if Kant is perceptive in exposing the defects of "monkish" humility, he is equally insistent on the idea that virtue integrally depends on genuine humility (VI, 485). The latter, he says, is "the limitation of the high opinion we have of our moral worth by comparison of our actions with the moral law" (*Lectures*, 127). Kant's repeated warning to compare ourselves not with others but only with the moral law itself is not simply a warning against moral egoism (137). Those who do otherwise fail to appreciate the ideality of the moral law and hence misunderstand the nature of morality altogether: "A man of true merit is neither haughty nor a snob; he is humble, because he cherishes an idea of true worth so lofty that he can never rise high enough to satisfy its demands" (238). Those who, in contrast, derive moral self-esteem by comparing their own behavior with that of others are not only "detestable"; by taking others as the measure of their own moral worth, they replace the idea of morality with an empirical standard (127, 136). Kant adds other elements to his critique of moral arrogance: the contempt it displays toward others, even the most vicious ones, denies their moral personality and capacity for free change (VI, 464). Moreover, he adds, those who are unduly satisfied with their moral perfections tend to the unpractical, thinking to promote the welfare of the world by empty wishes and romantic ideas. None of these claims, however, is as important as the statement that "the less strict our view of the moral law, . . . the more arrogant we are likely to be" (*Lectures*, 135). More precisely, moral arrogance exhibits a failure of understanding of the nature of morality; "for no one who has the law explained to him in its absolute purity can be so foolish as to imagine that it is within his powers fully to comply with it" (128).

The fact that humility is essential to genuine understanding of the moral law connects naturally with Kant's conviction that human virtue is a matter of struggle.[51] Pristine innocence is not the greatest of moral conditions, for this may as easily result from weakness or fortune as from character. What inspires respect, and even awe, is that virtue which has been won through struggle. The *Anthropology* baldly states that "there is *no merit* in doing what is easy" (VII, 148); the *Doctrine of Virtue* describes struggle as part of the concept of virtue:

The very concept of virtue implies that virtue must be acquired (that it is not innate); for man's capacity for moral action would not be virtue were it not produced by the *strength* of his resolution struggling with such powerful inclinations to the contrary. Virtue is the product of pure practical reason, insofar as reason, aware of its supremacy (on grounds of freedom) wins ascendancy over the inclinations. (VI, 477)

As Kant is aware, this idea is an old one; in several works he quotes the poet Haller as saying:

> The world with all its faults
> Is better than a realm of will-less angels.

Kant's interpretation of these lines begins to show the lengths to which he will take this view:

> Thus a philosophical poet assigns a higher place in the moral gradation of beings to man, so far as he has to fight a propensity to evil within himself, nay, just in consequence of this fact, if only he is able to master this propensity, than to the inhabitants of heaven themselves who, by reason of the holiness of their nature, are placed above the possibility of ever going astray. (VI, 64)

Note that Kant does not view holiness to be a sort of perfect virtue. Rather, he holds struggle to be so essential to the notion of virtue that he denies that holy beings are virtuous (*Lectures*, 244).

The spirit of ceaseless striving that we saw embodied in theoretical reason's search for the Unconditioned is even more essential to the moral realm. It is not only the concept of virtue that requires a notion of neverending struggle; the moral worth of the world is said to depend on the conflict "in which, after some defeats, moral strength of mind may be gradually won" (V, 147). Kant's idea is not merely that holiness – complete fitness of the will to the moral law – is impossible for any being in the world of sense. The *Lectures on Ethics* speculate that God might have made us morally perfect and happy:

> But happiness would not then have been derived from the inner principle of the world, for the inner principle of the world is freedom. The end, therefore, through which man is destined to achieve his fullest perfection is through his own freedom. God's will is not merely that we should be happy but that we should make ourselves happy, and this is the true morality. (252)

As so often, Kant appeals to freedom as that which gives value to all our actions. Here he uses the idea to ground the common belief that virtue is most valuable where acquired through pain and striving. Strength to resist temptation, not imperviousness to it, is what constitutes moral worth. Kant even speculates that it is for this reason that Christianity insists on the Incarnation: "it is a limitation of human reason, and one which is inseparable from it, that we can conceive of no considerable moral worth in the actions of a personal being without representing that person, or his manifestation, in human guise" (VI, 64–65). This too is the reason why we are moved by extreme examples of moral temptation, by those who would lose their lives rather than commit an injustice: "Virtue is here worth so much because it costs so much" (V, 156).

If true virtue is the product of struggle, it is something of which its bearer can never be certain. To know that you will follow the moral law regardless of every future temptation is a metaphysical impossibility; to pretend to know it is a grave moral flaw. Our understanding of the ideality of the moral law produces humility; our awareness that it is possible to undertake the struggle for virtue produces self-respect. Both, Kant has told us, are necessary for moral character. But this reveals that moral character itself is critically dependent on the absence of knowledge. To claim knowledge of one's bad character is to succumb to perverse ambition or black despair. To claim knowledge of one's good character is to engage in selfrighteous-ness, which, by its very process of development through comparison with others, ignores the ideality of the moral law. In either case, knowledge would preclude the struggle toward moral progress that is essential to the concept of virtue. The preservation of virtue itself depends on our inability to know, ever, whether we are truly virtuous.

Once again, Kant's need to deny knowledge in order to make room for faith resonates further than could have been expected. Religion would become idolatry, science scholastic metaphysics, and virtue ugly fanaticism if we were granted certain knowledge of the objects to which those endeavors strive. In Kant's terms, if pursuit of the Unconditioned is that which fuels every meaningful human activity, the attempt to declare it to be reached undermines them all.

So Kant concludes the second *Critique* with a reminder of the moral significance of a philosophical critique of practical reason's limits. Without it, "Morals began with the noblest attribute of human nature, the development of which promised infinite uses, and it ended in—fanaticism or superstition" (V, 162). Clarity about our lack of knowledge of moral character is crucial for the practice of morality itself. If true humility is an essential component of virtue, proper awareness of our own uncertainty is crucial for the process of becoming virtuous. All we can know is the directive for our behavior; the attempt to seek more knowledge not only leads us away from the task of seeking virtue but positively undermines it:

> In general, if we limit our judgement to *regulative* principles, which content themselves with their own possible application to moral life, instead of aiming at *constitutive* principles of a knowledge of supersensible objects (insight into which, after all, is forever impossible to us), human wisdom would be better off in a great many ways, and there would be no breeding of a presumptive knowledge of that about which, in the last analysis, we know nothing—a groundless sophistry that glitters for a time but only, as in the end becomes apparent, to the detriment of morality. (VI, 71)

In light of these claims, how are we to understand the *Doctrine of Virtue*'s designation of "Know yourself" as the first commandment of all duties? It is noteworthy that Kant immediately supplements the word 'know' (*erkenne*) with two others: *erforsche* and *ergründe*. Best translated as "explore," "investigate," "probe," and "fathom," they suggest that the moral self-scrutiny here demanded will be part of the process of the struggle for virtue just described, not a search for knowledge in an ordinary sense. The *Doctrine of Virtue* tells us that the point of self-examination is precisely to dispel fanatical self-contempt on the one hand and moral arrogance on the other. Chapter 5 will explore Kant's injunction to self-knowledge in more detail.

V. Facts of Reason

Kant himself initially sought the sort of justification of the moral law that his later works showed to be impossible.[52] Some readers followed him by seeking in his writings a deduction of the categorical imperative that would provide the certainty that is given for the categories. The foregoing should have suggested that all such attempts are doomed to failure. The search for a proof of the objective reality of the moral law ignores Kant's efforts, in the first *Critique*, to define and delimit the notion of objective reality as that which belongs to objects of experience, the products of understanding and sensibility. The moral law, as one of the ideas of reason, is another sort of thing entirely and hence cannot be given the sort of deduction appropriate to objects (V, 46). Further reflection shows that such a deduction makes even less sense for the moral law than for the other ideas: a proof that the moral law necessarily applies to experience would undercut the freedom that is its basis. As I argued in section IV, even certain knowledge of a much weaker claim would be self-defeating. Uncertainty about whether we or anyone else in fact obeys the moral law is essential to maintaining a moral character.

In a powerful article, "Themes in Kant's Moral Philosophy," Rawls has shown why attempts to ground still weaker claims are bound to fail. Kant's doctrine of the Fact of Reason, Rawls concludes, expresses his abandonment of the possibility of a deduction of the moral law.[53] Now if, as Rawls argues, the Fact of Reason just means that the moral law is authoritative for us, it is an expression of the claims I have made about the ideas of reason in general, namely, that it is their role to set ends and standards for experience, not the other way around. This is what it is the nature of reason to do. The second *Critique* thus holds no answer to the moral skeptic or to one who seeks a proof that the moral principles of reason are universally valid. Kant has done all he can do to establish a conception of reason as that which determines standards of judgement: the Fact of Reason *is* just the fact that reason, not experience, establishes what ought to be. Thus, the question of whether reason is objectively practical can have no other answer than the development of a particular notion of reason and the analysis of the notion of objectivity provided by the first *Critique*: "For Kant there can be no question of justifying reason as such. . . . The constitution of reason must be self-authenticating" (Rawls 1989, 102).[54] The goal of this study is to display this self-authenticating or coherentist account of the justification of reason. By examining the nature of regulative principles and showing that as directives for behavior rather than items of knowledge, they are not the sorts of thing for which objective justification is coherent or desirable, I have hoped to make the absence of such justification for the moral law seem less problematic.[55]

Yet if Kant believes that the Fact of Reason—and the general account of reason that supports it—is all that can be offered to address the question whether reason is objectively practical, he still feels bound to show that, as he puts it, reason is subjectively practical. For without proof that human beings are able to act from the spirit of the law, "since with all our efforts *we cannot completely free ourselves from reason in judging*, we would inevitably appear in our own eyes as worthless and depraved men" (V, 153; my italics). This passage shows that even after the question of the moral law's validity—its authority as a standard of judgment—has been settled, or rejected, Kant feels bound to address a more pressing concern. At stake is the question whether all human beings will be able to act according to the commands that reason sets. The question whether we are moved to action by principles of reason or whether passion and self-interest are always motivational is a very old one. As recent scholars emphasize, the very recognition of the moral law as the supreme norm implies, for Kant, the existence of a motive for following its dictates.[56] The view of reason in general as the faculty that sets ends to all our activities should help to strengthen that claim by providing its broadest context. If reason's idea of the Unconditioned is that which, by itself, provides a motive for our action elsewhere, the claim that it does so in morality gains considerable plausibility.

Yet it is unsurprising that we should seek a more specific response just where the need for reason becomes most urgent. Kant's very abstract discussion in the second *Critique* can seem especially disappointing in view of the political implications of this question, which were explicitly drawn in his day.[57] Conservative thinkers used Hume's insistence upon the impotence of reason in a variety of ways. We have already discussed the importance of the Humean claim that only custom and experience provide courts of appeal and Kant's construction of a theory of reason in which, by contrast, reason sets standards of judgment. Yet Hume's view involves another component that may seem even more troubling. If one allowed, as Hume did not, that reason might provide some criteria for judging the rightness of actions and institutions, what grounds do we have for supposing that people will be able to meet them?

A number of Kant's conservative critics argued specifically that while enlightened and privileged people might guide their actions by moral principles, the vast majority of humankind is moved only by passion and self-interest. If it offers a less consistent picture of human nature, this version of Hume's view may be all the more compelling for seeming to rest on indisputable evidence. Its political consequences are clearly opposed to all those which Kant sought to establish. If only a few enlightened leaders are capable of acting according to reason's principles, it follows that paternalistic government, using institutions of religion to manipulate the masses' passions and institutions of punishment to control them, is the only appropriate government.

In this context Kant's need for a response becomes urgent. At issue is not the universal validity of practical reason's commands but the universal capacity to fulfill them. Kant must show, in answer to conservative skeptics, that even the most ordinary of people are capable of meeting the standards reason sets.

It is thus, I believe, no accident that just at that point in the second *Critique* where we might hope for a proof of the moral law Kant offers a curious and striking example. After asking how consciousness of the moral law is possible, Kant asks us to consider a man who claims he cannot resist temptation when opportunity is present; but were a gallows to be erected in front of the bordello on which he would immediately be hanged after gratifying his lust, he would quickly find his love of life sufficient to overcome any sensual temptation.[58] Yet the same man, when asked whether the threat of immediate death would be sufficient to lead him to commit an injustice, would hesitate. Note that it is the uncertainty that Kant holds to be crucial. Everyone must admit that he does not know whether he would possess the moral strength in such a situation to choose death rather than injustice, yet everyone knows, just as firmly, that it would be possible for him to do so (VI, 49). The possibility that we could, for the sake of the moral law, defy the most fundamental of natural desires—love of life itself—discloses our freedom. This revelation cannot be proof of the moral law whose deduction was vainly sought (V, 47). Yet it shows us something about ourselves that nothing else could do.

Kant returns to such examples often, giving them central place in his discussions of moral education. These discussions themselves, though relatively brief, must be seen as crucial, since Kant holds that the concept of virtue, involving the struggle for progress just discussed, implies that virtue is not innate but acquired (VI, 477). In discussing moral education, Kant repeatedly condemns all attempts to teach virtue by pointing out its advantages. In thereby mixing self-interest with duty, he argues, they have failed to recognize a crucial feature of moral motivation, namely, that the more purely morality is represented, the more deeply it inspires and moves us. For only when morality is represented as free of—indeed opposed to—every advantage can we gain an awareness of ourselves as free and reasonable beings. This awareness inspires awe; only the concept of duty can reveal it. Hence, Kant argues, teachers of morality should take just the opposite of the usual course: by taking great care *not* to point out the advantages of virtue, they exalt its dignity in the only manner that provides true moral motivation.

How is the teacher to do this? Both the second *Critique* and the *Doctrine of Virtue* suggest the same sort of method. Drawing on the natural propensity of "even business people and women" to take an exact, subtle, and lively interest in arguments concerning moral character, Kant suggests that educators use the biographies of ancient and modern times to explore the duties they seek to instill (V, 155). This is not to abandon his claim that morality cannot be derived from examples. Moral principles must be erected on concepts; but "these concepts, as they are to become subjectively practical, must not remain objective laws of morality which we merely admire and esteem in relation to mankind in general. Rather, we must see the idea of them in relation to man as an individual" (V, 158). Thus, examples do not serve as models but as proof that it is really possible to act in conformity with the moral law (VI, 480). Our souls, Kant says, are strengthened by the realization that human beings have been capable of acting from pure practical reason.

This realization can only come through the most extreme of situations. Kant's suggestion that a ten-year-old should be brought to the veneration of morality through hearing the story of Anne Boleyn may seem quaint or outdated, drawn from a time when children were commonly raised on Plutarch. We may be increasingly tempted to seek psychological or self-interested causes of actions that earlier ages accepted as unambiguously noble, though Kant views such temptation as an attempt to lighten the burden of humiliation that such examples cause us to suffer (V, 78). Yet each of us, I would claim, has one hero—in history or in fiction—whom we believe to have defied death rather than acquiesce in injustice and whose actions we do not try to explain in empirical terms (though we may try to provide such explanations for the heroes of others). Such examples lift us above the world of sense (V, 106, 159). When considering them, a discussion of the psychological causes of decision will seem merely shabby. The thought of these extraordinary actions reveals to us something that Kant may obscure by talk of a noumenal *world* but that is in fact quite comprehensible: by overcoming even love of life for a value higher than it, human beings can bid farewell to the causal chain. Thus, the moral law displays our absolute freedom.[59] That our minds are filled with awe at this capacity is, Kant believes, a moral fact. Moral views that ground all motivation in empirical interests have no way to account for it. The categorical imperative—the formalization of ordinary moral consciousness—cannot explain how this is possible, but it marks, acknowledges, and discloses this possibility.

Such examples should be central in moral education, because they reveal for everyone the possibility that pure reason can be subjectively practical. Everyday cases of moral conflict can be explained in many ways. Kant emphasizes the extraordinary (and perhaps not coincidentally, political) situation because it alone provides decisive grounds for rejecting the empiricist's conception of moral motivation. In the *Doctrine of Virtue*, Kant's hypothetical pupil, ending his instruction by summarizing the hardship that may attend the moral life, is brought naturally to the following question:

> What is it in you that can be trusted to enter into combat with all the forces of nature within you and around you and to conquer them if they come into conflict with your moral principles? Although the solution to this question lies completely beyond the capacity of speculative reason, the question arises of itself; and if he takes it to heart, the very incomprehensibility in this self-knowledge must produce an exaltation in his soul which only inspires it the more to hold its duty sacred, the more it is assailed. (VI, 483)

The pupil who has come this far will perforce answer the question by acknowledging that it is his pure practical reason that can be trusted to engage in this task. His answer is an answer to conservative claims that for most people, principles of reason are not reliably motivational. Further, the contemplation of that power made possible only by such examples lends support to reason's authority; the revelation of the possibility that pure reason can be subjectively practical adds weight to our conviction that pure reason is objectively practical. While increasing conviction, the fact that knowledge of our capacity to act according to the moral law reveals our freedom does nothing to *prove* the validity of the law itself.[60] For what cannot be proven is the vision of the human being, based on a notion of autonomy, upon which the moral law depends. Kant believes that we cannot reject this vision and retain our self-respect; hence, most transgression of the moral law involves deception, a refusal to acknowledge the grounds of one's action. By forcing us to examine the maxims of our actions, the categorical imperative confronts us with the contradiction between the conception of ourselves on which our self-worth depends and the actions that conflict with it. Anyone who seriously undertakes such self-examination must, Kant believes, try to choose the actions that uphold a vision of the self most clearly revealed in the examples that display our ultimate freedom.[61] As section IV suggested, the knowledge disclosed in such examples is of a rather peculiar kind. That the result of these thought-experiments is a confirmation of possibility, not fact or necessity, reveals much about Kant's notion of self-knowledge. The call to self-knowledge is a call to engage in a process that should lead us to acknowledge the appropriateness of Kant's vision of the self and attempt to bring our actions in harmony with it.[62]

It is this concept of the person that provides the constraints on agreement that have vainly been sought as a transcendental derivation of the moral law. Here again, Kant's procedure is self-supporting: it is not by some independent objective good but by the free and public process of reflection and discussion that conflicts will be decided. Where we disagree about what constitutes treating people as ends in a particular context, we cannot appeal to criteria independent of that process itself. Impartiality is not achieved by reference to a standpoint higher than that of the viewpoints in such disagreement but by taking the viewpoints of others into account, through progressive enlargement of perspective. So O'Neill writes:

> Reason, on this account, has no transcendental foundation, but is rather based on agreement of a certain sort. Mere agreement, were it possible, would not have any authority. What makes agreement of a certain sort possible is that it is agreement based on principles that meet their own criticism. The principles of reason vindicate their authority by their stamina when applied to themselves. (1989, 38; see also Arendt 1982, 42−43)

In the context provided by Kant's notion of reason as a whole, it should be clear that this process cannot be viewed as a makeshift one, the replacement for a transcendental source of agreement that is unhappily unavailable. Kant's point is that any purported good that could provide such a foundation would endanger the freedom on which agreement must be based. Only decisions established by a procedure that is itself free and egalitarian can issue in applications of the moral law that is valid for free and equal persons. Only such a process is appropriate for beings who were "made to stand erect and face the heavens."

Notes

1. For discussion of some of Kant's uses of Rousseau's notion of false needs, see Velkley (1989, 199).

2. See Rawls (1980−87).

3. There is, of course, a considerable literature devoted to refuting Schiller's claim as a misunderstanding of Kant's ethics; even at the individual level, Kant has a much more sophisticated account of moral psychology than Schiller suggests. One of many passages in which Kant himself fully anticipates the Schillerian objection can be found in "The End of All Things": "Love is . . . an indispensable complement to the incompleteness of human nature (needed in addition to that which reason prescribes through the law): for what someone does unwillingly is done so poorly; even with sophistical excuses concerning the concept of duty; that this latter, without the entrance of the former, is not very reliable as a drive" (A519). Schiller himself recognized that "the great sage of the world [i.e., Kant] tried to guard against any such misinterpretation," though he believed his work required it (Schiller 1910).

4. This discussion does not imply that the principle of maximizing general happiness can only serve conservative political ends; Bentham forms the powerful counterexample. But Mill's famous attempts to avoid the conclusion that utilitarianism might lead to a decrease in human freedom and dignity led, of course, to his abandonment of classical utilitarianism.

5. See Rawls (1980−87). This point is one that Kant asserts rather than argues, but it is difficult to imagine what an argument for it would look like. It is interesting to note that Kant's conception of human nature is simply a revision of the Greek definition of the human being as the rational animal. The difference, of course, is that Kant has redefined reason so that freedom, not knowledge, is its central goal (see VII, 322). The second *Critique* tells us instrumental reason alone could not raise us above "mere animality"; if reason served only

those purposes which in animals are met by instinct, there would be no difference between us and the other beasts (V, 61).

6. For an examination of the trouble that Kant's discussion of noumenal and phenomenal selves has caused and an attempt to defend his account of freedom without them, see Allison (1990).

7. For a discussion of the notion of right as a revolt against nature, see Shell (1980, 113–15).

8. See Beiser (1992, 39).

9. Arendt shows that this view was held not only by philosophers but by participants in the revolution itself (1982, 45). Beiser (1992) argues that although Kant's philosophy had achieved academic recognition before the 1790s, it only became popular–and notorious–because it was widely perceived as supporting the Jacobins. He notes that among the many German liberals united in promoting ideals of freedom of speech and press, separation of church and state, and equality of opportunity, only Kant and Forster showed any sympathy for the Jacobins. Beiser quotes Kant's colleague at the medical faculty, J. D. Metzger, as follows: "There was a time in Königsberg when anyone who merely spoke of the Revolution was registered in the black books as a Jacobin, but Kant never let himself be frightened, and he would speak a word for the Revolution at the highest tables" (Cited in Vorländer, 1924, II, 221).

10. See Beiser (1992, chap. 2).

11. The only traditional Kant interpretation that sufficiently emphasizes the importance of this set of issues is that of Hermann Cohen. In his *Kants Begründung der Ethik*, he argues that the question of the reality of the moral idea, which he calls the only question of ethics, remained untouched from Plato to Kant: "For Aristotle, the idea was folly. . . . His world of ethics lies completely within the horizon of his experience" (1910, 3) According to Cohen, Aristotle thus turned ethics into a discipline of pragmatic psychology, which it remained until Kant took up Plato's question of the reality of the idea of the good. But see also Beiser (1992, 4) and Beck (1960, 48–49, 124).

12. For a discussion of the status of the postulates of practical faith, see chap. 4; for a similar discussion of the statement "World peace is possible" as a regulative idea, see Korsgaard (1989b).

13. The following discussion will abstract from the metaphysical aspects of Kant's discussion of freedom; but on the latter, see Allison (1990) as well as Korsgaard (1989a). Beiser, however, claims: "It is important to recognize that Kant's new concept of autonomy was formulated primarily in a political rather than a metaphysical context. What disturbed Kant was not the problem of determinism but that of oppression. Tyranny and injustice are the threats to freedom, not the causality of the natural order" (1992, 30).

14. The passage should be tempered by comparison with the plea for education with which the *Lectures on Ethics* closes: "But so far no prince has contributed one iota to the perfection of mankind, to the worth of humanity, to inner happiness; all of them look ever and only to the prosperity of their own countries, making that their chief concern" (*Lectures*, 253). For a detailed discussion of Kant's relation to the censors, see Beiser (1992, chap. 2).

15. For further discussion of Kant's replies to the objections against granting political freedom, see Saner (1973, 238).

16. Velkley notes that "Kant's 'idealism' has as one of its ingredients some of the 'realism' of Machiavelli, Hobbes, and early modern thought. . . . Thus Kant writes that the moral philosopher must first have knowledge of men as they are before he can assert how they should be" (1989, 191). For further discussion, see chap. 4.

17. Korsgaard (1989b; n.d.) stresses the importance of the fact that Kant's moral standpoint is a practical one, constructed from the perspective of the agent who seeks a justification not for believing an action to be the right one but for doing it. Attention to the structure of Kant's notion

of theoretical reason shows this to be true not merely of practical reason but of reason in general.

18. For a good discussion of practical reason and the Unconditioned, see Korsgaard (1986b). This account, given in the *Groundwork*, is slightly complicated by the second *Critique*'s description of the highest good as "the Unconditioned in the practical realm." For further discussion, see chap. 4.

19. See, in particular, the writings of Rawls, Korsgaard, and O'Neill.

20. Marx's description of Kant as the philosopher of the French Revolution surely points to this suggestion. Among the Kant scholars who have argued for some version of this claim are Arendt, Saner, Velkley, and Yovel. Beiser argues that all German philosophy of the late eighteenth century "was dominated and motivated by political ends" (1992, viii). O'Neill (1989) also explores political elements of the first *Critique*.

21. For some of the countless eighteenth-century descriptions of Kant's philosophy as "Jacobin," see Arendt (1982), Beiser (1992), and Gulyga (1985).

22. Gulyga, in particular, often emphasizes Kant's love of irony.

23. The following discussion has been deeply influenced by John Rawls. See Rawls (1980; 1980–87).

24. For further discussion of this point, see chap. 4; on egalitarian aspects of Kant's conception of the person, see chap. 5.

25. For further discussion, see Wright (1987).

26. It is likely that the Hegelian charge that Kant's views were atomistic itself influenced the tendency to focus on the largely individualistic examples of the *Groundwork*, rather than considering the wider social implications of the categorical imperative. Against this tendency Yovel writes, "Discrete moral actions will not do; the overall face of the world must be reformed in a totalizing effort, in which further sectors of human life and experience are reshaped in light of the moral idea and brought under its dominion" (1989a, 147). This statement, as well as Kant's argument for the duty to enter civil society, seems to conflict with Yovel's earlier conclusion that "even to the best of states cannot be attributed a moral value per se" (1980, 189). While Kant maintains a distinction between juridical and moral obligation and asserts, as Yovel points out, that good citizenship is possible even in a "race of devils," this does not support the strong distinction between moral and political progress for which Yovel's earlier work argues. For the obligation to enter into political organization at all is founded only on the idea that such organization furthers its members' moral development — even though (some aspects of) that organization may be undertaken by those who have not yet attained the autonomy that is its purpose. Although Yovel acknowledges that Kant uses social contract theory to argue for a nonutilitarian foundation of the state, his failure to identify the free self-development that that state is to promote, with increasing consciousness of the moral law, may have led to a stronger separation of politics and morality than Kant's texts warrant.

27. A demand for free and compulsory universal education would seem to follow from, among other things, the third example of the *Groundwork*. If the maxim to cultivate all one's natural powers is universalizable, the state should create conditions in which this cultivation is possible. In this instance, as in others, Kant would ultimately rest a demand for (the possibility of the realization of) political equality on the presupposition of moral equality. It has also been argued that many passages in Kant's work, such as the third juridical attribute in the passage just quoted, lead to support of a democratic socialist form of government as the only means to sustain the kind of thoroughgoing autonomy required by the categorical imperative; capitalism, by contrast, cannot treat all people as ends in themselves. While I find these applications of Kant's moral theory compelling, they clearly go beyond the scope of this book. But see Cohen (1910), O'Neill (1989), and van der Linden (1988).

28. See Kant's own discussions in "What Is Orientation in Thinking" "What Is Enlightenment?" and "On the Old Saw." See also van der Linden (1988) and Sullivan (1989).

29. Sullivan emphasizes a letter to Mendelssohn in which Kant wrote, "Although I am absolutely convinced of many things I shall never have the courage to say, I shall never say anything I do not believe" (1989, 245). Unfortunately, just this text seems to undermine Sullivan's claim; for Kant not only withheld written support but wrote several texts that deny its moral permissibility.

30. Curiously, Beiser seems to ignore the most interesting aspect of his own argument in concluding that Kant, in the end, betrayed his own radical political ideals (1992, 53). If Kant's discussion of the means to political change are, as Beiser argues, tailored to the demands of his time, we need not regard them as principled conflicts with his theoretical views. Beiser's conclusion that Kant finally "compromised with the status quo" also rests on a view of the postulates of rational faith that will be challenged in chapter 4; but this discussion underlines the difficulty and, I believe, the philosophical irrelevance of the attempt to impose consistency on the statements Kant made concerning the revolution.

31. The *Metaphysical Elements* does say that the argument against revolution holds whether or not the social contract was a historical fact (VI, 318–19); but it is hard to see how this can be maintained. No doubt, this is the reason why Kant warns, immediately after making this statement, against speculations about the origin of state authority "that threaten the state with danger if they are asked with too much sophistication" — another statement that conflicts with much of his work.

32. See van der Linden (1988). Korsgaard (1986a) provides an excellent way of rejecting Kant's conclusion about lying to a murderer within an expanded Kantian framework. Korsgaard's concluding remarks on Kant's discussion of the permissibility suggest the obvious extension of her discussion to the question of revolution.

33. See, for example, Rawls's statement: "It should be noted that this content can never be specified completely. The moral law is an idea of reason, and since an idea of reason can never be fully realized, neither can the content of such an idea. It is always a matter of approximating thereto, and always subject to correction" (1989, 254).

34. Compare, for instance, O'Neill's claim that the "complete morally relevant description of any act is not a mechanical task" (1975, 28). In chapter 2 I argued that principles of relevance and selection, in particular — which are crucial to scientific inquiry — must remain regulative and hence cannot be antecedently specified.

35. In addition to the well-known court metaphors in the first *Critique*, see the extended description in VI, 438 on conscience as both accuser and judge at the bar of justice. See Saner (1973) and Wright (1987) for discussions of Kant's description of reason as "permanent judge and permanent defendant at an endless trial" (Saner 1973, 258). For a discussion of the use of other legal paradigms in the first *Critique*, see Henrich (1989).

36. See the writings of Korsgaard, O'Neill, and Rawls.

37. Here I follow Rawls's discussion of the categorical imperative procedure.

38. See Sullivan (1989, 150).

39. As Korsgaard (n.d.) argues, a theoretical justification of morality cannot, in fact, meet the practical questions at stake in the demand for moral justification; the questioner seeks a reason to do the action, not to believe that it is the right one.

40. The following discussion considers only pure practical reason, ignoring Kant's interesting and complex discussions of the relationship between it and empirical practical reason.

41. Rousseau, of course, forms the exception to this claim. See Arendt (1982; 1977) and Sullivan (1989). Cohen, on the other hand, reminds us that Plato assigned a higher place to the Form of the Good than to that of the True and traces Kant's assertion of the primacy of the practical to this aspect of Plato's thought (1910, 300).

42. Konhardt argues that if theoretical interests were primary, the moral personality, which is the distinctive characteristic of humanity, would be lacking and there would be only a difference of gradation between us and other animals (1979, 237). But this claim is hardly obvious; classical philosophy argued that it was just the possession of theoretical reason that distinguished us from the beasts.

43. Sullivan argues for the cognitive superiority of practical reason (1989, 102−3).

44. For further discussion, see chap. 4.

45. In different ways, Gulyga, Konhardt, and Korsgaard tend to suggest that the differences between theoretical and practical reason are more fundamental, in this regard, than a coherent account of reason as a whole can allow.

46. This is part of the reason for Kant's insistence that the morality of an action is not to be found in its consequences, which are, of course, often beyond our control. For a discussion of how Kant deals with the moral problems raised by this fact, see the examination of the Highest Good in chapter 4.

47. For further discussion, see Korsgaard (1992; 1989b, 224).

48. For a discussion of the difficulties in Kant's account of the freedom of immoral actions, see Korsgaard (1989a) and Allison (1990).

49. See Rawls (1989, 73).

50. O'Neill writes: "Agents are not simultaneously their own spectators. In contexts of action they cannot go behind their own maxims and beliefs. We can make right decisions, but not guarantee right acts" (1975, 127). See also Korsgaard (n.d.).

51. For some discussion of this idea in Kant's ethics, see Schneewind (1992, 318). The idea certainly goes back to the New Testament and reaches perhaps its literary peak in Goethe's *Faust*.

52. For a study of Kant's attempts to provide a deduction of the moral law, see Henrich (1973). As we saw in the previous chapter, Kant was also initially unclear about the possibility of a deduction of the theoretical ideas of reason.

53. For the claim that the Fact of Reason *means* that no deduction of the moral law is possible, see also Konhardt (1979, 219).

54. See also O'Neill (1992; 1989, 64−65).

55. Korsgaard (1989a; n.d.) also emphasizes what she calls Kant's radical split between the theoretical and practical points of view and discusses why a theoretical demonstration of ethics is not, in fact, what we need. I share Korsgaard's conviction that the claims of practical reason are not ontological ones and that many errors have been made by viewing Kant's ethics to require them. The differences that Korsgaard characterizes as those between theoretical and practical reason are, however, ones that I believe must be ascribed to understanding and reason as a whole. This is not, I believe, a distinction that is only of interest to Kant scholars or those committed to a particular account of faculty psychology. For Korsgaard's account leaves open the question why practical reason should be viewed as reason at all. Without an account of the regulative nature of theoretical reason, the self-supporting, coherentist justification of reason as a whole is lost, leaving practical reason on shakier, more isolated ground than is necessary.

56. See Allison (1989, 125) and Korsgaard (1986b).

57. Here again, I am indebted to Beiser's work (1992, 5, 43, 283−85, 298−99, 306). See also MacIntyre (1988, chap. 17).

58. The example, by the way, is taken straight from Rousseau (1979, 325). For discussion of the importance of the example, see Allison (1990, 242−43) and Rawls (1989, 111−12).

59. Korsgaard (n.d.) suggests that the world of activity is just the noumenal world. I believe her view to be fundamentally correct. The point here is simply that this fact is revealed in a particular way in cases where people are forced to choose between death and injustice. While Kant does not call such cases theoretical proofs of our absolute freedom, he uses them to suggest that they remove all doubts about it.

60. See also Hermann (1989, 136).

61. What Kant describes as the hypothetical possibility that someone might deliberately choose to disobey the moral law has become much more alive for us; yet it is possible to consider even those most modern expressions of radical nihilism as confirmation of Kant's views. Dostoevsky's Underground Man, for example, must be possible: the decision to reject the moral law in order to prove one's freedom must, if obeying the moral law is a matter of free choice, be a possible one. Yet Dostoevsky's description of a being filled not simply with (sensuous) unhappiness but self-hatred may be seen as a representation of Kant's point: he who consciously chooses to disobey the moral law must despise himself, for he has not respected the humanity in his own person. Kant believes that doing this so deeply undermines the bases of self-respect that we would not choose to do so were we to be aware of the destruction of our personality to which such a decision would lead.

62. Something similar is suggested by Rawls (1989, 113).

4

The Structure of Faith

Perhaps the most decisive aspect of Kant's work, for the subsequent history of philosophy, is his argument that questions concerning God, human freedom, and immortality involve objects beyond the realm of human knowledge. These questions had been, when not the main object of philosophical endeavor, the points around which all other philosophical inquiry revolved; no wonder that Kant's placing them outside the province of philosophical speculation seemed to his contemporaries to be "all-destroying." Yet through the Critical Period, Kant insisted that while showing all speculative attempts to determine these matters to be fruitless, he had nevertheless provided arguments to show that we are absolutely justified in assuming a "rational faith" in the existence of God, freedom, and immortality:

> The enigma of the Critical Philosophy lies in the fact that we must renounce the objective reality of the supersensible use of the categories in speculation and yet can attribute this reality to them in respect to the objects of pure practical reason. This must have seemed an inconsistency so long as the practical use of reason was known only by name . . . The inconsistency vanishes because the use which is now made of these concepts is different from that required by speculative reason. (V, 5)

Nothing in Kant's work exhibits his conception of reason so clearly and so problematically as does the notion of rational faith. Fully aware of the historical significance of the notion, Kant returned to explain the nature of its justification throughout the Critical Period. Most readers, however, have viewed those arguments to be the weakest ones in his entire philosophy. Heine's description of them is worth quoting at length:

> God is, for Kant, a noumenon. According to his argument, that transcendental being which we hitherto called God is nothing other than a fiction. It arose through a natural illusion. Yes, Kant shows that we can know nothing at all of God, and indeed that every future demonstration of his existence is impossible. Let us write Dante's words "Leave hope behind!" over this section of the *Critique of Pure Reason*. . . .
> You thought we could go home now? Not on your life! There's still another piece to be performed. After the tragedy comes the farce. Up till now Immanuel Kant had been the unrelenting philosopher, he stormed the heavens, he put the whole garrison to the sword, the sovereign of the world swims unproven in his blood, there is no more mercy, no grace, no reward in the next world for abstemiousness in this one, the immortality of the soul is in its last gasp—it rattles, it groans—and old Lampe, a distressed spectator, looks on with his umbrella under his arm, and cold sweat and tears run down his face. There Immanuel Kant takes pity and shows that he is not

merely a great philosopher but a good man, and he thinks it over, and half kindly, half ironically, he says: "Old Lampe needs a God, otherwise the poor man can't be happy—but human beings should be happy in the world—practical reason says so—all right, then—practical reason may guarantee the existence of God, too." In the course of this argument Kant distinguishes between theoretical reason and practical reason, and with this, as with a magic wand, he revives the corpse of Deism which theoretical reason has put to death.

Did Kant undertake their resurrection not merely because of Old Lampe but because of the police? Or did he really act out of conviction? (1981, 601–4)

This view of the postulates of practical faith, expressed with equal vehemence if less wit, has become the standard one, uniting critics of Kant who held nothing else in common. For empiricists, Kant's arguments were an embarrassing concession to personal piety or public order, inconsistent with the rigorous demands of the rest of the Critical Philosophy. For Absolute Idealists, Kant's discussion revealed his fundamental failure to achieve knowledge of the objects of philosophy. Nearly every critic held Kant's claim to have denied knowledge in order to make room for faith to be an effort to protect the postulates of rational faith from the encroachments of the claims of knowledge. Thus placed according to the requirements of Kant's system beyond the realm of knowledge, the postulates became inaccessible to refutation as well as justification, and hence are as arbitrary and dogmatic as the claims of any ordinary fanatic.[1]

The standard view of the postulates makes them not only untenable but not even particularly original. Kant's statement that the discovery of the antinomies engendered the Critical Philosophy can be read to place him squarely in a rationalist theological tradition dating back to the Middle Ages.[2] Thus, the antinomies would have shown him that none of the propositions upon which religion is based can be proved or disproved by pure reason; he then constructs an epistemology to explain why this is the case; and finally, he offers a notion of faith that allows us to think but not to know the things that, he says are the objects of reason's deepest concern. Kant's unfortunate comparison of the Critical Philosophy to the police may reinforce such a view (Bxxxv): by protecting society against the dangers of proofs of atheism and materialism, transcendental idealism secures a realm in which we may peacefully believe the propositions necessary for temporal rectitude and eternal happiness. Were this kind of reading of Kant's project correct, his originality would be largely a question of scope, consisting in the systematicity and depth of the (negative) theory of knowledge constructed to support the claim that the truths necessary to religion cannot be known by reason. Neither the problem nor the solution would differ markedly from those posed by medieval rationalist theology.

Yet even Kant's discussion of the antinomies gives ample indication of the difference between his position and a traditional one. This introduction of the notion of transcendental illusion marks a turning point. Traditional views rested content with the ascertainment that reason leads to contradictions in this sphere, before urging the necessity of faith. In insisting that these contradictions are natural to reason and providing a diagnosis of reason's tendency to them, Kant points the way to a new conception of reason, not merely a rejection of it. Reason's failure to achieve knowledge of its objects combined with the inevitability of its attempts to do so indicates the necessity of a fully different understanding of the nature of reason:

> The observations and calculations of astronomers have taught us much that is wonderful; but the most important lesson that they have taught us has been by revealing the abyss of our *ignorance*, which otherwise we could never have conceived to be so great. Reflection upon the ignorance thus disclosed must produce a great change in our estimate of the purposes for which our reason should be employed. (A575/B603)

This reconception of reason provides a completely new possibility in the traditional debate concerning faith and reason. All parties to that discussion had viewed reason and faith as two separate sorts of entities, even when they were at pains to show that they need not be in opposition. By distinguishing between reason and knowledge, Kant opens the way for a faith that is not only not irrational (like that of Maimonides and Thomas Aquinas) but is central to the very notion of reason itself.

The previous chapters should have prepared the foundation for these claims. In the context of his conception of reason as a whole, Kant's notion of rational faith is both profoundly original and surprisingly convincing. Only by understanding his critique of rationalism and the idea that reason is a matter of knowledge can we regard the postulates as rational.[3] In the absence of a general conception of reason, it is natural to view the postulates of rational faith as instances of failed knowledge and hence, at best, as makeshift replacements for genuinely justifiable statements. If the postulates are not seen as special cases, however, but as one instance of Kant's general reconception of reason, they become far more compelling.

Though Kant initially spoke of three postulates, my discussion will focus on one. His arguments for the need to believe in God are far more plausible than his arguments for immortality, and there are indications that his own recognition of this fact led him to abandon the latter in his later work.[4] For different reasons, I shall ignore his discussion of human freedom. Though initially described as a postulate of faith, freedom is later seen to have a different status from the other postulates. Freedom is realized every time we act morally; while this does not give us superior knowledge of it, it makes the demand for knowledge less pressing.[5] By confining my examination to Kant's arguments for rational faith in God's existence, I hope to exhibit most clearly the structure of the notion of rational faith itself.[6]

I. The Pantheism Controversy

All of the material required for Kant's notion of rational faith can be found, at least in embryo, in the first edition of the first *Critique*. The later writings, however, most of which were written in response to early criticism, express his position most clearly and explicate the peculiar kind of justification the notion requires. This is particularly true of the essay "What Is Orientation in Thinking?" Kant's contribution to the eighteenth century's most significant debate about the respective claims of reason and faith. The pantheism controversy forced Kant to clarify his criticisms of rationalism and Humean fideism; through it, we can discover the most succinct and lucid statements Kant ever made about the structure of the notion of reason toward which, I have argued, his work is directed. Hence, it is important to examine the background of the pantheism controversy, which began with a biographical quarrel.[7]

The young F. H. Jacobi, upon hearing that Moses Mendelssohn was engaged in writing a book about Lessing's character, made it known that Lessing, in his last year, had revealed to Jacobi that he was a Spinozist. Mendelssohn, the model for the title figure of Lessing's play *Nathan the Wise*, had been Lessing's closest friend for thirty years. The charge of Spinozism was equivalent to the charge of atheism; Mendelssohn was bound to defend his dearest friend from such an accusation. Jacobi, he returned, failed to understand Lessing's irony and love of argument; at most, he wrote, Lessing could be said to hold a sort of purified pantheism that is fully compatible with religion and morals. Jacobi disagreed, offering his reminiscence of a conversation with Lessing as proof. Heated words were exchanged by mail, becoming even more heated when Jacobi published the private correspondence without Mendelssohn's permission. The debate was clouded by questions of personal breaches of faith, as well as by undertones of anti-Semitism; when Mendelssohn died five days after delivering the manuscript of his last salvo, "To Lessing's Friends," to his publisher, his friends were quick to accuse Jacobi of causing Mendelssohn's death.

The fact that the controversy did not die with Mendelssohn but widened to include every major German thinker of the late eighteenth century indicates that its significance went far beyond the factual questions of Lessing's last views or even the questions of the proper exegesis of Spinoza, with which most of the Mendelssohn–Jacobi correspondence is filled. Jacobi's intention in beginning the controversy was to use Lessing as means to proof of his own views: every consistent use of philosophy leads to atheism, therefore speculative reasoning must be abandoned for a leap of faith to positive religion. If he could establish that Lessing, the universally respected thinker of the German enlightenment, held Spinozism to be the only consistent philosophy, Jacobi would deal a devastating blow to the very notion of Enlightenment itself. Jacobi does not rest his case with Lessing, however, but goes on to analyze Spinoza as well as Leibniz in an often very persuasive manner, in order to prove his view, which he summarized in the following assertions:

1. Spinozism is atheism.
2. Cabalistic philosophy is, as philosophy, nothing other than undeveloped, or new, muddled, Spinozism.
3. The Leibnizian–Wolffian philosophy is no less fatalistic than the Spinozan and leads the unremitting investigator back to the principles of the latter.
4. Every method of demonstration results in fatalism.
5. We can only demonstrate similarities, correspondences, conditionally necessary truths. Every demonstration presupposes something already demonstrated, whose principle is revelation.
6. The principle of all human knowledge and agency is faith. (*Hauptschriften* 1916, 173–80)

If Jacobi's contribution to the pantheism controversy can be viewed as the first thoroughgoing attack upon the classical Enlightenment, Mendelssohn's can be viewed as its swan song. It was clear to the last heir of Leibnizian rationalism that every value upon which his life and work had been based was at issue in the controversy. Both the attempt to guide the Jewish people away from a position conditioned by dogmatism and rejection of modern culture and the attempt to persuade the rest of the world to accept them were predicated upon Mendelssohn's unwavering belief in a universal human reason that, if properly developed, would overcome superstition and prejudice by leading all people to those truths upon which a humanitarian society could be based. Mendelssohn's proofs of the immortality of the soul, which are now remembered as the objects of Kant's critique but earned him the title of "the German Socrates" in his day, seemed clearly to demonstrate the support that the right use of speculative reason could give to moral and religious beliefs. More generally, the identity of interest between the labors of speculative reason and the furthering of moral and religious ends was the cardinal assumption of the Enlightenment. Hitherto, this identity had been disputed by forces of the ancien régime and could be dismissed as precisely a relic of the prejudice and superstition that the Enlightenment would overcome with time. Jacobi, by claiming that the very principles upon which the Enlightenment was based led to nihilism, was the first to present the specter of the Enlightenment undoing itself from within. Mendelssohn was quick to see Jacobi's challenge as a dangerous new form of *Schwärmerei* and to embark, despite his failing health, upon a defense of human reason and philosophy, "my most faithful companion, my only solace in the adversities of this life" (1979, 5).

A certain portion of the controversy involved disagreement about the implications of Spinozism. While allowing for variants, however, most of the parties quickly agreed that a genuine Spinozism, properly understood, entailed the denial of a personal and independent cause of the world and the existence of final causes, or efficacy of free will. This was summarized by Jacobi's assertion that Spinozism is atheism. Jacobi's efforts, then, are devoted to showing that Spinozism cannot be disproved by rational means. The spirit of Spinozism, Jacobi writes, is the principle of sufficient reason; its greatest merit is its rigorous and consistent use of it. Had Leibniz, whose system contains more Spinozistic elements than any other, been equally scrupulous, he would have come to the same conclusions (*Hauptschriften*, 85–86). Every possible method of demonstration is based on the principle of sufficient reason and must, if rigorously applied, result in fatalism.

It is in this sense, then, that "there is no other philosophy than the philosophy of Spinoza" (*Hauptschriften*, 78) The principle that lies at the basis of all philosophical explanation, used consistently, implies the most unwelcome of Spinoza's conclusions; for an independent God who is the creator of the world implies something that is the cause of itself. Similarly, freedom of the will, human or divine, requires a will that acts spontaneously, without a prior cause, thus violating the principle of sufficient reason. Here, however, Jacobi asserts: "I have no conception which is more heartfelt than that of final causes; no livelier conviction than that I do what I think. . . . Of course, I must thereby assume a source of thinking and acting that remains thoroughly inexplicable" (89).

The belief in final causes, or freedom of the will, and in an intelligent personal God, are the deepest, most natural of human convictions. Atheism, continues Jacobi, develops later in human history as well as in the history of every individual, for it requires reflections that are contrary to the natural inclinations of every human being (224). If we accept these convictions, we must acknowledge that there are limits to the powers of human reason, for reason not only cannot explain, but contradicts, these deepest of human beliefs. These beliefs cannot, accordingly, be grounded in philosophy but must be accepted by a leap of faith.[8]

Jacobi's conception of faith was a general one, derived, in many ways, from Hume, to whom he paid tribute with the title of his first book. It is through faith, he wrote, that we know that we have a body and that other bodies and thinking beings exist outside us. There is no other way to real knowledge of existence, for the only objects revealed by reason are chimeras. Human beings must rely on faith not merely for the truths of religion but for nearly every vital piece of knowledge (170). Every proof made by reason presupposes something already proven, which cannot itself be grounded in reason but must rest upon revelation. Jacobi's conception of faith, then, is not really a challenge to an existential decision but a contribution to philosophical questions about justification. For Jacobi, there is no genuine decision to be made (279). If we follow our real convictions, we will accept our natural beliefs in the existence of God and freedom of the will. If reflection on the sources of those beliefs leads us to turn our backs on reason and philosophy, nothing of consequence has been lost. Not only does the consistent use of reason and philosophy undermine the truths of morality and religion; reason cannot even provide us with the simplest of truths upon which we rely every day.

For Mendelssohn as for many others, Jacobi's renunciation of reason – expressed, as it often was, in the most reasonable and well-argued terms – threatened to justify every possible form of revelry and fanaticism. Mendelssohn's goal, then, was to show that the rejection of Spinozism does not require a leap of faith but could be carried out by fully rational means. In the *Morgenstunden* and in his letters to Jacobi, he sets out to disprove Spinoza's basic principles. The details of his arguments need not concern us here, for Mendelssohn himself was clearly dissatisfied with them. Most readers of the documents of the pantheism controversy have felt that the moral victory was Mendelssohn's. It is difficult to remain unmoved by the uprightness and decency with which he returned Jacobi's provocative and often underhanded behavior.[9] Yet alas, this very decency threatens to become pathetic once Mendelssohn's doubts regarding his own methods are made clear.

For, he writes, should speculative reason lead us to unwelcome conclusions, we must resort to common sense – *bon sens*, or *gesunden Menschenverstand* – to lead us back to the desired paths. In Mendelssohn's first critique of Jacobi, he wrote, surprisingly, "Your leap of faith is a wholesome method of nature" (*Hauptschriften*, 1916, p 114). The impression that Mendelssohn thereby conceded far too much of Jacobi's position is thoroughly confirmed by the later writings. Jacobi doesn't know me, he writes in his last essay, and may have heard me described as a *Vernunftling* who concedes everything to reason and nothing to faith (305). Resisting this description, Mendelssohn continues, in moving terms, to assert the importance of faith. The primitive and childish natural wonder at the glories of creation has all the evidence of a geometric proof of God's existence. Natural faith is the starting point for a belief in God, and everyone who is unspoiled by sophistry must acknowledge the truths of natural religion. The business of speculation, Mendelssohn continues, is to provide rational foundation for the truths of common sense: "As long as both healthy common sense and speculation are on friendly terms, I follow them where they lead me; but as soon as they depart from one another I look to orient myself and try to bring them back, where possible, to the point from which we began" (308).

Mendelssohn asserts that when speculation departs from the beliefs of common sense, such as that in the existence of final causes, it is high time for speculation to orient itself according to sound common sense (314). If human beings, he writes, have intentions and final causes, then it is undeniable that these things exist in nature as well—fully begging Spinoza's question whether it is not equally ridiculous to posit final causes in the one as in the other. One has only to open one's eyes, says Mendelssohn, and observe any work of nature with the least degree of attention to be fully confident of the existence of final causes (316). The difference between this assertion and Jacobi's "I have no conviction that is more heartfelt than that of the existence of final causes" is difficult to discern. Mendelssohn does mention one of Spinoza's arguments against the existence of final causes but does little more to refute it than to deny that anyone could have ever asserted this seriously.

It is impossible to see a significant difference between Mendelssohn's position, once his appeal to common sense is accepted, and Jacobi's insistence upon faith, particularly as Jacobi's description of faith stresses its role in orienting us in all areas of everyday life. If common sense provides both the starting point and the corrective, should one prove necessary, for the labors of speculation, what is the real role of reason in Mendelssohn's philosophy? Concerning final causes, Mendelssohn writes that the only genuine question is whether they are capable of being proved apodictically or whether they must be derived from induction. This question, he writes, has no influence upon religion or morality but is both useful and pleasant for speculative minds and therefore deserves to be considered carefully and exactly (316–17). In one blow, Mendelssohn concedes the thrust of Jacobi's point: the use of reason and the enterprise of philosophy can be at worst dangerous, at best insignificant, to the welfare of the vast majority of human beings. In his eagerness to present a moderate and reasonable position, as free of the possibility of fanaticism through the glorification of reason as of that through faith, Mendelssohn unwillingly exposes all of the weaknesses of the classical Enlightenment.

The philosophical disagreement between Mendelssohn and Jacobi, for all the excitement surrounding it, seems to reduce to a matter of tone. Both hold the same beliefs—that in the existence of a personal creator and that in the existence of final causes—to be necessary to religion and morality. Both hold these beliefs to be natural and obvious to every human being who has not been corrupted by speculation. While Mendelssohn holds these beliefs to be provable by the right use of speculation, basing this assertion on the confidence that God must have been able to give human beings the power to know the truths upon which their unhappiness is founded (324), he is unwilling to grant reason a trustworthy or significant role in establishing them. Thus, his charge that Jacobi's rejection of reason opens the floodgates of fanaticism and zealotry rings terribly hollow, its force resting merely upon the weight of Mendelssohn's considerable position as a central figure of the German Enlightenment. But this only raises the question of whether that Enlightenment itself possessed a philosophically solid and coherent position upon which to base its attack upon the hated forces of superstition and darkness—a question posed more or less obliquely throughout Kant's work.

If the differences between Mendelssohn and Jacobi are short on philosophical content, how are we to regard the differences between their positions and that of Kant? It is crucial to note that both Mendelssohn and Jacobi — in private as well as public writings — appealed to Kant as support for their views. The preface to *Morgenstunden* expressed the hope that the work of defeating *Schwärmerei* would be completed by a "greater power, such as that of a Kant, who hopefully will rebuild with the same spirit with which he has torn down." In the letter that he enclosed with the copy of *Morgenstunden* sent to Kant, Mendelssohn complained that the fanatics and proselytizers of philosophy were becoming more violent than those of positive religion. While appealing to Kant's lifelong hatred of *Schwärmerei* in every form, Mendelssohn thereby underestimated the original and radical elements in Jacobi's position. Jacobi's use of Kant's work to support his own views was more adroit. In *Against Mendelssohn's Accusations*, he cited the first *Critique*'s most important passages on faith before asking:

> "I have reviled reason" — because I assert that one cannot apodictically demonstrate the existence of God according to the teachings of the theists nor satisfactorily refute the objections to it? "I am a *Schwärmer* and want to promote blind or miraculous faith" — because I assert that one can only *believe* in God, and only *practically* make oneself resolved in this faith? How, for what reason? And Kant, who has been teaching the same thing for more than six years, has not reviled reason, is not a *Schwärmer*, and does not want to promote a blind or miraculous faith? (*Hauptschriften*, 349 – 51)

Jacobi concluded his citations with a footnote:

> I have no intention of hereby wishing to degrade the Kantian philosophy to my own, nor of elevating mine to the Kantian. It is sufficient for me that this Hercules of thinkers must stand in greater damnation with regard to the indicated points, according to my opponents, than I do and that this can be seen as clearly as the bright midday sun. (352)

Jacobi's insistence upon the limits of human knowledge seems to echo Kant's own. The appeal to a practical, morally grounded faith in God, immortality, and freedom of the will is expressed even more forcefully by Kant. To be sure, Kant's writings, like the texts of the classical Enlightenment, are filled with the description of reason as "the very highest faculty" and praise of its proper use, as well as with contempt for fanatics and enthusiasts. But here one must ask whether this is more than empty and obsolete verbiage, the use of the word 'reason' to legitimize a procedure that has nothing essential to do with reason at all. Is the difference between Jacobi and Kant, too, merely a matter of rhetoric and one that, moreover, gives Jacobi the advantage of being more forthright?

These were questions that engaged supporters of both Mendelssohn and Jacobi as they urged Kant to make a contribution to the debate that would support their own positions.[10] Though Kant's voice had acquired considerable weight in the six years since the first *Critique*'s publication, the significance of the Critical Philosophy seemed undecided. Could it be used, despite its denial of knowledge, to support the rationalism on which the Enlightenment had depended? Or was it, as Jacobi claimed, the decisive step in undermining all such projects? Kant's texts seemed to provide support for both claims, and despite considerable prodding, he hesitated for months before making a public statement. This hesitation was not, I believe, accidental, nor simply due to the enormous pressure of work: even those of Kant's students who urged him to state his views and clear his name were unsure of what those views entailed. In "What Is Orientation in Thinking?" he succeeded in clarifying the systematic differences between his views and those of rationalism and empiricism.

Those differences rest upon Kant's insistence on the necessity of a critique of reason. Although it was the respective claims of reason and faith that were at issue in the pantheism controversy, neither Jacobi nor Mendelssohn considered the precise determination of the nature of reason to be of philosophical interest—a fact already suggested by the ultimate similarity of their positions. Jacobi's indifference to this determination was expressed in his assignment of a myriad number of tasks to the reason he described as Kantian, an indifference that became even more pronounced in his later works, where he uses the term 'reason' (called 'a spiritual eye for spiritual objects') to designate the faculty performing those functions he had so provocatively assigned to faith. For Jacobi as for Herder (whom he quotes with approval), it is enough that this faculty "speaks loud and clearly," directing our assent to those propositions essential to our temporal and eternal welfare.[11] Nor was Mendelssohn, for all his concern to defend the supremacy of reason, less careless in his alternating descriptions of it. Kant's claim that determining the nature of this organ and distinguishing it precisely from others must take place before any philosophical problems could be resolved was, of course, the basis of the first *Critique*. The pantheism controversy allowed him to explain the consequences of that determination as well as to explicate his conception of reason as regulative by seizing on the idea of orientation.

Mendelssohn had introduced the idea at the beginning of the pantheism controversy, writing that where speculation, failing to provide sure guidance, leads to conclusions incompatible with morality and religion, something else must step in to guide the thinker in his activities. Thus, Mendelssohn assumed from the outset an activity that is both more vital and more reliable than the acquisition of knowledge. The admission that something other than reason could provide this orientation was, Kant argued, fatal, for it opened the way for the dethronement of reason and the establishment of *Schwärmerei*. Before arguing that only reason is capable of providing orientation in thinking, Kant begins by trying to specify the notion of orientation itself. Orientation is not merely defined as finding a direction or, more generally, as finding one's way about but as finding an ascent within a given area of the world (VIII, 135). In trying to define the notion that Mendelssohn uses so blithely, Kant relies (perhaps too heavily) upon the original, geographical meaning of finding one's way in physical space. If I look at the sun at midday, Kant writes, I can find north, south, east, and west. I cannot, however, do this by observation alone; to determine these directions, I rely upon a subjective feeling that tells me the difference between right and left, for which there are no external criteria. Without this subjective feeling, even the astronomer would be unable to establish direction should the data of experience be changed and, for example, all the stars that are now placed in the east removed to the west without change of constellation and relationship to one another. Orienting oneself in space—be it a room, a darkened street, or the heavens themselves—

requires, in addition to empirical observation, a capacity that is grounded in, and directed toward, the subject. This capacity is present in everyone, though it can be further developed by practice (VIII, 135).

Even in purely mathematical space, Kant argues, physical objects of intuition are insufficient to provide the orientation that we need to guide our movements. How much more is this the case in what Kant calls logical space, that is, in thinking, particularly in those realms where objects of intuition are wholly absent! Kant's geographical examples are meant to show that the objects of experience could be so ordered as to be indistinguishable by mere perception without the help of another, subjective capacity. This subjective capacity is all the more essential where thought leaves the boundaries of experience and has to deal with objects that it must think and can never know. These are the objects of metaphysics: God, the soul, and the world as a whole. So Kant concludes: "Thus to orient oneself in thinking means: to determine oneself in holding-to-be-true [*Fürwahrhalten*] by a subjective principle of reason where objective principles are inadequate" (VIII, 136). That the objective principles of knowledge are inadequate in the realm of metaphysics has been shown, for Kant's purposes, in the first *Critique*. Of course, not every instance of inadequate knowledge justifies a judgment according to subjective principles of reason: in most cases, ignorance, if it acknowledges itself as such, has every right to remain blissful. Here Kant introduces the notion of a need of reason. Provisionally, Kant proposes, there are situations in which reason must make a judgment in order to orient itself, although all grounds that are ordinarily the basis of the possibility of judgment — the application of a concept to an intuition — are lacking.

> Here enters the right of a need of reason to presuppose and assume something as a subjective ground which it may not pretend to know on objective grounds; and consequently to *orient* itself in thought, in the immeasurable space filled for us with the thick darkness of the supersensible. (VIII, 137)

The judgment that reason thereby makes must be logically free of contradiction; its object must be thinkable through pure concepts of the understanding even though no intuition is possible. This condition is by no means sufficient: there are many possible objects for which reason has no need. Kant begins to explicate the idea of a need of reason by introducing the idea of a conditional need. If reason, for example, wants to investigate and explain the apparent purposiveness in the world, it must assume the existence of a first cause of the world. Although no proof of such a first cause is possible, reason is allowed to assume its existence as an aid to explaining certain appearances that are otherwise incomprehensible.[12] This need of reason is theoretical and hence conditional: the explanation of the natural world is not a human necessity. The needs of practical reason, by contrast, are unconditional. These do not concern judgments we should like to make given certain (natural) interests but those which every human being is required to make. Because we are under obligation to the moral law, we must make whatever judgments are required to orient us in fulfilling it. Practical reason, Kant argues, requires the idea of an independent highest good, in which morality is united with the greatest possible happiness insofar as this is granted in proportion to the first (VIII, 139). This cannot be the motive of moral behavior, but it is needed in order to sustain moral action. Now given the lack of visible correlation between morality and happiness, the only way in which this highest good is conceivable is through the assumption of a highest intelligent being who orders the world so that happiness will turn out to be proportional to virtue. Practical reason, then, has a right to assume the existence of such a being. For in order to persevere in moral action, human beings must be able to conceive the object of their actions as a realizable goal. This argument will be discussed shortly.

It is rational faith, Kant says, that grounds these judgments. By this term, Kant indicates those beliefs which are founded only on the data of pure reason. Other beliefs, provided they are rationally formulated, may become knowledge through a progressive accumulation of evidence: my belief, based on a reliable witness, that Kant lived and died in Königsberg, will become knowledge if all reports confirm it. Rational faith, by contrast, can never become knowledge, because it is not founded upon evidence at all: its basis is a necessary and subjective need of reason. As long as we are human, Kant writes, it will remain so (VIII, 141). That is, as long as we are human, we shall be incapable of attaining knowledge of the objects of faith; as long as we are human, we shall depend on these beliefs to orient our lives.

Kant calls rational faith in the theoretical realm hypotheses of reason, those in the practical realm, postulates—adding that the postulates of practical reason are in no way inferior to knowledge in degree although they are fully different in kind. Postulates of practical reason are as certain and unchangeable as propositions resulting from the most rigorous proofs, for no evidence can be obtained that would shake them. It is rational faith, Kant says, which is the ground of all faith and indeed of revelation (VIII, 142). The concept of God cannot come from any authority or experience, for no experience is adequate to it; at most, experience can suggest and confirm an idea of God that must first be present in reason itself.

It may be asked where Kant derived his certainty that reason, rather than some nonrational capacity, is in a position to fulfill the task of orientation. "What Is Orientation in Thinking?" asserts that this must be the case lest fanaticism be given the upper hand but provides no argument to show how this is possible. What would Kant reply to an obdurate Jacobian who insisted that reason was incapable of providing orientation because it is simply, by nature, the faculty of supersensible knowledge, but with an immeasurably weaker capacity than the rationalists supposed?

It is important, first, to note that no such question was raised during the debate, precisely because no one other than Kant recognized the importance of determining what reason was nor even of acknowledging the degree to which the most basic assumptions about it conditioned the entire controversy. Second, Kant's strength lies in the fact that he had recognized this importance and had already provided a description of the nature and function of reason. That is, the answer to this question would be nothing less than the *Critique of Pure Reason* itself. The description of reason as the source of orientation is simply a metaphor for the notion of reason as regulative. Kant returns to the notion of orientation, if not the word, in an interesting remark in his *Anthropology*: "The two expressions 'to know the world' and 'to know one's way about in the world' are rather far removed in meaning, since in the first case we only understand the play we have witnessed, while in the second we have participated in it" (VII, 121). Yet the idea that reason is essentially participatory and active, is I have argued, at the basis of the Critical Philosophy. If reason's major function is one not of obtaining knowledge but of providing regulative ideas that guide us in constructing science and sustaining a moral life, no special argument is needed for the claim that reason is in a position to take over the activity of orientation whose importance both Mendelssohn and Jacobi exalted.

II. Faith and Knowledge

The present section will explore the justification of rational faith by examining the differences between Kant and Leibnizian rationalism in detail. Many passages of "What Is Orientation in Thinking?" commend the spirit of Mendelssohn's endeavor, giving little indication of the profound distance that separates it from Kant's. This lends support to the so-called tragic view of Kant, which regards his intellectual life as the progressive but incomplete abandonment of the rationalist aspirations of his youth. For such a view, Kant's task in "What Is Orientation in Thinking?" would be to find a middle ground between two extremes—one of them unattainable, the other unbearable. Thus, Kant would be regarded as believing Mendelssohn's attempt to achieve knowledge of the supersensible to be a worthy but impossible goal. His strategy would be to posit a faith of reason that, though less satisfactory than Mendelssohn's purported knowledge, nevertheless provides some bulwark against the arbitrary, irrational faith that Jacobi propounds.

Such a reading, while not uncommon, fully fails to capture the scope of Kant's critique—a failure that is, to be sure, often furthered by Kant's own description of his project. His point is better taken as follows. The bankruptcy of traditional rationalism leaves two possible alternatives: either an accession to Jacobi's rejection of reason or a reconception of the notion of reason itself. Kant is hesitant to acknowledge the latter alternative as a construction of a new conception of reason, describing it as an investigation that has for the first time precisely determined the nature and function of reason (VIII, 134). But this sort of description, common to nearly every founder of a genuine philosophical revolution, should not prevent us from seeing the radical character of Kant's position. This explains why the essay under consideration is directed toward Mendelssohn; Jacobi, obliquely acknowledged as a man of talent and humanitarian feeling, is barely mentioned. Kant holds his position to be clearly false but uninteresting to attack. It is Leibnizian rationalism, as represented by Mendelssohn, that is in real need of critique, for it is this that unwittingly provides the starting point for the road to fanaticism.

The most basic assumption of that rationalism is the idea that reason's proper task is the knowledge of the objects of metaphysics and that reason (aided or purified by the proper method) is capable of providing this knowledge in the highest degree. Only after accepting the first *Critique*'s arguments for the inadequacy of speculative reason as an instrument of knowledge will we be able to understand reason's true function. Mendelssohn, Kant wrote, would have come to recognize this had not his age and habits made it impossible to give up the deep-seated assumption that reason's task was to provide knowledge of objects. The danger in this assumption is not so much that reason would have no function at all should it turn out to be false, though Kant once suggests this (VIII, 134). Even more seriously, Mendelssohn has fully conceded that there is an activity that is more important than the attainment of (supersensible) knowledge. If reason is devoted to the latter, then some other, nonrational faculty must do the work of orientation. Thus, even without accepting Kant's contention that knowledge of God is impossible, the rationalist has already degraded reason to a subordinate position in acknowledging something other than this knowledge to be vital.

To establish a real difference between his own position and that of Mendelssohn, Kant must show that rational faith is not merely rationalism with an intellectual conscience. Rational faith must be shown to be a truly self-sufficient sort of assertion, differing from knowledge in all its forms. His first attempt to do so occurs in the distinctions between faith and opinion, which is partial knowledge, made in the "Canon" of the first *Critique*.[13]

Kant begins by distinguishing between truth—the objective property of an assertion—and holding-to-be-true (*Fürwahrhalten*), which is an occurrence in the subject. The distinction is one between the validity of a judgment on the one hand and the act of judging and the means of its justification on the other. There are, he continues, three ways of holding a judgment to be true with conviction: opinion, which is subjectively as well as objectively insufficient; belief, which is subjectively sufficient but objectively insufficient; and knowledge, which is both subjectively and objectively sufficient (A822/B850). A statement is subjectively sufficient if the causes on the basis of which it is held would be sufficient to enable any reasonable being to make the same assertion in a similar situation. A judgment is objectively sufficient, on the other hand, if the grounds upon which it rests involve knowledge of an object (according to the criteria that have been laid out in the first part of the *Critique of Pure Reason*). Objective and subjective sufficiency come together in judgments of knowledge, where cause and ground are identical; both are lacking in matters of opinion. Only with faith, where the two diverge, does the question of objective and subjective sufficiency become a matter of interest.

Opinion, Kant makes clear, is would-be empirical knowledge. Matters of opinion are those of which there are no principled limits to knowledge but of which we simply happen to lack knowledge. Opinion is to be distinguished from fiction by the requirement that *something* be known by which the judgment secures an (incomplete) connection with truth (A822/B850). A complete connection, which turns opinion into knowledge, can be effected by the addition of more grounds of the same kind that originally distinguished opinion from fiction. Opinion is not permissible in judgments of pure reason, which are made a priori or not at all. It is legitimate, however, as a preliminary judgment about matters of experience and is usually the first step toward empirical knowledge. To be legitimate, opinion must be recognized for what it is and, as such, can make none of the claims that are justified by assertions of knowledge. Opinion is uncertain and wavering and allows of merely private validity.

Kant is at great pains to distinguish opinion from faith and insists that ordinary discourse, which uses the words interchangeably, confine its use of 'faith' to the very particular conditions he will stipulate (IX, 67).[14] The difference between having been to Rome and having been told about it is not, he writes, a difference between knowing and believing that Rome exists. This is rather a difference between knowing and opining; if my informants are sufficiently reliable and numerous, it is merely a difference between two sources of knowledge. Unlike matters of opinion, matters of faith are those of which knowledge—and even estimates of probability—are impossible to obtain. Faith must be free of logical contradiction, but it has no relation to any of the other conditions that are valid for normal judgments. It is not based upon evidence of any kind but upon a need of reason. Faith is not, like opinion, partial knowledge; it is distinguished from opinion (and thus from knowledge as well) not in degree but in kind. Indeed, in degree of conviction, faith is in no way inferior to knowledge: faith is unshakable because we know that no knowledge could be relevant to its refutation. On the other hand, no knowledge can further its confirmation: unlike opinion, nothing can be added to belief to turn it into knowledge: "The pure rational faith can never be converted by all the natural data of reason into knowledge because . . . the grounds of assent are of such a kind as not to be objectively valid at all" (VIII, 141).

These features of rational faith, however, are just those which awoke suspicions. Kant thus far distinguished opinion from faith only by defining faith as a substitute for knowledge where knowledge is, in principle, impossible. This would make the difference between faith and opinion an accidental difference of subject matter but not of kind. Here faith merely appears to be dogmatic opinion—like opinion, a substitute for the knowledge that could not be achieved, unlike opinion only in being more secure, since the matters of which it treats afford no possibility of refutation.

Kant insists, however, that the difference between faith and opinion is a difference in kind and rests on their relation to action: "It is only from a *practical point of view* that the theoretically insufficient holding of a thing to be true can be termed faith" (A823/B851). Even more clearly: "The term 'faith' refers only to the guidance which an idea gives me, and to its subjective influence in the furthering of the activities of my reason which confirms me in the idea, and which yet does so without my being in a position to give a speculative account of it" (A827/B855).

Faith, then, not only has a necessary relationship to action but has so little theoretical content that it *refers* only to the guidance it gives to action. Opinion and knowledge, Kant suggests, often have a mediate relationship to action, but this is something quite different from the direct connection between faith and action. Faith is a condition on the attainment of an end that has been chosen. Statements that are held to be true in the form of faith are held only insofar as they are necessary to attain such an end: they are only justified as such, and they have no more content than is required to achieve this purpose.

As explication Kant introduces a concept that he terms "pragmatic faith," said to be analogous to rational faith: "The physician must do something for the patient in danger, but does not know the nature of his illness. He observes the symptoms, and if he can find no more likely alternative, judges it to be a case of phthisis" (A824/B852). Here it seems more accurate to say that the doctor *treats* the patient for phthisis; his judgment that this is a case of phthisis involves no more (but no less) than this. Faith is the minimal holding-to-be-true required to take the action that the situation demands.

Kant notes two differences between pragmatic faith and rational faith. First, the physician's lack of knowledge is contingent: another physician, in the present or the future, could observe the same symptoms and make a surer diagnosis, which might even achieve the status of knowledge. Rational faith, on the other hand, is appropriate only in those situations where we are certain that knowledge is impossible. Second, the physician's end is contingent: he need not take this case, he may pronounce the patient to be incurable, and so on. Rational faith concerns ends that are absolutely necessary: we have no legitimate alternative to obeying the moral law. Thus, pragmatic faith is contingent, and rational faith necessary, in a double sense.

While this example nicely illustrates the idea of faith being held insofar as it is necessary for action, it poses a problem that is not dispelled by Kant's assertion that rational faith is more necessary than pragmatic faith. The example suggests no structural difference between having faith that a patient has phthisis and opining the same thing, save the assertion that this faith is necessary for the medical treatment of a patient in danger. Yet surely the *knowledge* either that the patient has phthisis or that the diagnosis is completely false would be the best of all forms of holding-to-be-true in this case. Even should we suppose that it were impossible to make a positive diagnosis of phthisis, this would be a matter for regret. We would regard the medical profession's reliance on faith in such cases as a sorry substitute for knowledge and as confirmation of the view that medicine has not yet achieved the status of a full-fledged science. Kant's example suggests that the difference between opinion and faith is that the latter is appropriate to situations where practical demands permit us to hold things to be true to which we have no other right. We must act, and we are allowed to use whatever means are at hand for pragmatic purposes; if knowledge is unavailable then we must make do with something else. Yet in Kant's example of pragmatic faith, it is clear that knowledge would better serve the *pragmatic* purposes that are served in the absence of knowledge by faith. Thus, the example only supports the general view of rational faith as failed knowledge. Kant's assertion that it only functions where this failure is necessary does little to mitigate the problem.

Fortunately, as is so often the case, Kant's view is more subtle and sound than his illustrations of it. His best attempt to distinguish faith from opinion lies in the argument that faith, unlike opinion, is not interchangeable with knowledge. We have seen that opinion is a substitute for knowledge where knowledge happens to be unavailable. For Kant it is equally unquestionable that opinion should be replaced by knowledge whenever possible. Faith, by contrast, is not permitted where knowledge is the desideratum. Conversely and even more importantly, judgments of faith are not satisfactorily replaceable by judgments of knowledge. Though opinion, faith, and knowledge are described as three ways of holding a judgment to be true, opinion and knowledge form a continuum where faith has in fact no place. While the argument for this claim is nowhere set out as clearly as one might wish, Kant's texts are full of indications for it. I will show that in situations where rational faith is justifiable, judgments of knowledge would be neither necessary nor sufficient nor desirable. Hence, the example of pragmatic faith in which knowledge of the correct diagnosis would be the most desirable solution is simply misplaced.

Kant is firm in denying that rational faith can resolve the questions of speculative reason: "The subjective grounds upon which we may hold something to be true, such as those which are able to produce faith, are not permissible in speculative questions, inasmuch as they do not hold independently of all empirical support" (A823/B851). Speculative questions are genuine requests for knowledge. Empirical considerations would thus be relevant in deciding them. What is lacking in speculative matters are the conditions that could provide empirical ways of determining, for example, whether the world has a beginning. In the absence — even the permanent absence — of such conditions, we cannot decide as we please: speculative questions *as such* can only be resolved by providing the knowledge that they demand. If such knowledge is impossible, faith cannot be put in its place. Rational faith provides no clue as to the nature of the objects it postulates; as we have just seen, faith refers only to the guidance that an idea gives us. Since this is far from being the knowledge that speculative reason seeks, Kant insists, the strictures of the Critical Philosophy are in no way violated by the postulates of rational faith. We can have something resembling an opinion concerning speculative issues, but this is a very inferior version of the knowledge that is sought and can, at most, play the role of a private occupation (IX, 66–67; VIII, 141).

Faith cannot be substituted for knowledge, because assertions of faith, though apparently having the form of claims to knowledge, do not really have knowledge as their end. It might be thought that this only entails that knowledge of the objects of faith is unnecessary: assertions of faith, though resembling knowledge claims, are actually satisfied by some weaker claim on the world. Properly expressed, this is indeed one outcome of Kant's discussion; he argues elsewhere that the postulates of faith *need* not be known: "It is only a necessary need of reason to presuppose, not to demonstrate, the existence of the highest being, and so long as we are human, it will remain so" (VIII, 141).

We have seen that faith is necessary and justified only insofar as it is required for action: we are licensed to postulate the existence of God, immortality, and freedom as conditions of our obedience to the moral law. This postulation is not merely less determinate than are claims of knowledge: it does not, like judgments of knowledge, determine an object at all, but rather the will of a subject (B167). This faith does not involve, for example, even a hypothesis about the character of the objects involved, nor does it open the possibility of any synthetic statements about them. Kant holds these sorts of features to be unnecessary for the sole purpose that the postulates are to fulfill.

We come closer to understanding the nature of rational faith when we consider the idea that knowledge of the objects of faith is not only unnecessary but insufficient. Rational faith, that is, performs a function that knowledge cannot fulfill. This idea appears most clearly in "What Is Orientation in Thinking?" Now all parties to the debate had agreed that in addition to knowledge, something called orientation was necessary. Kant's point is that this is not merely because knowledge in this realm is logically impossible; more interestingly, knowledge is logically incapable of fulfilling the task at hand. He begins to specify this in the long footnote which concludes the essay: "Thinking for oneself means to search for the highest criterion of truth in oneself (i.e., in one's own reason) and the maxim of always thinking for oneself is *enlightenment*" (VIII, 146).

The appearance of pious banality first offered by this sentence is immediately offset by the sentence following it, in which the radical nature of Kant's notion of thinking for oneself becomes evident: "But there is not so much in it as those suppose who make enlightenment a matter of *knowledge*" (VIII, 146).

Knowledge, Kant continues, is merely a negative principle for the use of the whole faculty of thought. That is, thinking for oneself presupposes a recognition of what one knows and does not know (what is not known must be clearly acknowledged as such, and cannot be assumed), but this is simply the minimal condition upon thinking: "Often he who is thoroughly rich in knowledge is the least enlightened in the use of it" (VIII, 146).

It is, then, the right use of knowledge, not its acquisition, that makes up thinking for oneself. The democratic tendency of this conception is clear: Kant emphasizes that thinking for oneself can be well undertaken by those without much knowledge. But what is this process? Although "What Is Orientation in Thinking?" provides no more than the metaphors of spatial orientation to explicate the notion of orientation, we can refer to the conclusions of the previous chapters for help. We have seen that principles of knowledge are inadequate to constitute science; for "What *use* can we make of our understanding, even in respect of experience, if we do not propose ends to ourselves?" (A816/B844).

Regulative principles of reason are required to set ends within experience, a fully different task from those of the understanding, which is merely capable of recording experience. This discussion must be born in mind when considering Kant's claim that the essential difference between opinion and faith involves the immediate relationship between faith and action. It is not the case, as the example of pragmatic faith misleadingly suggested, that this relationship is constituted by the fact that the demands of action licenses faith that would otherwise be unjustified. Rather, faith *is* the function of guidance, or orientation, that all action requires. If knowledge is insufficient to provide this guidance in theoretical science, where it is available, then Kant's argument against Mendelssohn cannot merely be that speculative knowledge is unobtainable. Even the same insight into the supersensible world as we have of the sensible world would not give us what we need, for it would remain mere insight, a passive perception of fixed realities lacking a link to action.

If constitutive principles cannot be substituted for regulative ones in the realm of science, they appear much more inadequate in those matters where rational faith has a role; what is needed is a guide to *moral* action, which requires a kind of thinking that is fully autonomous. "What Is Orientation in Thinking?" stresses the mechanical character of knowledge: "Everybody must believe a fact which is but sufficiently confirmed, just as he must believe a mathematical demonstration, whether he will or not" (VIII, 146).

Insofar as knowledge, the acquisition of facts, is a process of acceptance of truths that (if we are minimally rational) is forced on us "whether we will or not," it is simply second-rate. Note that this example treats both the knowledge of empirical facts and a priori proofs as equal in this respect, implying that despite their independence from the constraints of the empirical world, none of the attempts at a priori proofs of God's existence is more free or sublime than the most ordinary of empirical assumptions. Both involve assent to beliefs that are forced upon us from without. "What Is Orientation in Thinking?" goes so far as to describe superstition as "the subjection of reason to facts" (VIII, 145). The source of superstition, Kant suggests, is not so much that the supposed facts to which it adheres turn out to be false: the very process of basing something so crucial as faith upon the acceptance of facts (whether actually true or not) is slavish. The acceptance of faith, including the living of one's life according to the best of moral principles—if done as accession to received facts, instead of the use of one's own reason—is mere superstition. On the other hand, the so-called freethinking that is merely a rejection of (the same) received facts involves, for Kant, as a simple negation, the same process that leads to superstition. What is known as freethinking, he writes, is the independence of reason from its own needs (VIII, 146). As such, it is merely the absence of self-criticism. Genuine freedom in thinking is "the subjection of reason to no other laws than those which it gives itself" (VIII, 145). Given Kant's prior discussion of reason's own laws, this definition of freethinking will ensure that genuine freethinking leads not to atheism but to the only acceptable faith in God. The holding of such a faith on the basis of tradition or revelation is mere superstition. Real faith, Kant argues, is the only sort of holding-to-be-true that is sufficiently free to assert the existence of God, immortality, and freedom as practical postulates: "for since it cannot, as things of faith, be grounded on theoretical proofs (like facts) it is a free holding-to-be-true and only as such compatible with the morality of the subject" (V, 453; see also XX, 298).

This structural insufficiency of knowledge leads to Kant's strongest argument for the existence of a self-sufficient real faith. While both Mendelssohn and Jacobi, like many others, insist that faith in God and immortality is necessary for human morality, neither is concerned to examine the nature of this necessity. This failure, Kant holds, leads to the assertion of a kind of faith that is, in fact, at odds with a genuine autonomous morality. Real faith, he argues, is the only kind of holding-to-be-true that is acceptable for these postulates: positive knowledge of them would have consequences that would be disastrous for morality. Knowledge of the reality of the highest good, in which happiness was apportioned to virtue by God's will, would indeed secure obedience to the moral law: no one would dare transgress it. But, Kant says, this would no longer be *moral* activity.

This idea first appears in the *Critique of Practical Reason*, where Kant writes that were we to have the knowledge we seek,

> instead of the conflict which now the moral disposition has to wage with the inclinations and in which, after some defeats, moral strength of mind may be gradually won, God and eternity in their awful majesty would stand unceasingly and before our eyes (for that which we can completely prove is as certain as that which we can ascertain by sight). But because the disposition from which actions should be done cannot be instilled by any command, and because the spur to action would always be present and eternal, reason would have no need to endeavor to gather its strength to resist the inclinations by a vivid idea of the dignity of the law. Thus most actions conforming to the law would be done from fear, few would be done from hope, none from duty. The moral worth of actions, on which alone the worth of the person and even of the world depends in the eyes of the supreme wisdom, would not exist at all. The conduct of man, so long as his nature remained as it now is, would be changed into mere mechanism, where, as in a puppet show, everything would gesticulate but no life would be found in the figures. (V, 147)

Kant's idea, as simple as it is breathtaking, is repeated in all of the later writings on rational faith. The postulation of the highest good is necessary as an object of our moral striving: the hope of its realization keeps us from wavering despair. Were this postulation changed to knowledge, our very nature would change. The object of virtue would become identical with its motive; it would no longer be possible to act righteously for its own sake, for all obedience to the moral law would be done out of fear of (eternal) punishment. The concept of morality itself would perforce disappear. In its place would be the simplest kind of empirical practical reasoning—the calculating of risks and the weighing of alternatives to secure the least costly means to (eternal) happiness. We would, that is, "be virtuous out of sensuous impulses" (XXVIII, 2.2, 1084) Just as a theological physics would be an *Unding*, no longer describing laws of *nature* but the arrangements of God's will, so the resulting theological ethics would no longer be ethics but merely a listing of God's commands (V, 484−85). Both would be, from the point of view of justification, fully arbitrary.

This argument contains a critique of all forms of positive theology far more devastating than the theoretical incoherence of which they were accused in the first *Critique*. The very attempt at a positive theology, conceived as a necessary basis for morality, is accordingly as destructive to genuine religious feeling as it is to morality itself. True religion, Kant says, cannot consist in knowledge of what God does to make us blessed but of what we must do to be worthy of being blessed (VI, 133). Any religion that puts the (alleged) knowledge of God—whether historical or a priori— before moral commandments is, Kant suggest, mere idolatry, the attempt to influence a higher being for our sensuous satisfaction, temporal or otherwise. Only a religion based on rational faith, Kant writes, "is of pure moral value, for it is free and uncoerced by any threat (whereby it can never be upright)" (VI, 182).

Knowledge of God's purposes would not produce genuine reverence but pathological fear. The theoretical certainty that the speculative thinker seeks would, if it could be found, produce law and order at the cost of turning the universe into a police state so thorough that every concept of responsibility and value would be lost.

In the second *Critique* he uses this argument as a confirmation that "the inscrutable wisdom through which we exist is not less worthy of veneration in respect to what it denies us than in what it has granted" (V, 148). In the *Lectures on Philosophical Theology*, he is even clearer:

> Our faith is not scientific knowledge, and thank heaven it is not! For God's wisdom is apparent in the very fact that we do not *know* that God exists, but should have faith that God exists. For suppose we could attain to scientific knowledge of God's existence . . . all our morality would break down. In his every action, man would represent God to himself as a rewarder or avenger. This image would force itself on his soul, and his hope for reward and fear of punishment would take the place of moral motives. (XXVIII, 2. 2, 1083−84)

The idea that human reason's peculiar fate is the endless search for knowledge that it is incapable of achieving is the starting point of the Critical Philosophy. Only in this argument does Kant suggest grounds for this being not the fate of a Sisyphean hell but one that could be allotted by a benevolent God. Attainment of that knowledge would destroy the possibility of morality, the failure to seek it would mean the loss of every creative human endeavor. Nor can it be said that Kant offers this argument as consolation for what he elsewhere describes as the permanent humiliation of speculative reason in its failure to achieve its goal (A795/B823). For Kant, the idea that morality depends on practical reason's ignorance of the rewards of its actions is fundamental to the very idea of morality.

If knowledge of the objects of faith would be neither necessary, nor sufficient, nor desirable, then rational faith is not a poor substitute for knowledge; it is not a substitute for knowledge at all. It is not the impossibility of knowledge that is paramount here, though the realization of this impossibility is the first step to the discovery of reason's real function. Far more important is the positive undesirability of speculative knowledge in the supersensible realm. Once this is clear, it becomes impossible to view Kant as a sadder or wiser version of Mendelssohn: for Kant, the destruction of the hopes of speculative reason is no tragedy. In the "Canon of Pure Reason" he writes:

> The whole equipment of reason, in the discipline which is entitled pure philosophy, is, in fact, determined with a view to the three above-mentioned problems (i.e., God, freedom, and immortality). These, however, themselves in turn refer us yet further, namely, to the problem *what we ought to do* if the will is free, if there is a God and a future world. As this concerns our attitude to the supreme end, it is evident that the ultimate intention of nature in her wise provision for us has indeed, in the constitution of our reason, been directed to moral interests alone. (A801/B829).

This passage, echoed by many others, asserts that the entire effort of human reason is motivated by the need not for a speculative, but for a practical, solution to the problems it necessarily raises. It suggests that the charge that regulative principles are failed constitutive ones must be turned on its head. If the whole equipment of reason is motivated by—and, when properly used, directed to—the practical, then the search for constitutive principles providing knowledge of the supersensible is more appropriately described as an instance of failed regulative principles. Speculative philosophy seeks knowledge where the real need is for orientation.

III. Faith and Fanaticism

This exposition leaves unanswered the general question raised in the introduction to this book: If it can be successfully established that Kant's conception of reason is genuinely distinct from his conception of knowledge, what remains to make it recognizable as a conception of reason? All forms of the common charge against the notion of rational faith—that it is the dogmatic preservation of traditional beliefs freed from all the constraints of truth that Kant so carefully established—can be contained in this question. To put the question historically, if it has been made convincing that Kant is sufficiently distinct from the tradition represented by Leibniz and Mendelssohn in that he repudiates rather than mourns the rationalist hope of a solution to the "three greatest problems of reason" through the attainment of speculative knowledge, what separates him from a Jacobian affirmation of faith unhampered by any ties to reason at all? If Kant's attachment to reason is only nominal, rational faith is merely bad faith. What distinguishes Kant's assertion, inaccessible to proof or refutation, of the existence of God, the immortal soul, and human freedom from the ungrounded *Schwärmerei* that he condemns?

Kant's answer to this charge can be seen as twofold. First, having undermined the view of the postulates of rational faith as instances of failed knowledge by showing them to fill a sort of role different from knowledge, he has undermined the very possibility of assimilating them to the traditional debates about the respective claims of reason and faith. Second and more directly, he describes the features of rational faith that give it a genuine claim to be nonarbitrary, thus preserving the core that we require in anything that could count as a notion of reason.

The charge of wishful thinking—and with it, the suggestion of purest irrationality—was first made against Kant's notion of rational faith by the young Thomas Wizenmann during the pantheism controversy.[15] Wizenmann had compared Kant's postulate of God's existence on the basis of human reason's need for God to "the example of a man in love, who has fooled himself with an idea of beauty which is merely a chimera of his own brain and who now tries to argue that such an object really exists somewhere" (V, 143−44).[16]

What distinguishes Kant's argument from such a procedure, whose manifest arbitrariness undermines the very possibility of rational discourse? Kant replies as follows:

> I concede that [Wizenmann] is right in all cases where the need is based on inclination, which cannot postulate the existence of an object even for him who is beset by it, and which even less contains a demand valid for everyone, and which is, therefore, a merely subjective ground of wishes. Here we have to do, however, with a need of reason arising from an objective determining ground of the will, i.e., the moral law, which is necessarily binding on every rational being; this, therefore, justifies a priori the presupposition of suitable conditions in nature and makes them inseparable from the complete practical use of reason. (V, 144)

Rational faith, then, originates in needs that are common to every rational being, since it concerns the conditions of obedience to the moral law, which is valid for every rational being. The swiftness with which Kant answers Wizenmann's objection must be explained with reference to his general views about reason and inclination. Kant takes it to be clear that while all people have fundamentally similar rational capacities, their desires vary widely (A831/B859). One of Kant's arguments for rejecting moral theories based on the satisfaction of desires is that desires differ; while the desire for happiness is universal, Kant holds it to be too indeterminate to have content apart from particular desires included under it (V, 34−35). Only a moral theory based on reason, he argues, is sufficiently universal to provide a moral framework that, discounting such desires, can impose harmony upon the world. Hence, in stipulating that rational faith is founded upon a need of reason, Kant stipulates that it be based on a need that is universal and unvarying, ruling out the possibility of a belief that each person formulates individually at will. So he states that the moral argument is "valid for human beings as rational beings in the world in general, and not simply a way of thought which happens to be adopted by this or that human being" (XX, 306). If Kant is somewhat lax in explicating the notion of a need of reason, it is not because he found it particularly problematic but because there is nothing mysterious about the notion at all. Once any talk of faculties is granted, the statement that reason has needs is just the statement that human beings have needs of different kinds; there is no more cause to argue for the claim that reason has needs than for the claim that inclination does. Kant does say that the fact that reason is the source of ideas creates problems for reason: the definition, limitation and employment of the ideas become the basis of the needs of reason (V, 142). But this process is no more puzzling than the development of the needs of inclination: it could just as easily be said that the structure of inclination poses problems which become needs to be satisfied. Since, for Kant, it is the possession of reason that distinguishes us from animals, the needs of reason are just those universal needs which human beings have in addition to those we share with other animals.

Kant not only requires that only needs of reason may provide the basis for rational faith; not even every need of reason suffices to do so. Only the needs of practical reason can form the foundation for rational faith; theoretical reason's needs must remain unsatisfied. I have suggested one reason for this claim: reason's theoretical needs are needs for knowledge and can only be satisfied as such. Since rational faith is not a substitute for knowledge, there is simply no way in which it could satisfy those needs. A second reason for Kant's stipulation that only practical reason can provide the foundation of faith is that theoretical needs are not sufficiently important. Only that which Kant calls an absolutely necessary need of reason is strong enough to ground faith.

The distinction between needs that are absolutely necessary and those which are merely necessary need not be problematic. We ordinarily weigh needs as well as desires—distinguishing, for example, between those things needed to support life at all and those which are necessary to sustain a decent life. Aware of Rousseau's sophisticated distinction between true human needs and those created by society, Kant knew that there will be differences of agreement in such matters. Nevertheless, there is, for Kant, only one absolutely necessary need of reason, and this is the furthering of the highest good. Only those things which are conditions of the possibility of achieving this end are, therefore, allowed to be postulated as rational faith. Thus, even though Kant holds the exploration of nature to be of enormous value and often suggests it to be an end that is common to all rational beings, it is not a sufficient basis for rational faith. The conditions of scientific inquiry are not arbitrary—they are not peculiar to some rational agents but spring from a genuine need of universal reason—but they are nevertheless contingent. Morality is absolutely necessary and science is not. This claim itself is a moral one; the argument for the superior importance of morality cannot be made on other grounds (see chap. 3, sec. III) Here Kant depends on it to assert the primacy of the needs of practical reason. As was shown in chapter 2, Kant argues that the needs of theoretical reason are sufficient to provide the basis for an analogue of rational faith insofar as it is necessary to further scientific inquiry. This analogue, however, is relative only to the contingent purpose it serves. Kant argues that it has even less content, as well as less necessity, than the postulates of rational faith (V, 477–78).

If rational faith is universal in origin, arising from the greatest needs common to every human being, is it universal in application? Does it claim the assent of every (rational) human being? The answer to this question will be crucial in refuting the suspicion of *Schwärmerei*, for a defining feature of rational assertion is its claim upon the agreement of all rational people in normal circumstances. Kant's position on this issue is not entirely clear. Many passages assert that the postulates are universally binding:

> It is a duty to realize the highest good as far as it is in our power to do so; therefore, it must be possible to do so. Consequently, it is unavoidable for every rational being in the world to assume what is necessary to its objective possibility. The assumption is as necessary as the moral law, in relation to which alone it is valid. (V, 144)

The "Canon of Pure Reason" states: "Once an end is accepted, the conditions of its attainment are hypothetically necessary. This necessity . . . is sufficient, absolutely and for everyone, if I know with certainty that no one can have knowledge of any other conditions which lead to the proposed end" (A824/B852).

We know Kant to hold that the postulates fulfill this condition. More generally, Kant has classified faith as a judgment of conviction, while defining the distinction between persuasion and conviction as one between the judgments that are only binding on a particular subject and those which are valid for everyone "provided only he is in possession of his reason" (A820/B848). Similarly, he describes belief as "assertoric" (IX, 66) and writes that asserting a statement means declaring it to be necessarily valid for everyone (A821/B849). These and many other passages seem to allow us to conclude that the postulates have absolute and universal validity.

A small but definite number of passages, including one quoted by Jacobi as support for his own views, appear to deny this: "No, my conviction is not logical but moral certainty; and since it rests on subjective grounds (of the moral sentiment) I must not even say '*It is* morally certain that there is a God, etc.' but "*I am* morally certain, etc.'." (A829/B857). The *Logic* is even more explicit: "Faith, then, because of its merely subjective grounds, does not yield a conviction that can be communicated and commands general acclaim, like the conviction that comes from knowledge. I myself can be certain only of the validity and immutability of my practical belief" (IX, 70).

The apparent inconsistency expressed here can, I think, be resolved with reference to Kant's insistence that real faith be absolutely free. The *Critique of Practical Reason* states that "commanded faith is an absurdity" (V, 144). If this is the case, the postulates cannot demand universal assent in the way that a mathematical proof does. The *absurdum practicum* argument by which they are justified claims the assent of everyone not insofar as they are theoretically rational but insofar as they are practically rational, that is, moral beings. This is and must be a matter of free choice. Equally, as we saw, it is a fact about which no one, including the subject himself, can have knowledge. This privacy requires that everyone must carry out the *absurdum practicum* argument himself.[17]

This suggests that the main difference between the justification of rational faith and that of other statements lies in the role that authority is able to play in each case. In his discussions of knowledge, Kant asserts that there is no epistemological difference between the testimony of one's own experience and that of reliable witnesses. Given appropriate information about your character and capacities, I would act irrationally in rejecting your claim on my assent to knowledge that you are in a better position than I to possess. In matters of faith on the other hand, intellectual superiority is insignificant: There can be no authorities of faith because there are no moral authorities. "I therefore can only say: *I* find myself compelled, through my end according to the laws of freedom, to adopt a highest good in the world as possible, but I cannot compel anyone else by reason (faith is free)" (IX, 69).

This discussion suggests that the passages just cited do not undercut the claim that the postulates are universally binding. Since the *absurdum practicum* argument is valid for us insofar as we are practically rational beings, Kant holds it to have, in fact, universal validity. The restriction of the justification of real faith to the individual subject is meant instead to preclude the possibility that it could be imposed on the basis of grounds external to the subject's own practical reason. Where assent can be commanded by a priori proofs, it can also be commanded by political force, for knowledge permits — or requires — authority to play a role in determining the validity of the statements in question. So Kant writes:

> The Christian faith, as a *learned* faith, relies upon history and insofar as erudition (objectively) constitutes its foundation, it is not in itself a free faith (*fides elicita*). . . . But if it is to be valid for all men, including the unlearned, it is not only a faith which is commanded but also one which obeys the command blindly (*fides servilis*), i.e., without investigation as to whether it really is a divine command. (VI, 164)

By removing the postulates from the realm of knowledge — a priori or historical — Kant removes them from a realm in which authority is appropriate. Thus, it becomes not merely reprehensible but impossible for anybody but the individual to determine his or her own faith. Faith, Kant says, permits no imperative (VII, 42; XX, 298). Again, "A commanded faith is a nonentity [*Unding*]" (V, 144)

Precisely the fact that the determination of faith rests on nothing but the use of pure practical reason with which we are all equally endowed makes the postulates more, not less, binding than traditional assertions of dogma. This should become clearer in further discussion.

Now these stipulations surely rule out the example that Wizenmann chose: the procedure of justification used for rational faith cannot, like the hopes of a man in love, establish the reality of particular inclinations. Still, they may not suffice to remove the suspicions upon which the objection was founded. Rational faith is not the cavalier assertion of the propositions that we would like to be true; it must be founded on the very deepest of needs common to human reason. But let it be granted that we all have such needs, granted that they are crucial, granted even that they could only be satisfied by rational faith. Can this be enough to warrant our assertion of any statements? Kant's defense of rational faith seems to rule out the possibility of individual fantasy but not that of mass delusion. He never seems so much as to consider the possibility that the doctrine of rational faith might license the systematic and universal substitution of illusion held to be necessary to stave off unpalatable truth. This disregard is especially unnerving in the face of the fact that since shortly after Kant's death, it is precisely faith in God and immortality that have been variously understood as the result of just such widespread and systematic delusion. Kant's emphasis upon the universality and the importance of the needs upon which rational faith is based may seem to beg the most important questions at issue. Is he not simply saying that we are permitted to hold statements to be true if we *all really* need to believe so?

This objection, natural as it is (and Kant would hold it to be a natural expression of reason's drive to the constitutive) fails to recognize that rational faith, like other regulative principles, does not concern truth conditions at all. Hence, to accuse Kant of allowing us to believe what we wish to be true is beside the point. If understood as a statement about Kant's justification of rational faith as referring to human needs and not the facts of the external world (the latter being, of course, the normal route to the justification of knowledge), then the objection is, in some sense, correct. Kant's justification *is* based solely on his analysis of human possibilities, not the claims of external reality; this was what was meant by stating faith to be subjectively, but not objectively, sufficient. But to object to this justification, one must object to it in all its radicality, as a whole. To suppose that Kant somehow managed to overlook that his defense of rational faith was based on an analysis of the subject that would be wholly illegitimate in justifications of knowledge is as arrogant as it is naive. Rather, as I have argued, this defense is a piece of a general, self-supporting regulative notion of reason.

It is noteworthy that neither Jacobi nor any of those writers who, following him, could be accused of irrationalism made use of anything resembling Kant's argument. Far from acknowledging that their faith rested on subjective grounds, they commonly appealed to an immediate intuition of God, which, though nondiscursive and often incommunicable, was said to provide as direct and certain a connection with God as any of the less private forms of knowledge. The point is not that Kant argues that this kind of appeal is doomed to failure because, for example, no (sensory) intuition of God could be adequate. More importantly, this makes clear that it is not the form of justification—in an argument from subjective needs to an assertion of faith—that is for Kant the source of *Schwärmerei*. What are Kant's real worries when he speaks of the dangers of fanaticism?

The essay "On a Recently Raised Distinguished Tone in Philosophy" answers this question with more than usual clarity. Here, too, Kant criticizes the substitution of alleged insight for philosophical reasoning, because the former is unable to provide results that are valid for everyone (VIII, 401). But here it is not only the uncertainty that attaches to such private validity but the elitism entailed by these procedures that comes to the fore. The essay is full of scorn for those who claim to be in possession of a special mystical insight into the objects of metaphysics: their presumption may be based on classical erudition, but this merely belongs to the culture of taste (VIII, 403). Their activities cannot be indulged, "because they elevate themselves above their brothers, and harm the inalienable right of everyone to freedom and equality in matters of pure reason" (VIII, 394). The danger of fanaticism is not its lack of solid grounding: this could be a cause for amusement or contempt but hardly, by itself, for concern. Kant's worry is rather the tendency to impose these beliefs, however grounded, on others.

A major source of the emotions surrounding the pantheism controversy was Jacobi's approving use of Lavater, the Swiss mystic who, a decade earlier, had scandalized the German Enlightenment by challenging Mendelssohn to refute Christianity or convert to it. In this context, the danger that some people will use (nonrational) notions of faith to force particular conceptions of religion upon others is very immediate.[18] The notion of rational faith must be so constructed as to not only be immune to this kind of abuse but to provide some protection against it. The stipulations that rational faith be based upon universal needs and that it involve fully free affirmation serve to protect "the inalienable right of everyone to freedom and equality in matters of pure reason." Kant's final guarantee against fanaticism lies in the regulative nature of real faith. He explains:

> To the extent that a religion propounds, as necessary, dogmas which cannot be known to be true through reason but which are nonetheless to be imparted

uncorrupted (as regards essential content) to all men in all future ages, it must be viewed (if we do not wish to assume a continuous miracle of revelation) as a sacred charge entrusted to the guardianship of the learned. For even though at first, accompanied by miracles and deeds, this religion, even in that which finds no confirmation in reason, could obtain entry everywhere, yet the very report of these miracles, together with the doctrines which stand in need of confirmation through this report, requires, *with the passage of time*, the written, authoritative, and unchanging instruction of posterity. (VI, 163)

Note that Kant holds every dogma of revealed religion, whether it appeals to reason or more mystical sources, to require the development of this sort of authority. With the claim to religious authority comes, of course, the claim to the right to legislate in matters of faith. Thus, the very form of traditional religion, namely, its basis in the assent to certain propositions about the nature of God, provides the starting point for fanaticism: "The pure rational faith, in contrast, stands in need of no such documentary authentication but proves itself" (VI, 129).

This description is not quite adequate: the advantage of rational faith in this regard is not that it proves itself but that it does not consist of propositions that need to be proved. Rational faith contains no dogmas at all, for its "purpose is not to determine God's nature but our own" (VI, 431). Its lack of theoretical content serves not merely to deprive speculative philosophers of the opportunity to build theological systems but to deprive every type of inquisitor of the possibility of coercing those who do not assent to his dogmas. With rational faith, there is no fact of the matter about which other people could be in error.

Kant's insistence on rational faith's immunity to religious dogma accounts for the *Religion*'s painstaking discussion detailing exactly what part of traditional Christian dogma is permissible in rational religion. As he writes:

Everyone can convince himself, through his own reason, of the evil which is in human hearts and from which no one is free; of the impossibility of ever holding himself to be justified before God through his own life-conduct and at the same time, of the necessity for such a justification in his eyes; of the futility of substituting churchly observances and pious compulsory services for the righteousness which is lacking, and over and against this, of the inescapable obligation to become a new man; and to be convinced of all of this is part of religion. (VI, 163)

As soon as Christianity goes beyond these convictions to assert other propositions, whether historical (e.g., that Jesus was resurrected and ascended to heaven) or not (e.g., concerning the nature of the Trinity; VI, 140) it ceases to be rational religion and becomes a faith that must be commanded (VI, 164).

Kant's concept of rational religion has been criticized for denying recognition to aspects of religious experience that are, of necessity, arational, if not irrational. To discuss this question in detail would lead us far from our goal.[19] It is important to note, however, that if Kant did not emphasize such aspects, he did not deny them, even asserting that "there are also many mysteries in rational religion" (XXVIII, 2.2, 1120). What is crucially rational about rational religion is that it is founded on nothing that cannot be derived from the individual use of pure practical reason unaided by interpretation or authority. And this, he has argued, amounts to two regulative postulates without theoretical content, gaining significance only through their function in sustaining our moral life. While this presumably leaves room for many forms of private nonrational religious experience as well as the pursuit of opinions about the nature of that experience, it decisively disallows their use in any official, coercive function. The doctrine of rational faith warns, moreover, against the impiety of such a use:

> Moral theology is thus of immanent use only. It enables us to fulfill our vocation in this present world by showing us how to adapt ourselves to the system of all ends, and by warning us against the fanaticism—and indeed the impiety—of abandoning the guidance of a morally legislative reason in the right conduct of our lives in order to derive guidance directly from the idea of a Supreme Being. (A819/B847)

Thus, Jacobi's initially promising attempts to assimilate rational faith to his own irrational appeal to faith must be unsuccessful. Kant's doctrine cannot be accused of irrationalism because it constrains the use of rational faith to needs that are universal to every individual human reason and is based upon an argument that is applicable by (and only by) every individual human reason. Furthermore, the postulates do not permit the theoretical content that is necessary to the delusion of masses or the compulsion of minorities. Here, it becomes clear that Kant's prohibitions on the theoretical use of the postulates are not merely a matter of paying lip service to his own epistemology. The repeated statements that we have practical, but not theoretical, grounds for asserting the postulates and that their use is restricted to practical, but not theoretical, ends are based on the idea that the postulates, as regulative principles, are not open to the kind of abuse that constitutive principles allow. The attempt to imagine a group of fanatic subscribers to rational faith founders from the start, for the faith that serves them as orientation does not possess the sort of content about which they could be fanatical. This should become apparent in examining, finally, Kant's arguments for the necessity of the postulates.

IV. The Highest Good

The second *Critique* tells us that the investigation of the Highest Good is the real task of philosophy. This striking claim cannot simply be understood by reference to the role played by the Highest Good in Kant's ethics, however significant. Nor is it sufficient to point to its position as the linchpin of Kant's rational religion or even to the idea of the Highest Good as the negative principle of history (Yovel 1980, 72–80). The importance which Kant assigns to the notion of the Highest Good is understandable only in the context of his identification of the Highest Good as the Unconditioned in the practical realm (V, 107–114). The object of all of practical reason's endeavors is a state in which the greatest possible virtue is joined with the greatest possible happiness. Such a state would be completely intelligible, nothing further could be sought. The question of the Highest Good thus returns us to the broadest question of the principle of sufficient reason: whether and how there is reason in the world.[20]

Until quite recently, most commentators tended to ignore the notion of the Highest Good in the belief that it was in serious contradiction with the rest of Kant's moral theory, which flatly rejects any teleological conception of ethics. But recent

nphasized Kant's distinction between the Highest Good as the object of the
e categorical imperative (the Unconditioned, or good in itself, in another
e determining ground of the will.[21] If the Highest Good is not a motive for
action but an end of action constructed by reason itself, then it is not merely consistent
with the rest of Kant's moral philosophy but forms an important part of it. Properly
understood, the Highest Good plays a significant role in moderating Kant's alleged
rigorism.

The fact that we need an end of action is once described as "man's own fault" (VI,
3). Kant sometimes seems to suggest that this need arises in connection with, if not as
a consequence of, the insufficiency of our virtue:

> All men could have sufficient incentive if (as they should) they adhered solely to the
> dictation of pure reason in the law. What need have they to know the outcome of their
> moral actions and abstentions, an outcome which the world's course will bring
> about? It suffices for them that they do their duty, even though all things end with
> earthly life and though, in this life, happiness and desert never meet. And yet it is one
> of the inescapable limitations of man and of his faculty of practical reason (a
> limitation, perhaps, of all other worldly beings, as well) to have regard, in every
> action, to the consequence thereof. (VI, 7)

But if Kant regards our caring about the consequences of our action as a
limitation, it is one to which he is willing to give credence, thus displaying both the
complexity and the humanity of his moral view. Not Kant but duty is rigorous and
must be so defined. Once Kant has done so, however, he turns to consider the
conditions under which it is possible for human beings to be moral. The formulation
of those conditions, unlike that of the concept of morality itself, may take human
needs and limitations into account. In Kant's system of ethics, the Highest Good fills
the gap between the rigor of the concept and the conditions of its fulfillment.

This idea is introduced by way of a critique of ancient attempts to translate the real
problems posed by the Highest Good into a verbal problem, by identifying virtue and
happiness. Recognizing that reason has a need to find a connection between virtue
and happiness, both Epicureans and Stoics sought to make that connection analytic.
The former postulated the identity of happiness and virtue by supposing that furthering one's own happiness is all there is to virtue; the latter postulated the identity of
happiness and virtue by insisting that the consciousness of one's virtue is the only
genuine happiness. Although each posited a different principle as the fundamental
one, their approaches were equally reductionistic. By insisting on the identity of
happiness and virtue, they attempt to deny the possibility that the pursuit of happiness
and the pursuit of virtue could conflict with one another, a possibility whose
confirmation hardly requires the authority of a moral philosopher. In a word, both
seek to deny that duty is *hard*. If the Epicurean seeks to deny this by refusing to
acknowledge a duty which exists independently of our own exercises in prudence
while the Stoic assures us that we are missing no real happiness if we are certain we
have done our duty, both are equally flying from the central fact of moral experience.
This fact, the permanent threat of conflict between being happy and doing one's duty,
is what Kant designates by the expression "the heterogeneity of the two concepts of
the highest good"; and he is surely correct in accusing both the Stoics and the
Epicureans of attempting to reduce a genuine conflict to a conflict of words (V, 112).

Kant does not hold Epicureanism even to qualify as a candidate for a possible moral theory; his criticism of the principle that happiness is virtue is clear and brief. Less well known and much more interesting is his criticism of Stoicism:

> They not only exaggerated the moral capacity of man, under the name of "sage," beyond all the limits of his nature, making it into something which is contradicted by all our knowledge of men; they also refused to accept the second component of the highest good, i.e., happiness, as a special object of human desire. Rather, they made their sage, like a god in the consciousness of the excellence of his person, wholly independent of nature. (V, 127)

This passage is of great importance for countering the supposed rigorism of Kant's ethics. The Stoics, Kant holds, were correct in naming virtue as the first principle of the highest good. Yet in making it the sole principle of the highest good, they not only presuppose a degree of human virtue that is belied by all experience. More important, they posited a moral psychology that cannot—and Kant implies, should not—apply to human beings; for it contains a denial of our own (sensuous) nature, which has its own claims and needs. The sage described by the Stoics, "wholly independent of nature," is "like a god." Now God, Kant tells us, has no need of an ethics at all, since his will is determined automatically to the good. But this is to say that God is not subject to the conflict between the pursuit of happiness and the pursuit of virtue that constitutes the human moral struggle. In denying the existence of this struggle by attempting to define it away, the Stoics run the risk of blasphemy. They do not, in any case, produce a doctrine that could or should be of relevance to the human moral situation. For if, as we saw, it is precisely this struggle that constitutes moral value itself, the sage of the Stoics is not even an appropriate human ideal.

To understand this, it is important to note that the happiness in question is not individual. Even those most virtuous among us who can forgo a personal reward for our actions must be disheartened by the fact that our best efforts to relieve others' suffering so often go astray.[22] This reflects the natural tendency of naive moral consciousness to posit what Kant calls a synthetic connection between virtue and happiness. Thus, virtue, we think, should be the cause of happiness: those who conscientiously observe the moral law for its own sake should somehow be rewarded with happiness, thus achieving the Highest Good. Were this the case, "freedom, partly inspired and partly guided by moral laws, would itself be the cause of general happiness, since rational beings, under the guidance of such principles, would themselves be the authors both of their own enduring well-being and of that of others" (A810/B838).

The problem is not only that this solution is refuted by most of human experience, whose history is full of examples of the sufferings of the just. Kant's idea is, further, that virtue is not the kind of thing that could, of itself, be the cause of happiness; for "happiness contains whatever (and no more than) nature can obtain for us; but virtue contains what nobody but a person himself can give to or take from himself" (VIII, 283). Virtue concerns the determination of practical reason and nothing else; since we as free beings can determine our own wills, we are capable of being virtuous. Happiness, however, concerns events in the natural world; these are not within our control. This was one reason why the consequences of our actions can play no role in constituting their moral worth. Hence, we cannot cause happiness by being virtuous, because being virtuous involves the determination of human will and not the order of nature. This is, Kant believes, not an accidental problem:

> The moral law commands as a law of freedom through motives wholly independent of nature and of its harmony with our faculty of desire (as incentives). Still, the acting rational being in the world is not the same as the cause of the world and of nature itself. Hence, there is not the slightest ground in the moral law for a necessary connection between the morality and proportionate happiness of a being which belongs to the world as one of its parts and as thus dependent on it. Not being nature's cause, his will cannot by its own strength bring nature, as it touches on his happiness, into complete harmony with his practical principles. (V, 125)

There is not the slightest ground within the moral law for a connection between these fully heterogeneous elements. Only a being who was nature's cause, in a position to arrange the natural world accordingly, could ensure that being virtuous had happiness as its effect. Though Kant's argument may draw its strength from the observed absence of rewarded virtue, his point is that virtue by itself cannot be the cause of something that depends upon thousands of contingencies beyond reason's control.

Kant's discussion of the need for a necessary connection between happiness and virtue is put in formal terms that may seem artificial. Rather than viewing Kant as *positing* a necessary proportionality between happiness and virtue, we might see him more immediately as responding to a complaint about their disproportionality that is at least as old as the Book of Job.[23] While the relation between virtue and happiness may seem, in moments of cynicism or hopelessness, to be inverse, soberer observation suggests that they simply coexist at random. The absence of a systematic connection between happiness and virtue is at issue in every serous moral critique; our indignation when the wicked flourish, our despair when the righteous suffer have their source here. Kant would argue that both indignation and despair presuppose a need of reason to find, or create, a necessary connection between happiness and virtue. Our deepest, most immediate moral reactions are based on the assumption that such a connection should exist. The bitterness we feel at the contemplation of (what we call) innocent suffering reflects reason's need to see happiness connected with worthiness to be happy. Kant writes:

> As soon as men begin to reflect about right and wrong, . . . this judgment is inevitable: that it cannot be indifferent whether a man has behaved fairly or falsely, justly or violently, when up to his life's end he has (at least visibly) met with no happiness for his virtues, no punishment for his vices. It is as if they perceived a voice within saying that the issue must be different. And so there must lie hidden in them a representation, however obscure, of something after which they feel them-selves bound to strive, with which such a result would not agree. (V, 458)

Kant does not argue for the claim that reason has a need to see happiness apportioned to virtue nor is it easy to imagine how he might do so; his strategy is merely to show that it is this assumption that underlies naive moral intuition as well as most of religious and philosophical tradition. His claim is not that something is (let alone must be) the case in the world we know but that reason has a need for it to become so. At issue is not a statement about the world but a demand that we make upon it. More recent social theorists may refer to childhood experiences of reward and punishment to provide psychological explanations of how those demands are developed. But knowledge of how we come to acquire them does not make them disappear. The search for a necessary connection between happiness and virtue is the search for (complete) justice. In presupposing such a connection, reason simply "rebels against the thought that the present state of reality is final and that undeserved misfortune and wrongdoing, open or hidden—and not the self-sacrificing deeds of men—are to have the last word" (Horkheimer 1977, 2).

The timeless nature of this need is sometimes obscured by Kant's examples. The *Critique of Judgment*, for example, states, "We believe we perceive the traces of a wise providence even in evil when we see that the wicked evildoer does not die before suffering the well-deserved punishment for his crimes" (V, 449). In "On the Failure of All Philosophical Attempts in Theodicy," Kant writes of the "jubilation" that accompanies the observation of such a punishment, immediately reconciling the observer to heaven, and even calls this the only kind of purposiveness that one can hope to observe in the world (VIII, 260). Such passages may lead one to ask whether, even supposing that human reason may have had such needs, it wouldn't be preferable to try to do without them. Shouldn't we try to redefine the highest good as simply the greatest amount of virtue and the greatest amount of happiness and abandon the insistence on their connection as a relic of an age that was at ease with naive conceptions of reward and punishment?

There are two answers to this question. First, it seems motivated by a reluctance to accept some of Kant's remarks about punishment that strike us as primitive not only, I suspect, because our attitude toward individual criminals may have become more humane but because the crimes that pose real theoretical problems are so massive that the concept of proportional punishment becomes absurd. Without discussing this development in detail, I think it can be said that Kant's doctrine is, in practice, compatible with the impetus to this objection. Kant would be the first to emphasize that judging persons to be wicked, as well as determining the appropriate proportionality between virtue and happiness, vice and misery, is not our business but God's. Nonetheless, he would argue, it is impossible to will that the wicked be made as happy as the truly virtuous. Nor is it possible for reason to regard the happiness of the righteous as accidental; though ignorant of the mechanisms by which happiness is distributed according to virtue, reason must view this as a matter of reward.

Kant is not seeking a substitute for theodicy. This is not merely because he holds every theodicy, as a justification of God's ways to man, to require knowledge that transcends the limits of reason. Such claims come perilously close to those statements enjoining us to recognize that God surely has his reasons for the distribution of happiness in the world, which we cannot hope to understand. Such talk, he writes, is itself a form of theodicy and one of the worst: it is an apology that requires no refutation other than the abhorrence of every human being who possesses the least feeling for morality (VIII, 258). The key to the difference between Kant's position and that of traditional theodicy is expressed in his claim that through rational faith, the doubter is directed to have patience but is never satisfied (VIII, 262). The task of theodicy is to provide a justification that helps us to accept the world; Kant's goal is to encourage our demands upon it. All earlier treatments of the question of the Highest Good had the function, Kant holds, of discouraging reason's demand for a world in which happiness and virtue are connected. Both Stoics and Epicureans thought to resolve the problem by denying its existence; happiness and virtue are not disproportional because they are, in fact, identical. Leibniz, acknowledging the heterogeneity of happiness and virtue, asserted that God has, in fact (to the best of his ability), arranged them proportionally; appearances to the contrary are merely the result of our limited knowledge. Kant insisted upon the obstinacy of the appearances; to do otherwise would be a matter of empirical denial and political quietism. Yet the fact that the world we inhabit displays no connection between happiness and virtue presents a problem that can cripple practical reason's efforts to seek one. Kant goes so far as to state: "God's governance of the world in accordance with moral principles is an assumption without which all morality would have to break down; for if morality cannot provide me with the prospect of satisfying my needs, then it cannot command anything of me either" (XXVIII, 28.2, 116).

It is not, of course, the case that there would be no moral principles if there were no God. The moral law, eternal and unchanging, must be thought as (conceptually) prior to God. But "without a God and without a world invisible to us now but hoped for, the glorious ideas of morality are indeed objects of approval and admiration but not springs of purpose and action" (A813/B841).

Without God, we would be in the position of the Stoics, who had no hope for a happiness distinct from virtue: morality would be an object of praise but not of human possibility. To understand this, it must be clear that Kant's discussion of the Highest Good concerns not the motivation of discrete moral actions but sustaining moral resolution over the course of a lifetime. In any particular situation it must always be possible to act out of respect for the moral law, without regard to the success of our intentions; otherwise, morality would be heteronomous. Yet though we may begin by believing that sheer commitment to the moral law is enough to sustain us, the gradual revelation of suffering and failure can lead to despair. If experience seems infinitely to delay the connection that reason needs between happiness and virtue, then the Highest Good will come to seem impossible. And if the Highest Good is impossible, then the moral law, which has the Highest Good as its object, is directed toward an illusory end. Hence, if we continue to obey the moral law we must regard ourselves as fools; if we cease to obey it we are scoundrels. This, says Kant, is the antinomy of pure practical reason. While its structure is complex, the danger Kant perceives is not one that arises as the result of theoretical reflection. Rather, what he describes is the transition from youthful idealism to a "mature" cynicism and resignation that has come to seem such a part of the life passage that it barely receives notice.

For Kant, however, this passage is a threat; its existence becomes a problem for moral psychology. The purpose of rational faith is to prevent it by providing hope that our efforts to make the world other than it is will not be fruitless: we must believe that our efforts to attain virtue will be completed by God's ordering of the natural world. This is the sense in which the *Critique of Judgment* refers to rational faith as trust: "Faith is a trust in the achievement of an intention, whose promotion is duty, but whose possibility of completion is not something of which we have insight" (V, 472).

V. What May I Hope?

How does rational faith fill the need that Kant has shown must be satisfie
continue to act morally over the course of a lifetime? Initially, the answer ~~
easy: only a Being who was both perfectly virtuous and omnipotent *and* capable of
controlling nature could bring about the Highest Good. We are therefore licensed to
have just enough faith in such a Being as is needed to keep us going in moments of
despair. Since this faith is regulative, we know it will not permit the theoretical
content that would open the way to theological debate about the nature of God's
attributes and powers or even discussions of the relationship between God's causality
and human freedom. Rational faith is not knowledge but a principle of action. Yet in
order to serve as such, certain questions must be answered.

The first concerns God's role in human history. Yovel's excellent analysis of
this question shows that "what God guarantees is not the realization of the
Highest Good but only its ontological possibility, and this guarantee, moreover,
is furnished not by special action on God's part, but by his very existence" (1980,
96). This ensures that the postulate of God's existence will be a spur to human action, not an excuse for abandoning it. If only God could realize the Highest
Good, the human obligation to pursue it would be superfluous. Kant allows God
no direct influence on human history, and he insists that the manner in which we
are to obtain hope from the postulate of God's existence remains forever mysterious; for it is unclear not only what exactly God will do but even "whether he
will do *anything at all*" (VI, 139). However, even were Kant less severe in disal-
lowing miracles or providence, the realization of the Highest Good could hardly
depend on God alone. For its first condition is the greatest possible virtue, and
the promotion of this is an entirely human affair. The autonomy of reason demands that not even God could make us virtuous; only by doing all that we can
to become worthy of happiness are we entitled to hope that God will complete
the Highest Good by granting it. The notion of God, for Kant, is the notion of the
possibility of connection between reason and nature; reason itself remains in
our hands.[24]

If Kant's stern warnings may deter us from speculating about how this connection
might take place, they cannot prevent us from asking where. For the claim that the
Highest Good can only be realized by an intelligible Being may suggest that it can
only be realized in an intelligible world. This need not, of course, be the case; it is
perfectly possible that God could realize the Highest Good in the world of appearances, though we cannot do so. The realization of the Highest Good does not require a
supersensible world but only a supersensible being who can combine the effects of
nature and the effects of our freedom. Yet a number of passages show Kant leaning
toward the former view. For example:

> When we see ourselves obliged to seek at such distance — namely, in the context of an
> intelligible world — the possibility of the Highest Good which reason presents to all
> rational beings as the goal of all their moral wishes, it must appear strange that
> philosophers of both ancient and modern times have been able to find happiness in
> very just proportion to virtue in *this* life (in the world of sense) or at least have been
> able to convince themselves of it. (V, 115–16)

Kant himself was well aware of the dangers inherent in the suggestion that the Highest Good is only realizable in an intelligible world, for God was invoked to provide the possibility of hope for the success of our actions in this world. The idea that the realization of the Highest Good must be deferred to another, unreachable one is to substitute the lukewarm consolations of traditional theology for the liberating demand for social change. If the object of the moral law is unrealizable in this world, then our efforts to further it are doomed to futility. So Kant's later writings clearly state that "The final end of pure practical reason is the Highest Good insofar as it is possible in the world" (XX, 294).

The *Religion* states that the Highest Good is possible in the world (VI, 6) and describes the whole content of rational faith as the proposition "Make the highest good possible in the world your own final end!" Both Velkley and Yovel give compelling arguments to support the claim that Kant holds the Highest Good to be realizable in this world. While Yovel sees a shift from a transcendental to a historical realization between the first two *Critiques* and Kant's later work, Velkley argues that the historical emphasis is already present in Kant's earliest writings.[25] Surely both are correct in stressing the political and emancipatory intentions of the notion of rational faith. Its use in sustaining our commitment to moral action would be undermined if the Highest Good were not realizable in time. Hence, Kant must, it is argued, posit the Highest Good as a real, albeit distant, historical goal.

As appropriate as these arguments may be with respect to Kant's ultimate goals, they ignore a tension within Kant's own thought that I believe to be present throughout the Critical Period. This tension is denied in Velkley's claim that for Kant, evils have a cultural origin; if reason alone introduces injustice into the world, reason alone can rectify it.[26] Thus, the course and the goals of history become human — which is to say, political — ones. The rejection of theodicy is the first condition of emancipation. From this point of view, the secularization of the Highest Good is part of the general secularization of human ideals that took place during the Enlightenment and reached its height in Feuerbach and Marx. While Velkley has done a great service in emphasizing Kant's place in this project, I believe that he ignores Kant's own doubts about it — as traceable to Rousseau, perhaps, as was his enthusiasm. Here we should recall the reactions to the Lisbon earthquake, the watershed for an era that had yet to see the phenomena of the French Terror, not to mention Stalinism, and hence had more reason to be sanguine about human ability to overcome humanly caused evil. The problem of evil that occupied the Enlightenment was a different one: even if, through persistence and virtue, human actions could come to be governed by reason, natural ones seem irrevocably resistant to it.[27] There *are* earthquakes, floods, disease, disasters. Their existence raised a question about the rationality *of the world* in a way that will seem foreign to all but the most religiously raised of us. The search for the Unconditioned is a search for a world that is thoroughly intelligible, structured according to reason's laws. Restructuring human affairs according to those laws would go a long way toward achieving it; and since it is the only avenue open to practical reason, Kant quite rightly emphasizes it. Hence, he writes, we must proceed as though everything depended on us (VI, 100–101). Yet he knows it does not; while part of the answer to "What may I hope?" is historical, the notion of the Highest Good reveals a problem that history is unable to resolve. If the need to find reason in the world itself seems outdated, Kant's acknowledgement that we cannot do so is deeply modern.[28] And it is this acknowledgment that is missed by the attempt to view the Highest Good in purely secular terms. Nothing else in Kant's work exposes so clearly the gap that he believes to separate reason from nature. Morality, the product of pure practical reason, is free of all natural conditions, happiness is wholly dependent on the natural world (V, 453). Our desire to become the authors of our own happiness is a desire to overcome that separation. But despite suggestions to the contrary, Kant's notion of the Highest Good is not a means by which to do so.[29]

Kant's denial of the possibility of the unity of reason and nature is expressed in his rejection of the "analytic" solutions to the problem of the Highest Good; his whole argument against them rests on the claim that virtue and happiness are too fundamentally heterogeneous to be unifiable. Rational faith is the means that permits us to live with the consciousness of this separation, allowing us to hope that the world will become a place more appropriate to reason's needs. Yet if the search for the Unconditioned, in science and in the social order, is an expression of reason's need to become at home in the world, reason's coming of age involves the realization that this need will never be fulfilled. But this, we will see, is the task of Critical Philosophy.

If Kant (often) held the overcoming of the gap between the claims of reason and the claims of the world to be impossible, the idea that the actual needs of reason might change is a possibility closer to hand. I believe this is suggested by passages such as the following:

> Since the promotion of the highest good and thus the presupposition of its possibility are objectively necessary (though only as a consequence of pure practical reason) and since *the manner in which we are to think of it as possible is subject to our own choice*, in which a free interest of pure practical reason is decisive for the assumption of a wise Author of the world, it follows that the principle which here determines our judgement . . . is a faith of pure practical reason. (V, 146; my italics)

Since rational faith does not concern the objects themselves but our moral needs and capacities, Kant might well allow that the content of the postulates could change while the form of the argument for their necessity remained the same. Thus, it might be the case that reason's needs have changed to the point that we do not, two hundred years after Kant, need to represent to ourselves a personal God to sustain our moral convictions but can make do with some more general assumption. The extreme indeterminacy of Kant's postulate of God's existence lends weight to this idea. Yovel argues that God, for Kant, has no theological meaning: "As a postulate of practical philosophy, the statement 'God exists' is equivalent to the statement that 'there must necessarily be something' (in the structure of the world or of man) that makes the realization of the highest good through human activity possible" (1980, 126).

Might this very minimal postulation of God's existence be replaced by the postulate that the world as a whole is progressing toward the best? There is some reason to think so. Kant connects the latter postulate with the former one and holds its assertion to be a need of practical reason (XX, 307).

"On the Old Saw" presents a moral argument for the need to believe in human progress that exactly mirrors the *absurdum practicum* argument, strongly suggesting that practical reason could substitute faith in human progress for faith in God. Doing so would, of course, require abandoning the need for a unity of reason and nature that the search for the Unconditioned had expressed, but for many, that is what modernity requires. If some of reason's needs can change, they can also be abandoned. Total intelligibility may not be a goal; it is no longer inconceivable to human reason that the world may not be comprehensible as (potentially) the best of all possible ones. One learns to make do with less. If Yovel is correct, this is all that Kant's argument entitles: "*If all that man needs in order to act is the bare assurance that his efforts are not doomed to futility, then this assurance is also all that the postulate may assert objectively*" (Yovel, 1980, 277). Some days, even this assurance will seem a great deal.

Curiously, Yovel describes the form of inference that allows us this postulate as based on "no other grounds than Kant's overriding optimism" (1980, 297). Yet optimism was hardly a feature of Kant's own character.[30] Nor does anything reveal Kant's distance from the classical Enlightenment more than his denial that experience confirms the idea that the world as a whole is progressing toward a better state. Knowledge of this claim is not only impossible for human but also for divine reason; here there is no difference between God's eye and our own (VII, 83–84). This is, of course, because the question is not yet decided; but Kant believes that "the history of all times cries loudly against" the assumption that humanity is progressing (VI, 20). The *Religion* dismisses "modern optimism" in a masterful passage:

> If we wish to draw our examples from that state in which various philosophers hoped preeminently to discover the natural goodliness of human nature, namely, from the so-called state of nature, we need but compare with this hypothesis the scenes of unprovoked cruelty in the murder dramas enacted in Tofoa, New Zealand, and in the Navigator Islands, and the unending cruelty (of which Captain Hearne tells us) in the wide wastes of northwestern America—cruelty from which not a soul reaps the slightest benefit—and we have vices of barbarity more than sufficient to draw us from such an opinion. If, however, we incline to the opinion that human nature can better be known in the civilized state (in which predispositions can more completely develop), we must listen to a long melancholy litany of indictments against human-ity: of secret falsity even in the closest friendship, so that a limit upon trust upon the mutual confidences of even the best friends is reckoned a universal maxim of prudence in intercourse; of a propensity to hate him to whom one is indebted, for which a benefactor must always be prepared; of a hearty well-wishing which yet allows of the remark that "in the misfortunes of our best friends there is something which is not altogether displeasing to us"; and of many other vices still concealed under the appearance of virtue (to say nothing of the vices of those who do not conceal them), and we shall have enough of the vices of culture and civilization (which are the most offensive of all) to make us rather turn our eyes away from the conduct of men lest we ourselves contract another vice, misanthropy. But if we are not yet content, we need but contemplate a state which is compounded in strange fashion of both the others, that is, the international situation, where civilized nations stand toward each other in the relation obtaining in the barbarous state of nature (a state of continued readiness for war)—a state, moreover, from which they have taken fixedly into their heads never to depart. (VI, 33)

Little could be further from Enlightenment assurances about the prospects of the world that we know. Kant not only denies that we can know the world to be progressing to a better state; we have every reason to doubt it. And this doubt leads us to a moral hopelessness whose structure involves more than simple complaints about the difficulty and scarcity of virtue. Experiencing virtue as involving worthiness to be happy, reason demands a connection between happiness and virtue. But we have seen the analytic connections to be hollow; and experience daily belies the possibility of a synthetic one, whether effected by a personal God or the vaguer, more distant tendencies of history. Hence, no moral law appears to have a realizable end and directing our lives according to any such law seems merely ridiculous.

Thus, optimism becomes not a chance trait of character or a result of particular experience but a moral obligation. Between hope and hopelessness there is no middle ground; the answer to "What may I hope?" cannot be *nothing*. If maintaining hope is a condition of our obedience to the moral law, we must find a way to do so. Some will find the idea that we could be morally required to adopt an attitude troublesome; from what we know of Kant's character, he was particularly suited to appreciate how difficult this could be. No doubt, this played a role in accounting for the moral worth he assigns to struggle. In itself, optimism is no more a value than is innocence; both can be as easily the result of immaturity or foolishness as of virtue.

Here the distinction between regulative and constitutive principles, between the needs of reason and the obstinacy of appearances, becomes crucial. For a view that refuses to permit regulative principles permits only complacency or despair. The optimism of the Enlightenment is nihilism's easiest prey, no sturdier than the evidence upon which it is based. The regulative principle that the world is in progress to a better state is another matter. Taken as constitutive, this assertion must be self-defeating, leading to complacent acceptance or despondent resignation toward the world as it is. Understood as regulative, it is an unshakable demand that the world come to meet the claims that reason advances, permitting the hope that sustains all our efforts to make this so. Kant is surely right to hold that if we choose to live rationally—with the hope of bringing the world to meet the needs of reason—we must choose to believe this much.

Notes

1. Hegel's statement of this objection in *Faith and Knowledge* (1977, 55–96) was one of the first. Even so sensitive a modern commentator as Yovel views the postulates to be "irrational rather than nonrational; for they are not only ungrounded in any cognitive science, natural or metaphysical, they conflict with the very theory of knowledge and with the Critique at large" (1980, 296). Most recently and explicitly, Beiser has revived Heine's objection, arguing that with the introduction of the postulates, Kant "deeply betrays the radical spirit of his philosophy" (1992, 55).

2. Maimonides, and after him, Thomas Aquinas, argued that reason was incapable of deciding between the alternatives of the first antinomy and introduced the principle that when neither thesis can be proved or refuted by reason, we are justified on largely moral grounds in deciding the question according to faith. See Maimonides, *Guide for the Perplexed*.

3. Allan Wood's (1970) *Kant's Moral Religion* is a welcome exception to the standard view of the postulates, arguing that Kant's doctrine of rational faith is a systematic and profound attempt to deal with religious questions in rational terms. Wood's arguments, however, can be greatly strengthened if placed in the context of Kant's general view of reason.

4. See Wood (1970, 182). For statements of the problems in the argument for immortality, see also Yovel (1980, 113) and Korsgaard (1989b, 238).

5. For discussion of the changes in Kant's view of freedom, see chap. 3, sec. V, and also Allison (1990), Beck (1960), and Wood (1970).

6. The translation of *Vernunftglaube* is problematic, for the term expresses a unity between reason and faith that is missing in the English 'rational faith' — an expression better translated as *vernünftiges Glauben*', which Kant does not use. Moreover, *Glauben* is used to express both 'faith' and 'belief'. To maintain continuity and avoid awkwardness I have retained the standard translation, but the reader should be aware of its inadequacy.

7. For a thorough historical discussion of the *Pantheismusstreit*, see Beiser (1987), to which I am indebted on a number of points.

8. Jacobi's conception of a leap of faith does not involve the sort of notion of decision to be found in Kierkegaard, who took over the term. Nor does it rest on any particular theological problems or paradoxes. This is made clear in his first reply to Mendelssohn, who had written that Jacobi's recourse to faith as a means of overcoming doubt was fully in the spirit of Christianity, but "My religion knows no duty to settle doubt except by rational grounds and commands no faith in eternal truths" (*Hauptschriften*, 1916, 118). Mendelssohn conceived of Judaism as a religion based only on those essential truths which could be proved by pure reason alone. The rest of the religion, he held, involved a set of practices dependent upon historical revelation but having nothing to do with the truth or falsity of eternal propositions. Jacobi insisted that his argument for the necessity of a leap of faith was unrelated to the particularities of any religion: "My dear Mendelssohn, we are all born in faith, and must remain in faith, just as we are all born in society and must remain in society" (168).

9. See, for instance, the following passage from Mendelssohn's last piece: "As long as my friend was not accused of being a blasphemer, as well as a hypocrite, the news that Lessing was said to have been a Spinozist was rather a matter of indifference to me. I knew that there is a purified Spinozism which is compatible with everything practical in religion and morality; knew that this purified Spinozism is very well compatible with Judaism, and that Spinoza, despite his speculative teaching, could have remained an orthodox Jew had he not denied Judaism in other writings and thereby forsaken the law. . . . The doctrines of Spinoza are much closer to Judaism than to the doctrines of the orthodox Christians. If I could love Lessing and be loved by him when he was a strict follower of Athanasius, why not all the more, when he came closer to Judaism, and I perceived him as a follower of the Jew Baruch Spinoza? The names 'Jew' and 'Spinozist' could be neither so shocking nor so provocative to me as they may be to Herr Jacobi" (*Hauptschriften*, 1916, 295).

10. For a detailed discussion of the correspondence and political background of Kant's entrance into the debate, see Beiser (1987, 114–115).

11. See chap. 1, sec. VII.

12. See chap. 2, sec. VI.

13. The length of this chapter is no guide to its systematic importance; after defining a canon as "the sum total of the a priori principles of the correct employment of certain faculties of knowledge" (A796/B824), Kant describes the entire "Transcendental Analytic" as the canon of the pure understanding. Section 9 of Kant's *Logic* contains a similar discussion.

14. It must be remembered that *Glauben*, here translated as 'faith', also means 'belief', the translation Kemp Smith uses.

15. See chap. 2, sec. VII.

16. For a discussion of Wizenmann's work, see Beiser (1987, 109–113).

17. Kant's claim on universal agreement is, of course, a claim about potential, rather than actual, agreement; see Arendt (1982, 71–72) and O'Neill (1989). This is the case for every regulative principle, but the *absurdum practicum* argument provides the idea with body and

constraints not filled out elsewhere; for here Kant gives us directions for a process that each of us is meant – and able – to undergo. Our agreement is therefore free, but we have a clearer idea of how to produce it than in other cases. The possibility that one might carry out the argument and reject it is one that Kant must allow but considers very distant, since the conscious decision to reject the moral law that this would entail is incompatible with self-respect. See chap. 3, secs. IV–V.

18. See, in this context, Kant's letter to Mendelssohn upon the publication of the latter's *Jerusalem* (X, 322–26).

19. Of course, the difference between Jacobi's argument that speculative reason leads to atheism and must therefore be rejected in favor of faith and Kant's argument that it is inadequate to decide between the alternatives of theism and atheism and must therefore be set aside in favor of faith is clear enough. In the foregoing, I have tried to distinguish Kant from an imaginary version of Jacobi whose force does not depend on this argument.

20. Guyer describes the Highest Good as the ultimate form of systematicity (1989a, 166); see my discussion of the connection between systematicity and the principle of sufficient reason in chapter 2.

21. V, 109. See especially Rawls (1980–87) and Yovel (1980, chap. 1); see also Velkley (1989). It may be further noted that the function of the Highest Good is in keeping with the rest of Kant's notion of reason, whose task is to provide ends. Thus, Rawls's discussion of the Highest Good as an object constructed by practical reason out of its own principles is not a special case required by the formal considerations of Kant's ethics but the general role of reason in providing ends for human action. Kant's discussion of this issue is particularly clear in a footnote to "On the Old Saw" (VIII, 279).

22. Yovel distinguishes between the problem of the Highest Good at the personal and the cosmic level and claims that Kant's emphasis shifts from the former to the latter (1980, 48–55, 98–99). In fact, I believe, the latter (which Yovel describes as "a peculiar Kantian version of the problem of moral theodicy") is always with him, underlying his constant concern with the principle of sufficient reason and the Unconditioned itself.

23. In "On the Failure of All Philosophical Attempts at Theodicy" Kant claims the Book of Job to be an allegorical version of his doctrine of rational faith (VIII, 253–71). The friends of Job, he says, are those who attempt a theoretical/dogmatic theodicy; Job himself, living righteously and trusting in God to order the world accordingly, displays genuine rational faith. Kant asserts that the verse "Till I die, I will not remove mine integrity from me" (Job 27:5) forms a proof that Job's faith is based on morality and not vice versa.

24. The parallels between this discussion and that of teleology in the third *Critique* should be apparent. There, God was invoked to guarantee the "wholly fortuitous" connection between our cognitive capacities and the vast manifold of nature. The notion of God thereby grounds the possibility of the success of our efforts in explaining the world; it is hardly meant to curtail them (see chap. 2, sec. VI).

25. See Yovel (1980, 72) and Velkley (1989, 141–43).

26. See Velkley (1989, 80, 214). Velkley holds this view to be traceable to Rousseau. Yovel, too, ascribes to Kant the view that evil will abolish itself in the historical process; I believe that even Rousseau was more ambivalent about these matters than Velkley suggests.

27. Of course, the outburst of discovery and technology that we have come to call the scientific revolution was an attempt to break this resistance; Bacon is fairly explicit about just this aim. But the age which had nearly deified Newton was also the age most crushed by the Lisbon earthquake.

28. Perhaps it is not accidental that the problem of the Highest Good, which Kant described as the task of philosophy, was present in the ancients and not made explicit again until Kant; for the disharmony it reveals is inescapably modern. Though earlier thinkers may

have evinced this disharmony (one might view Leibniz as having evaded it), Kant is the first to state and accept it. In a criticism of the reductionism common to Stoics and Epicureans, he suggests something like this: "We cannot but regret that these men . . . unfortunately applied their acuteness to digging up an identity between such extremely heterogeneous concepts as those of happiness and virtue. But it fit the dialectical spirit of the times (and still sometimes leads subtle minds astray) to overcome essential differences in principle, which can never be united, by seeking to translate them into a conflict of words and thus to devise an apparent unity of concepts with other terms. This commonly occurs where the unification of heterogeneous principles lies either so high or so deep, or would require so thorough a revolution of doctrines accepted in a philosophical system, that men fear to go deeply into the real difference and prefer to treat it as mere diversity in formulas" (V, 112).

29. Both Konhardt and Velkley suggest that the goal of the Highest Good is to overcome the gap between freedom and nature.

30. On Kant's melancholy and pessimism, see Arendt (1982, 24−25). On his violent repudiation of the early essay on optimism, see Shell (1980, 18).

5

The Task of Philosophy

The first *Critique* tells us that all the interests of reason combine in three questions: What can I know? What should I do? What may I hope? A lesser-known passage of the *Logic* adds a fourth question—What is the human being?—and tells us that the first three questions are related to the last. Hence, Kant concludes provocatively, the whole field of philosophy could be reckoned to anthropology, whose business it is to tell us what is human (IX, 25).

By describing, in turn, the activities of reason in science, ethics, and religion, I have tried to delimit Kant's answers to the first three questions. In turning finally to philosophy, are we turning to the fourth? A passage from the *Conflict* strongly affirms this: "Philosophy is not a science of representations, concepts, and ideas, or a science of all sciences, or anything of the sort; but a science of the human being, his representation, thought and action; it should show the human being in all his components, how he is and should be" (VII, 69).[1] Yet many other texts suggest that Kant held a more traditional conception of philosophy, as just the sort of science of the sciences that this passage rejects.

I will argue that Kant's work reflects a tension between two wholly diverse conceptions of philosophy and hence of his own procedure, as well as whatever is to succeed it.[2] The first, which may be called a regulative conception, can be drawn from the anthropological remarks, the discussion of reason's search for self-knowledge, and the descriptions of philosophy as an ideal. The second, constitutive conception, is reflected in the determination to "put metaphysics on the sure path of a science" and to complete a necessary edifice that will never need to be revised. Unraveling the elements of these very different and ultimately incompatible tendencies is a daunting prospect. Kant's inability to give a satisfactory account of his own project was widely thought by his contemporaries to undermine its basis.[3] Kant's later readers have tended to ignore his clearly inadequate metaphilosophical discussions, since these are not developed enough to constitute two coherent accounts of the nature of philosophy, let alone one. This chapter, accordingly, will be both briefer and more speculative than the preceding ones. After presenting the elements in Kant's texts that can be used to elaborate his conceptions of philosophy, I shall describe the problems inherent in the constitutive one. I shall conclude by suggesting ways in which a regulative conception of philosophy could be developed to resolve, in a Kantian spirit, problems that Kant left open. Such a conception will prove crucial in completing an account of Kant's notion of reason, the most intimate of philosophical concepts, for no activity seems more characteristic of reason than the practice of philosophy.

I. The Urge to Metaphysics

Kant's inability to maintain a clear distinction between metaphysics and philosophy is the first indication of the inchoate nature of his metaphilosophical views. At first glance, his distinction seems to correspond to an intuitive one. Metaphysics is narrower than philosophy, both in scope and appeal: it is a (possible) science consisting of a priori propositions and is carried out by—and of interest to—a few specialists. Philosophy, by contrast, may include metaphysics but extends considerably beyond it. The *Fortschritte* assigns priority to philosophy because, unlike metaphysics, it is concerned with practical reason, with which we are all equally endowed (XX, 301). Philosophy's goal is the attainment of wisdom, which involves not simply knowing but furthering the essential ends of humanity (A840/B868). In this sense, Kant often speaks of the philosopher as an ideal that it would be arrogant to claim to have realized: the truly wise person would also be a truly moral person, exhibiting a complete unity of knowledge and virtue:

> For what counts . . . is not merely knowing *what* it is one's duty to do (because of the ends all men have by their nature this is easily stated); it is primarily the inner principle of the will, namely, that consciousness of this duty be also the *incentive* to actions. This is what is required in order to say of someone who joins with his knowledge the principle of wisdom that he is a *practical philosopher*. (VI, 375; see also A839/B867)

Hence, the idea contained in the concept of philosophy is never wholly attainable but serves as a goad to the unceasing search for wisdom that ought to take place. The absence of a fully developed metaphysics, by contrast, is a matter of historical accident: Kant believes that no one before him was able to find the clue on which a satisfactory metaphysics depends. Once found, however, he assures us that it can be completed simply, rapidly, and definitively. Accordingly, metaphysics must consist of synthetic a priori propositions, while philosophy can include both pure and empirical principles (A840/B868). Philosophy, Kant sometimes says, requires metaphysics, a system of pure rational concepts independent of the conditions of intuition; for without knowing the first grounds of duty, we can have neither certainty nor purity in teaching or implementing morality (VI, 375−76; see also VII, 114).[4] Metaphysics thus has a foundational purpose, but it seems clearly less important and universal than philosophy, in comparison to which metaphysics is a scholarly preoccupation whose fruits, whether spurious or sound, have only distant impact on the real interest of humankind (Bxxxii; XX, 261).

This set of distinctions is an attractive one, but it is not one that Kant maintains.[5] Indeed, just after carefully drawing such distinctions, he will assert that "the title 'metaphysics' may also, however, be given to the whole of philosophy" (A841/B809) and claim that the sole preoccupation of *metaphysics* is wisdom (A850/B878). In these and a number of other passages, metaphysics no longer appears as a small and foundational division of philosophy; rather, "metaphysics is actually the true philosophy!" (IX, 32). Moreover, most of his discussion of transcendental illusion and reason's unavoidable drive to speculation proceeds on the assumption that 'metaphysics' and 'philosophy' are virtually interchangeable. Kant's inability to retain a clear distinction between metaphysics and philosophy is, I believe, the result not of carelessness but of the fact that he does not have a systematic account of either. His temptation to identify metaphysics and philosophy stems from the constitutive conception of philosophy, which, I shall argue, cannot be maintained. For the present, however, let us follow Kant's most common practice of using 'metaphysics' and 'philosophy' as interchangeable.

One distinctive and enduring feature of Kant's view of metaphysics or philosophy is his belief that it is universal and inevitable. Here Kant is fairly unique in the philosophical tradition, which held philosophy to be the province of a small and educated elite. For Kant, by contrast, "The idea of [metaphysics] is as old as speculative human reason; and what rational being does not speculate, either in scholastic or in popular fashion?" (A842/B871). While insisting on the fruitlessness of traditional efforts to construct a science of metaphysics, Kant insists on the importance and necessity of a disposition to metaphysics in a manner far beyond the dreams of the most determined of traditional metaphysicians. The first *Critique* opens with a statement of the inevitability of metaphysics, "as prescribed by the very nature of reason itself"; his subsequent descriptions are hardly less extravagant. Metaphysics is compared to a favorite child and a beloved to whom one always returns after a quarrel (IV, 353; A850/B878). Though metaphysics may seem to be the most frustrating and dispensable of human intellectual endeavors, a battlefield of endless controversies with no visible progress or result, it is in fact the only one that we can never do without. The *Prolegomena* summarizes:

> That the human mind will ever give up metaphysical researches is as little to be expected as that we, to avoid inhaling impure air, should prefer to give up breathing altogether. There will, therefore, always be metaphysics in the world; nay, everyone, especially every reflective man, will have it and, for want of a recognized standard, will shape it for himself after his own pattern. What has hitherto been called metaphysics cannot satisfy any critical mind, but to forego it entirely is impossible; therefore, a *Critique of Pure Reason* itself must now be attempted or, if one exists, investigated and brought to the full test, because there is no other means of supplying *this pressing want, which is something more than a mere thirst for knowledge*. (IV, 367; my italics)

What is the pressing want that fuels our repeated attempts at metaphysics? What is the source of that disposition to metaphysics that Kant claims will persist even should all attempts to establish a science of metaphysics continue to fail? Kant maintains that it is a practical one. Metaphysics, he repeats, is concerned with three problems: the freedom of the will, the immortality of the soul, and the existence of God. Every other question with which it is occupied—such as the nature of substance, causality, or necessity—is undertaken only in order to contribute to a resolution of these (A3/B7, B395, and A797/B825–A804/B832; IV, 362; V, 4–13; XX, 291). Kant's claim is both a historical and an intuitive one: it was in fact the desire to resolve moral and theological questions that led to the development of metaphysics; and only questions of such essential weight could explain the continued preoccupation with apparently fruitless speculation. The "Canon" makes a further claim: the urge to metaphysics cannot result from reason's need to answer these questions speculatively, since a theoretical answer to these questions, even were one possible, would not be of much use (A798/B826).[6] Hence, he concludes, reason's interest in these matters must be entirely practical:

> The whole equipment of reason, in the discipline which may be entitled pure philosophy, is in fact determined with a view to the three above-mentioned problems. These, however, themselves, in turn, refer us yet further, namely, to the problem of what we ought to do if the will is free, if there is a God and a future world. As this concerns our attitude to the Supreme end it is evident that the ultimate intention of nature in her wise provision for us has, indeed, in the constitution of our reason, been directed to moral interests alone. (A801/B829)

Now this view could explain what Kant takes to be the universality of the urge to metaphysics prior to the *Critique of Pure Reason*. That urge is a misdirected attempt to find orientation in the ordinary matters that concern us most deeply — in particular, determining how to act morally if we are free to do so. Philosophy here appears as sublimation: unaware that its real needs are for guidelines in action, human reason exhausts itself in constructing (spurious) theoretical resolutions of its real problems. But this hardly accounts for what Kant maintains will be the persistence of the metaphysical disposition after the publication of his own work. For once we have recognized that the attempt to construct a speculative metaphysics is a diversion of our true needs, it seems natural to suppose that we should be able to relinquish the former and begin to fulfill the latter. The *Critique* should have taught us not only that knowledge of the objects of metaphysics is impossible but that our very desire for knowledge is misplaced. Having understood this process, it would seem that we ought to be able to give it up. Rather than continuing to indulge in metaphysical speculation (which, even if, per impossible, successful, would not give us what we need), we should turn our attention to giving reason genuine satisfaction by doing our best to realize the Highest Good. Passages such as the following strongly suggest this to be the outcome Kant expects his work to have: "Our criticism will easily discover the illusion to which . . . dogmatic procedure is due, compelling pure reason to relinquish its exaggerated pretensions in the realm of speculation, and to withdraw within the limits of its proper territory — that of practical principles" (A794/B822).

Yet he maintains that the disposition to metaphysics is inextirpable. One reason Kant suggests for this is the persistence of transcendental illusion: like the astronomer to whom the moon appears larger at its rising even though he knows it to be otherwise, we will continue to seek metaphysical solutions to our problems even after discovering them to be illusory:

> for here we have to do with a natural and inevitable illusion, which rests on subjective principles, and foists them upon us as objective . . . not one in which a bungler might entangle himself through lack of knowledge, but one inseparable from human reason, and which, even after its deceptiveness has been exposed, will not cease to play tricks with reason and continually entrap it into momentary aberrations ever and again calling for correction. (A298/B354)

Reason, in this passage, is inexplicably compelled to seek objective principles where its real need is for subjective ones — to reify the Unconditioned when it ought to be engaged in the practical task of trying to attain it. Now I have noted that the attitude that Kant asks us to maintain is a difficult one: in science, as in morality, the continued struggle to approach an idea while acknowledging it to be unattainable involves a balancing act of major proportions. In these descriptions of transcendental illusion, Kant seems to suggest that this effort is bound, at times, to fail. By positing knowledge, reason seeks a stance that seems more convenient or secure. Metaphysics thus appears to be the result of a perpetual weakness, even neurosis; Kant's assertion that this weakness is a natural part of the human condition scarcely makes it more attractive.[7] On this view, the task of critique, or philosophy, is very much akin to the therapeutic one ascribed to Wittgenstein: to continue to expose the distortions and errors to which reason is inevitably prone and perhaps to remind us of the way to a more satisfactory form of life.

But a different account of the source of the disposition to metaphysics is tentatively suggested in the *Prolegomena*:

> I think I perceive that the aim of this natural tendency is to free our concepts from the fetters of experience and from the limits of the mere contemplation of nature so far as, at least, to open to us a field containing mere objects . . .which no sensibility can reach . . .in order that practical principles [may be assumed as, at least, possible]; for practical principles, unless they find scope for their necessary expectation and hope, could not expand to the universality which reason unavoidably requires from a moral point of view. (IV, 362−63)

Here Kant outlines an idea that is most fully expressed in the late *Fortschritte*. Reason's urge to metaphysics is not the result of weakness or error but of the justified desire to leave the confines of experience for its appropriate place in the realm of ideas. For moral ideas *are* supersensible objects that cannot be fully realized in experience, but they alone are the legitimate objects of reason's concern. Here the failure that Kant attributes to metaphysics is smaller in scale: reason errs in assuming its goal to be knowledge of these objects. Yet in seeking metaphysics, it is correct in seeking for itself a field that is not confined to the merely empirical. The (future) task of metaphysics, then, properly understood, is to remind us of the real character of the ideas of reason, to uphold and maintain them in the face of skeptical claims of their emptiness or fictional nature. The *Fortschritte* describes the goal of metaphysics as the transition from the sensible to the supersensible realms; the purpose of the *Critique of Pure Reason* is to ensure that this transition is not a dangerous leap but an orderly expansion (XX, 273). For, he continues, it is freedom of the will that is the supersensible whose attainment is the real purpose of metaphysics (XX, 292). That freedom is the condition of our realizing the Highest Good, the goal of practical reason and philosophy; but this cannot be achieved without theory for the reasons discussed in the previous chapters. Reason's presentiment of the importance of these objects accounts for the persistence of metaphysics: we are correct in continuing to seek a path from the sensible to the supersensible, mistaken only in believing that path to be one of knowledge (XX, 294−95).

These ideas can only be adequately developed within a regulative account of the nature of philosophy. Kant's failure to provide such an account leaves them merely suggestive. Before attempting to expand them within such a framework, I will turn to describe his constitutive conception of philosophy.

II. The Sure Path of a Science

The best-known expressions of Kant's constitutive conception of philosophy are contained in the preface to the second edition of the first *Critique*. Here we find Kant's comparison of his enterprise to that of Copernicus and his survey of the origins of other scientific revolutions. Like them, he assures us, metaphysics, after centuries of "merely random groping," is finally on the sure path of a science. Kant names the features that ensure the scientific character of the new metaphysics. It will be absolutely certain, that is, a priori; indeed, it will consist entirely of synthetic a priori propositions (B18). It will not be a very extensive science but can and must be completed once and for all (Bxxiv, 23; XX, 321). It will have popular ramifications, but it remains the province of a small number of specialists (Bxxxii; VI, 379–81). It is modeled on (a particular conception of) the natural sciences, as can be seen not only in the examples of the B preface, but from the general structure of the *Prolegomena*, whose stated goal is to provide the possibility of a science of metaphysics by showing the possibility of pure mathematics and natural science—other fields based on synthetic a priori propositions (IV, 275). In contrast to the "Sisyphean labors" of past metaphysicians who toiled in realms as vast as they were ultimately empty, Kant's metaphysics is a modest but solid body of certain knowledge.

But in what does this body of knowledge consist? While the demands on the requirements of knowledge remain consistent within the constitutive conception of philosophy, Kant maintains two very different views about the content of the knowledge that is to be thereby provided. In the first, metaphysics is replaced by critique. Having learned the impossibility of knowledge of the traditional objects of metaphysics, reason (in the broadest sense) turns its attention to discovering its own laws, concepts, and principles. Kant's most striking expressions of reason's humility, as well as of his own self-confidence, support such a view. His assurance that there is not a single metaphysical problem that the *Critique* has not solved, since it has to deal with nothing but reason itself, expresses the idea of critique as the replacement of metaphysics (A xiii). So does the claim that the proud name of ontology must give place to the modest title of a mere analytic of pure understanding and the conclusion that the elements of reason suffice only for a dwelling house, not the contemplated tower reaching to the heavens (A247/B303, A707/B735). The claims that critique is a process of self-knowledge may be easiest to read in this vein. Kant's metaphysics consists in compiling an inventory of reason's own possessions and tracing reason's limits. Here arises the traditional claim that Kant replaces metaphysics with epistemology: transcendental philosophy is no longer concerned with objects but with their cognition.[8] This view gains support from Kant's repeated insistence that metaphysics is a small, self-contained and completable science in focus and scope. Rather than providing us with an understanding of God or the essence of things in general, it merely charts our own capacities for knowledge. Post-Kantian metaphysics will leave even less room for activity: since the elements of reason's structure have already been described, all that is left for future philosophers to do is to use the principles of critique to expose the illusions of future unrepentant metaphysicians as they arise. So Kant concludes, "The greatest and perhaps the sole use of all philosophy of pure reason is therefore only negative, since it serves not as an organon for the extension but as a discipline for the limitation of pure reason, and instead of discovering truth, has only the modest merit of guarding against error" (A795/B823).

And yet for nearly every passage that indicates that Kant held the critical philosophy to be a replacement of metaphysics, there is one containing an opposing conception of critique as propaedeutic to a new metaphysics. On this view, the spare achievements of the *Critique* are far from being the end of metaphysics. Rather, they are a methodological and foundational preparation for a metaphysics that is yet to be constructed. The task of the *Critique* is to decide the possibility of metaphysics; it is a treatise on method, not the system of the science itself (Axii, Bxxii). The *Prolegomena* tells us that metaphysics consists of a priori concepts like cause, whose validity must be shown before they can be employed with the certainty expected of a science; the legitimization of such concepts is therefore the most difficult and important task that could be undertaken in the service of metaphysics (IV, 260). Yet all the labors of the "Analytic" are merely preparatory, providing "the materials from which the intention is to carpenter our science" (IV, 368). The shape of that future science is hard to discern. Kant says it will contain a metaphysics of nature as well as of morals, which will, in turn, confirm the truth of the *Critique* itself (B xliii). In one passage Kant even says that the future system of metaphysics prescribed by the *Critique* will follow the system of Christian Wolff, who was peculiarly suited to raise metaphysics to the dignity of a science had it but occurred to him to prepare the ground first by examining pure reason itself (B xxxvi). Rather than shattering traditional metaphysics to pieces, Kant's goal seems here to be merely to reconstruct it on firmer ground.

The problems with the view of critique as propaedeutic to metaphysics are not simply that it poses an irreconcilable conflict to the more radical picture of critique as a replacement for metaphysics, for which there is equal support in Kant's texts. Nor are they exhausted by the fact that the works that Kant eventually presented as examples of postcritical metaphysics have seemed disappointingly secondary in significance when compared with the critical works themselves. While new scholarship continues to uncover considerable interest in both the *Metaphysical Foundations of Natural Science* and the *Metaphysics of Morals*, it remains difficult to regard them as the goal to which the entire critical effort was to lead. Even more troubling, I think, is that it is hard to regard them as metaphysics at all;[9] for Kant never wavered in describing metaphysics as concerned with the supersensible ideas of reason. Establishing a priori first principles of natural science or morality may be a project that is of interest or importance; but it does not seem to be, by Kantian lights, a metaphysical one. Hence, it remains incomprehensible how they could either subvert or satisfy the disposition to metaphysics that Kant declared to be universal. That Kant himself did not hold them to do so is suggested by the passages in later works describing metaphysics as an idea that is yet to be built (XX, 310).[10]

Attempting to reconcile these two very different accounts of the content of metaphysics seems as futile as the attempt to decide definitively for one of them. The ample support that Kant's texts provide for both views reflects his attempt to validate impulses contained in each of them and, I suggest, his ultimate dissatisfaction with either; for the deeper problem with both versions of the constitutive view was recognized, in some form, by the metacritics: no conception of metaphysics as a priori science seems to satisfy the foundational requirements that Kant imposes. This fact becomes explicit in "The Discipline of Pure Reason," a chapter of the first *Critique* that has been relatively neglected because it seems merely to repeat criticisms of traditional philosophy that Kant made elsewhere. Yet if we follow Kant's description of the "Discipline" as concerning not the content, but the method, of knowledge through pure reason, the chapter acquires more interest. Kant surveys what he designates as the only ways of proceeding scientifically in philosophy (A856/B884). His discussion of the differences between mathematics and philosophy is intended to demonstrate the uselessness of philosophers' attempts to imitate mathematical procedure. While Kant says these arguments undermine all dogmatic methods in philosophy, of whom he gives Wolff as an example, it is striking to note that every great systematic philosopher has sought to create a method modeled on features of mathematics or logic. Kant goes on to dismiss the skeptical mode of proceeding in philosophy not because its conclusions are false but because its method is as censorious, and hence dogmatic, as that of traditional metaphysics. In discussion of transcendental deductions in the final section of the "Discipline," Kant reminds us that their use is severely limited, so that his conclusion that reason should withdraw from the realm of speculation is unsurprising. The final page of the first *Critique* returns to this discussion of method and tells us that the critical path alone is still open, but the attentive reader should be bewildered about the nature of that path. For in arguing that neither of the other modes of "scientific" philosophy can succeed—because they rely on models of knowledge that are inappropriate in philosophy—Kant seems to be moving toward a position in which philosophy is no longer a matter of knowledge in the sense he seemed to require. With the strictures on method set out in the "Discipline," it becomes impossible to understand how Kant could have hoped to maintain a conception of metaphysics as a science of synthetic a priori propositions. Even if we accept the first version and view critique as the replacement of metaphysics, the most we can say is that metaphysics discovers a small set of synthetic a priori propositions: the law of causality, perhaps the categorical imperative, and so forth. The status of the investigations that result in those propositions remains fully opaque.

If neither version of the constitutive view is successful in meeting the foundational criteria Kant sets for a scientific metaphysics, they are equally unsuccessful in satisfying the urge to metaphysics, which Kant holds to be universal. This failure must be, for Kant, of major significance; for his distinctions between metaphysics as a disposition and metaphysics as a science rest on the assumption of a connection between them. If reason has a need that expresses itself in metaphysics, the (Kantian) science of metaphysics must do something to satisfy it, if not in the form that reason expected. Neither of the versions just sketched seems able to satisfy reason's need for metaphysics at all—the one because it seems to concern wholly different subjects, the other because its task seems to consist in little more than the repeated denial of the possibility of satisfaction. And if the constitutive conceptions are unable to satisfy reason's need for metaphysics, they are perforce unable to account for it except as the project of inexplicably repetitive delusion. Yet if anything seems to be a requirement on a successfully Kantian conception of philosophy, it is an account of that feature of philosophy which Kant so uniquely emphasized: the universality and persistence of human reason's urge to engage in it, in spite of not only the difficulty but the fruitlessness of all its traditional forms.

In these times it seems often tempting to ignore metaphilosophical questions altogether. The history of philosophy has rendered a verdict: it is not Kant's work that has been ignored for lack of a coherent metaphilosophical foundation but those of the metacritics who demanded one. In view of the kinds of difficulties I have outlined, most of Kant's readers are now inclined to view the absence of an acceptable account of the nature of philosophy as a gap in his work that must simply be accepted. Yet I believe there is good reason not to do so. This conviction results not only from belief in Kant's idea that reason is a unity: if the account I have given of the nature of reason's activity is appropriate for the fields already discussed, something like that account must work for philosophy itself. Even more importantly, many ideas in Kant's discussions of philosophy point toward a rejection of the constitutive conception of philosophy he elsewhere maintains and can be used to lead us toward a more appropriate, regulative account. To these we now turn.

III. Newton of the Mind

> Kant, though he had insisted on this distinction [between thought and knowledge] was still so strongly bound by the enormous weight of the tradition of metaphysics that he held fast to its traditional subject matter, that is, to those topics which could be *proved* to be unknowable . . . He remained less than fully aware of the extent to which he had liberated reason, the ability to think, by justifying it in terms of the ultimate questions. He stated defensively that he had "found it necessary to deny *knowledge* . . . in order to make room for *faith*" but he had not made room for faith; he had made room for thought, and he had not "denied knowledge" but separated knowledge from thinking. (Arendt, 1977, 14)

Arendt's remarks hold true for Kant's account of reason in general; as noted, Kant is often unable to maintain what Arendt calls the liberating quality of the regulative/ constitutive distinction that he himself discovered. This failure is especially apparent in his account of philosophy. For in the remarks that make up what I have called his constitutive conception of philosophy, Kant relies on far more conventional assumptions about what constitutes scientific quality than he does in his account of natural science. All of the antipositivist insights that contemporary philosophers of science justly attribute to Kant seem forgotten when Kant turns his attention to metaphysics.[11] In place of the idea of a continually progressing and revisable body of knowledge, we have a "small but elegant science" that can and must be completed once and for all times (XX, 320). Instead of a grounding through regulative ideas that shape scientific inquiry in myriad and mutually supporting ways, we are faced with a demand for absolute necessity through a set of synthetic a priori truths. Kant's idea of what it would take to make metaphysics scientific thus seems surprisingly regressive when compared to his account of the foundations of natural science. Yet our solution cannot be simply to urge a conception of metaphysics that is grounded in Kantian insights about the objectivity of natural science; the natural sciences have a clear-cut, if complex, relationship to the empirical. If, in chapter 2, I showed that relationship to be more intricate than traditional empiricism can account for, I did not question the fact that for Kant, as for contemporary philosophers, the empirical world forms the subject, content, and touchstone of legitimacy of the natural sciences. By contrast, the relationship of metaphysics to experience remains, to put it mildly, highly problematic. It was the questionable nature of such a relation that led Kant to follow traditional philosophy in declaring metaphysics to be a science of the a priori; but this demand, as we saw, could not withstand his own critical achievement.

An alternative for a Kantian metaphilosophy would best begin, I think, by discarding the word 'metaphysics', in the belief that Kant's arguments against traditional metaphysics also hold for any future attempts to construct a final, systematic body of a priori truths concerning the ideas that continue to occupy human reason. With it, we would discard the notion that philosophy, if it is to be sound, must imitate or become science. That doing so is not as contrary to Kant's own programmatic statements as it may appear is suggested not only by his (perhaps unwitting) attack on the possibility of every form of scientific method in philosophy in the "Discipline" but by another fact that has received far too little notice: Kant's "Newton of the mind" was Jean-Jacques Rousseau. As Newton had uncovered order and regularity behind the apparent disorder of the natural world, so Rousseau "was the first to discover beneath the varying forms human nature assumes the deeply concealed essence of man . . . After Newton and Rousseau, the ways of God are justified" (XX, 58.12–59.3). A discussion of the nature of Rousseau's method(s), of great interest in its own right, is hardly required in order to state that whatever they may be, they are far from what natural scientists consider scientific. Rousseau's works surely "show the human being in all his components, how he is and should be" – as one of Kant's texts describes the task of philosophy (VII, 69); but they just as surely eschew those procedures which were considered to be scientific ones even at the time they were written.[12] The comparison of Rousseau and Newton should thus give Kant's most enthusiastic invocations of scientific method in philosophy a rather different caste from what they have hitherto assumed.

Abandoning the term 'metaphysics' – and with it the attempt to transform philosophy into a (super)natural science – does not mean abandoning all attempts at justification. A regulative conception of philosophy cannot regard itself as a matter of propounding incommensurable and intuitive worldviews but must preserve something of the universalistic, Enlightenment impulse that is distinctively Kantian. Yet this is easily done when the focus of concern is shifted from the results of philosophy – the discovery of alleged truths – to the process of philosophizing itself. Support for so doing can be found in the passages that describe philosophy as an ideal that no one can properly claim to have achieved: "we cannot think of the *philosopher* as a man who *works at building* the sciences – that is, a scholar; we must regard him as one who *searches for wisdom*" (VII, 280).

If philosophy, as a doctrine of wisdom, is an idea, rather than an existing edifice, it follows, for Kant, that what can be transmitted and justified is a process of method – an activity of seeking, rather than a particular body of knowledge:

> We cannot learn philosophy; for where is it, who is in possession of it, and how shall we recognize it? We can only learn to philosophize, that is, to exercise the talent of

reason, in accordance with its universal principles, on certain actually existing attempts at philosophy, always, however, reserving the right of reason to investigate, to confirm, or to reject these principles in their very sources. (A838/B866)

Further support for the idea that it is the nature of the process of philosophizing, rather than its results, that should be the focus of justification can be found in the many legal metaphors that Kant uses to describe philosophy. The Critical Philosophy is seen as a tribunal, its participants a jury of fallible men (Axi, A751/B779, A476/B504).[13] And just as an impartial legal system concerns itself with achieving the conditions of a just process without seeking to determine any outcome antecedent to that process itself, so philosophy should be concerned with the legitimacy of its methods. What emerges from a legitimate method, and only what does so, will be legitimate philosophy, for it is the very process of the exercise of human reason that is at issue.

As might be expected, the criteria for the legitimacy of that process will be the same sort that validate regulative principles in other areas: "Reason has no dictatorial authority; its verdict is always simply the agreement of free citizens, of whom each must be permitted to express, without let or hindrance, his objections or even his veto" (A738/B766). The right of philosophy to submit everything else to its criticism—a right that Kant proclaims from the opening pages of the first edition of the first *Critique* to the final polemics of the *Conflict*—rests squarely on its democratic character. Philosophy may not rely on experts but must remain a free and open examination that everyone can (potentially) conduct (VII, 129; Axi). The fact that philosophy can and must sustain self-criticism is a guarantee of its right to engage in criticism of everything else. This is not merely because it ensures that the results of philosophy are open to continual correction; rather, it shows that philosophy expresses that freedom which consists in subjecting oneself to law, which is, for Kant, the supreme value.

Kant lists three maxims that are to be followed in the search for wisdom: to think for oneself, to think oneself in the place of others, and to think consistently with oneself (V, 294–95; VII, 200).[14] These maxims bear the familiar and often frustrating marks of all regulative principles: constraining inquiry without determining it, they cannot become more specific without sacrificing autonomy. As in other fields, Kant will require us to judge philosophical positions by applying principles of coherence, relevance, unity, and intelligibility that require judgment, that is to say, decision—not by mapping them onto the world. Here, I believe, it is not only because Kant holds that no important systematic claims are ever determined in the way that low-level claims of empirical knowledge are determined. If, as Yovel suggests, Kant's definition of autonomy is equally his description of critical philosophizing, the connection between the autonomy and the regulative character of philosophy must be particularly strong.[15] This view of philosophy makes the metacritics' demands unanswerable: the demand that the principles of Critical Philosophy receive a foundation from something outside themselves is not simply a demand that they surrender their autonomy but that they disappear entirely; for, as O'Neill writes: "Critique itself is at bottom no more than the practice of autonomy in thinking. Autonomy does not presuppose but rather constitutes the principles of reason and their authority (1989, 57). The principles of philosophy are regulative not only in form but—to put it paradoxically—in content, as well. Not only does philosophy require autonomy, like other legitimate forms of inquiry; philosophy *is* the requirement of autonomy, the maintenance of the idea of freedom itself. This means that part of the task of philosophy is to justify itself as a standard, to uphold the very idea of reasonableness as something toward which we should strive. Reason's justification of itself will be regulative; if philosophy is an idea of reason, nothing else makes sense.

IV. Self-Knowledge

Thus, we are led to Kant's description of critical philosophy as self-knowledge, the most difficult of reason's tasks. Part of the demand for self-knowledge is a demand for justification. Kant is not asking us to accept a standard of reasonableness on faith; given the dismal record of past philosophy, he believes it would be foolish for us to do so. A justification of reason that proceeds via self-knowledge is reflexive and self-supporting; but as we have seen, demands for a foundationalist sort of justification cannot be made appropriate to reason's nature.[16]

But the description of philosophy as self-knowledge may seem to founder from the start on a different problem entirely. The possibility of a priori knowledge of the self is crucially denied in the first *Critique*; on that denial rests much of the weight of the doctrines of transcendental idealism. It thus seems impossible to claim any sort of privileged a priori knowledge of the self while remaining within a Kantian framework. On the other hand, Kant maintains that reason's inquiry into itself is not a psychological one and insists that his project is fundamentally different from the "physiology" of reason produced by Locke. If the self-knowledge provided by philosophy can neither be a priori nor empirical, what sense can be made of it at all?

Rather than supposing Kant to have simply missed the glaring contradiction between his call to reason to undertake self-knowledge and his denial of either the possibility or the philosophical interest of traditional conceptions thereof, we might take this problem to be a clue to the fact that Kant is proposing a different sort of task entirely. I do not claim that Kant's view of reason's self-knowledge is a developed one; but this fact may be seen as a point of departure rather than of despair.[17] In beginning to work out a conception of philosophy as self-knowledge, we would do well to attend to Arendt's distinction between thinking and knowing, meaning and cognition, as well as Henrich's distinction between reflection and introspection.[18] Whatever the status of the self-knowledge provided by reason turns out to be, it will clearly be quite different from that provided by the other sciences that study the self—so much so that we would probably do well to call it "thought" or "reflection," rather than "knowledge."[19]

In seeking to distinguish philosophy from those sciences (in particular from psychology), we must, I think, reexamine the question of necessity on which previous attempts at distinction have foundered. Here I can do no more than sketch some issues such a reexamination must raise.[20] It was Kant himself, of course, who suggested that the difference between his investigations and psychological ones rested on a difference in necessity: psychological results are empirical, that is, accidental or contingent (Aix − x). But if in rejecting the demand that philosophy become metaphysics we have rejected the demand that its statements be a priori, this cannot be the way to maintain a distinction between philosophy and psychology. We might rather turn to the idea, which Kant himself leaves undeveloped, that one of the functions of the tripartite division of the faculties is to replace a notion of necessity that cannot survive a denial of insight into things in themselves. Thus, the truths of sensibility most resemble accidental ones, holding only for those creatures which possess our forms of sensibility. Truths of understanding are more fundamental; on these, Kant suggests, rest the differences between created beings and God. Only reason provides absolute necessity. But in what does this necessity consist? Not in the availability of insight into things in themselves, which Kant consistently denies; principles of reason, since regulative, do not concern insight at all. Nor should we seek to understand the kind of necessity provided by reason in any of the avenues provided by notions of possible worlds and the like; to do so raises the problems of subjecting reason to compulsion, which would undermine its autonomy. The pivotal role played by the notion of autonomy in Kant's work requires that necessity be detached from certainty. Rather, the necessity demanded and provided by reason is indelibly normative, the "necessity" expressed by the demand that something ought to happen, even if it never has. When we use the word 'reason', we express an ideal. The necessity embodied in the ideas of reason is not that contained in truths, a priori or otherwise, but that contained in a demand on what ought to be true.

[Exploring these thoughts could help us to explicate the distinction between the self-knowledge provided by philosophy and that provided by psychology and to understand why the former could be a (reflexive) justification for the notion of reasonableness itself.]In a suggestive article, W. H. Walsh proposes that philosophy and psychology be distinguished in terms not of degrees of necessity but of areas of investigation: philosophy studies the self insofar as it is rational, while psychology concerns the nonrational factors in the self, "which are responsible for the constant discrepancy between thinking as it is and thinking as it should be" (1982, 169). With this statement, Walsh signals that the designation of something as "rational" is not simply a descriptive claim: to define philosophy as self-knowledge of the rational is to say that philosophy studies not merely what human beings are but what they could and should become. And this is precisely how philosophy is described in some of Kant's later writings.[21] Thus, philosophy can become self-knowledge without collapsing into psychology not by means of a claim to greater certainty, which cannot be maintained without returning to the metaphysics that Kant himself destroyed. Nor does it need to imitate science in order to avoid the view of philosophy as mere cultural commentary, which would reject the call to Enlightenment so basic to Kant. Rather, philosophy's self-knowledge is distinct from that provided by psychology because it is moved by, and directed toward, a moral ideal, which can and must be justified through the process of philosophy itself. That the philosopher can and should be interested in all the elements of the human may be demonstrated by Kant's attention to matters ranging from mental illness to the proper number of guests at the dinner table.[22] But these subjects are of interest to the philosopher as philosopher, insofar as they shed light on the human defined not as rational animal but as one who shall become so (VII, 321 − 22; see also VII, 246).

The normative element in the call for self-knowledge is made explicit in the *Doctrine of Virtue*, where Kant describes the injunction Know Thyself as the first command of all duties to oneself (VI, 441). The Socratic idea of self-knowledge provides Kant with a paradigm but probably not as clearly as does Rousseau, who begins his *Second Discourse* with the remark that the inscription on the Temple at Delphi is the most important and most difficult precept of any moralist (129). The opening pages of that work concern the difficulty of self-knowledge, for the problems of "disentangling what is original from what is artificial in man's present nature" seem almost insurmountable. Rousseau's consequent resolve to "begin by setting aside all the facts, for they do not affect the question" (139) will seem outrageous; and, like much of Rousseau's prose, it is intended to shock. Yet the *Second Discourse* provides us with potent arguments against the abuse of the factual in the study of the human, of which two are the most important. First, Rousseau believes that many "facts" in this area are constructed; philosophers, as well as more empirical students of human beings, give us accounts of human nature in order to justify particular institutions as natural. Locke's account of private property and Hobbes's description of the state of nature without an absolute monarch are but the best-known examples of claims to factuality that are propelled by particular interests. Even more importantly, Rousseau anticipates Kant in warning against the danger of deriving 'ought' from 'is', heaping scorn on those who would conclude from the existence of slavery that government is not established for the benefit of the governed. We cannot, he says, offer fact as a proof of right: even indisputable facts only reveal to us what human beings have made themselves, not what they could and should be.[23]

If Rousseau's form of self-knowledge will not provide facts, what can we expect from it? The *Second Discourse* describes its inquiries not as "historical truths, but only for hypothetical and conditional reasonings; better suited to elucidate the nature of things than to show their genuine origin" (139). Rousseau's intention is to give us a sense of possibility. Unlike many students of the human, he does not disguise the moral impetus that propels his work: the goal of the *Second Discourse* is to show that the inequalities of present civilization are not necessary ones. To do this, he does not need to give us historical proof of a previous condition but only a plausible account of how inequality could have arisen. His goal is to jolt us out of assumptions regarding aspects of human "nature" that seem inevitable, part of the order of things. Knowledge is irrelevant in achieving this; for, as the *Emile* states poignantly, "We do not know what our nature permits us to be" (1979, 62). What is needed is instead an exploration of human possibilities insightful enough to correspond to what we already know about human nature yet open enough not to restrict or determine it. And this, of course, is one way to describe *Emile*, the book that moved Kant as no other. In describing how a child could be educated for freedom, Rousseau presents us with a stunning maze of observation, reflection, and conjecture about the mechanisms of our own enslavement and the means by which it might be undone. The insight into what we are that we may have won after reading it will be inextricably bound with an insight into what we could be. The goal of self-knowledge is an understanding of possibility; but this is not something to be gained only by studying facts. Throughout the *Emile*, Rousseau responds to the objection that human beings are not like the one he describes with the answer, "Not the ones you made." Kant will echo this idea in his discussion of Plato's *Republic* in the first *Critique*. That their claims are only testable in the attempt to put a new ideal into practice is clear to both Kant and Rousseau: this is the goal of their inquiries into the human.

These remarks can only be suggestive; further study of Rousseau's conception of self-knowledge and its importance for a Kantian conception of philosophy is needed. It is not difficult to see how Kant's conception of moral education is meant to explore and expand our notion of human possibility (see chap. 3, sec. V). I should like to close this section by sketching lines of inquiry by which we might see Kant's epistemological work as part of the project of self-knowledge that is given to us as a moral demand, though it may seem worlds away from that discussed by Rousseau. At the close of the "Analytic," Kant accuses those who complain that his view leaves us without insight into the nature of things of

> demand[ing] that we should be able to know things, and therefore to intuit them, without senses, and therefore that we should have a faculty of knowledge altogether different from the human, and this not only in degree but as regards intuition likewise in kind—in other words, that we should be not men but beings of whom we are unable to say whether they are even possible, much less how they are constituted. (A277/B333)

Here we see transcendental idealism's significance not in any of the proofs of any of the particular conditions of experience it may offer nor in its (now seemingly obvious) claim that any object that the mind represents must conform to the conditions under which it can be represented as an object. Kant's achievement is the simple posing of the question of whether there are conditions of human knowledge. Once the question is posed, it is hard to avoid something like the answer he has given. Yet in not raising the question, he claims, previous philosophers relied on a model of divine cognition to understand human cognition. Leibniz is explicit in supposing human knowledge to be a vastly weaker form of divine knowledge, as well as in proposing means by which we might approach the ideal of a knowledge unencumbered by human limitations and hence providing insight into things in themselves. But strikingly, Kant shows that even Hume's skepticism, in failing to recognize that there are conditions on our knowledge of those fleeting impressions that make up experience, assumes as a model another kind of knowledge to which we have no access. No less than the most devout metaphysician, the Scottish atheist relies on a model of knowledge that would be appropriate only for the divine. This is Kant's goal in introducing what he calls the problematic concept of an intellectual intuition, bound up with the idea of a noumenon itself—not in order to make positive statements about them but to show, by contrast, something about who we are (A254/B309–A257/B313). This example suggests that the demand for self-knowledge may be more important than any of its particular results. Crucial is that the question of self-knowledge be raised and the exploration begun; it is in doing so that Kant's deepest break with his metaphysical predecessors is completed.[24]

V. Coming of Age

The metaphor of coming of age occurs most prominently in "What Is Enlightenment?" but it is one that is present throughout Kant's critical work. Whether or not

Kant's regard for *Emile* influenced his choice of this metaphor may remain an open question, but it is certain that he used the figure of a child's growth to maturity to describe both a historical process of humankind and one that every individual reason must undergo. If the critical philosophy represents humankind's intellectual maturity, it is also the means by which all individuals attain their own. Here the identification of philosophy with self-knowledge becomes particularly striking, for Kant makes clear that enlightenment, not metaphysics, is required.[25] The metaphor similarly underscores the impossibility of providing rules that would determine critical thinking constitutively; if self-determination is essential to maturity, it is equally fundamental for reason's own development.

Unlike the legal and architectural metaphors that recur in Kant's writing, this one has received scant attention. Let us take a moment to examine his use of the idea of growing up to describe the history of philosophy. The childhood of pure reason is dogmatic, reflecting reason's unlimited trust in its own powers (A761/B789; XX, 264).[26] Dogmatic metaphysics, stemming, in large part, from theology, is characterized by children's unreflective self-confidence both in themselves and in the goodness of the world around them. The source of that self-confidence, Kant says, was reason's initial success (XX, 262). As young children experience their expanding capacities and, thereby, the increasing intelligibility of the world around them, they are liable to assume the limitlessness of both. The second step in the history of philosophy is one that Kant holds to be as natural as the first: this is skepticism, which Kant describes as a swing from boundless trust to boundless mistrust (XX, 263). Kant believes this step to be a necessary one, indicating that "experience has rendered our judgment wiser and more circumspect," but it cannot be final (A761/B789). It is easy to expand Kant's metaphor and describe this period as reason's adolescence.[27] The discovery that elders are liable to err produces the mixture of disappointment and exhilaration that characterizes the adolescent's inclination to doubt everything hitherto learned. This doubt is surely more mature than the boundlessly self-confident assertions of childhood, and Kant insists that it is a process of education and growth that reason must undergo (A754/B782). The attention that Kant devotes to this process reflects, perhaps, Rousseauean conviction in the importance and precariousness of the period of transition from childhood to maturity. That it cannot represent adulthood is due to the fact that it is not yet self-critical. Skepticism is represented throughout Kant's work as a reactive impulse, a pure if understandable response to the failures of dogmatism (XX, 263). In the wash of disappointment occasioned by those failures, the adolescent is unable to value the impulse that motivated them or arrive at a truly self-determined understanding of his own capacities. Both these tasks are required by adulthood, which is, unsurprisingly, Kant's metaphor for the Critical Philosophy.

If Critical Philosophy is the adulthood toward which the history of thought was directed, it is equally the process by which each of us can reach rational maturity. Through the self-knowledge it provides, we can learn the autonomous discipline in which freedom is found: neither entirely abandoning ourselves to the demands of others nor, reactively, rejecting all such demands, we begin to use our own reason, to think for ourselves. Kant's interest in the processes of education reflects not only the general convictions of the age of Enlightenment but a particular view of the task of philosophy. As Yovel writes, "Kant considers rational education and the free dissemination of ideas to be the genuine action of the philosopher, which can transform social and political reality no less than the personalities of his audience" (1980, 217). Kant suggests that each of us must pass through the phases that characterize the intellectual growth of humankind as a whole; there is no shortcut to maturity. As the falls that a toddler takes in the process of learning to walk are infinitely preferable to being permanently kept on leading strings, so must we expect error and disappointment while learning to think for ourselves. Kant's repeated denunciation of censorship stems in large measure from his belief that we must undergo certain intellectual developments—in particular, that skepticism which has been viewed as dangerous to society—in order to mature. So he dismisses the normally recommended course of withholding skeptical teachings from the young. While this might temporarily protect them from unwanted opinions by artificially prolonging their childhood, it leaves them all the more helpless in the long run for having had no opportunity to develop their own powers (A754/B782). In intellectual inquiry as in political practice, we can only become ready for freedom by exercising it. Hence, every kind of censorship is a foolish attempt to protect individuals, and humankind as a whole, from a developmental process by which alone they can mature.[28] Now these reflections should allow us to reject decisively the specter of misology that Kant had raised and to answer a question posed at a number of points throughout this book: In directing us from speculation to practice, is Kant urging us to abandon the intellectual? If we accept the idea that the practical is primary, must we regard thought as merely instrumental, at best? If philosophy involves a process of self-knowledge that is integral to coming of age, the answer to these questions is *no*. At the same time, we can begin to give an account of the persistence of the disposition to philosophy despite the destruction of traditional metaphysics. That disposition may involve illusion, but it is not propelled by it. To give up philosophy because it entails frustration and error would be to abandon the struggle for maturity, individual and collective, for the same reasons.

Kant is as clear in recognizing the costs of maturity as in rejecting those who would seek to avoid it. His version of the Fall names the expulsion from Eden—"the dismissal from nature's womb . . . the safe and harmless environment of child-care"—as the price of reason (VIII, 114). Kant's claim that we can no longer judge whether humankind has gained or lost by the process that took us from the tutelage of nature to the state of reason seems coy in view of the invective which shortly follows it. There he scorns those who express nostalgia for a mythical golden age as seeking a state in which to "fritter away their lives with childish games," a state he ascribes to the South Sea Islanders who recur in his writings.[29] All these statements are expressions of Kant's belief that it is the ceaseless search for the Unconditioned that gives value to human life. They also reveal how easy it is to unite Kant's insistence on the importance of critical philosophy with his strong antielitist denunciation of the metaphysician's claims. While insisting that the greatest philosopher cannot advance further than the most common understanding in regard to the essential ends of human nature, Kant expects the same task of both (A831/B859). The unity of reason is nowhere so clearly revealed as in Kant's conviction that the primacy of the practical requires not the rejection of philosophy but the practice of it.

Thus, we can complete the sketch of the explanation of the urge to philosophy suggested most clearly in the *Fortschritte*. Human reason is driven to seek the Unconditioned, the thoroughgoing intelligibility of the world as a whole. Coming of age requires not abandoning, but redirecting this search: from dogmatic metaphysics to empirical science, from a theodicy that affirms the social order to a political program that transforms it. It requires, in short, the recognition that reason's function is not constitutive but regulative. Philosophy was correctly driven by the search for the unconditioned, which is inseparable from reason itself; it simply needs orientation in doing so. Providing that orientation should be the task of a regulative notion of philosophy, which would proceed in two ways. The first involves a self-knowledge that explores *what we are and have been*, seeking limits and boundaries through a critique of previous attempts at philosophy and (thereby) of reason itself. The second explores *what we could become* by maintaining, validating, and expanding our notions of the possible. Its task is thereby to uphold a vision of the reasonable itself — as a goal that, like every idea, we should never claim to possess nor cease to desire.[30]

Such a conception of philosophy is fundamentally different from postmodern calls for an end to metaphysics because it is regulative, frankly directed toward the achievement of enlightenment. The Kantian answer to those who find its justification of that goal unacceptably self-supporting is available in the first *Critique*.[31] Those who assume that if philosophy failed to provide us with certain knowledge, it can, at best, become an instrument of play accept the traditional assumption that only constitutive claims ensure genuine reality. Their rejection of metaphysics is merely the disappointed mirror image of metaphysics itself. This is, I believe, the meaning of Kant's claim that skepticism is simply counterdogmatism (A755/B783). The skeptic uncritically shares the dogmatist's beliefs about the nature of reason and reality. His rejection of reason and philosophy is based on their failure to succeed in terms of an unexamined and untenable model. Hence, their attitude toward the hope of enlightenment that underlies every attempt at philosophy is as dogmatic as that of those who sought to fulfill that hope by constructing systematic metaphysics.

The regulative conception of philosophy that I have sketched is also, however, different from that described by Velkley, who states that Kant redirects the task of metaphysics to reason's practical goal of becoming at home in this world (1989, 145). If philosophy involves coming of age, it also involves an acceptance of loss of the unreflective sense of unity that children feel toward their world. Critical philosophy directs reason to acknowledge the depth to which it will never be at home in the world. Thus, Hegel succeeds in describing Kant's most essential thought: "I, as Reason or conception, and the things external to me, are both absolutely different from one another; and that, according to Kant, is the ultimate standpoint" (1974, vol. 3, 455). Kant insists upon the existence of a gulf between human reason and the natural world that is so fundamental that it can ever be fully overcome. Hegel was neither the first nor the last to find this thought intolerable. Indeed, one historian has written that "the history of post-Kantian philosophy largely consists in the quest for the unifying principles behind Kant's dualisms" (Beiser 1987, 91). This quest, I believe, has proved a failure and its failure rests on the inability to recognize the nature of the dualism that pervades Kant's work. That dualism is not an ontological matter: Kant displays little interest in questions of the nature and number of substances that make up the world. Such questions are paradigmatic, for him, of fruitless metaphysical speculation. His dualism is not, on the other hand, sufficiently addressed by the harmless statement that Kant's philosophy posits not two worlds but two standpoints. While it is certainly correct to deny that Kant postulates two worlds, the talk of standpoints fails to capture the conflict whose description lies at the heart of Kant's philosophy. A standpoint can be taken up more or less at will, put aside, exchanged for another, considered again. The fact that the "standpoint" of the needs of reason is not that of the claims of nature is a source of permanent conflict: the acknowledgment of the duality of reason and the world is, at the same time, the acknowledgment of their disharmony. It is this acknowledgment that strikes the reader as profoundly modern. Thus, Walter Benjamin described post-Kantian attempts to unify reason and nature as eleventh-hour reactionary flights from the *honesty* of Kant's dualism (1977, 32).

Yet this thought contains a core of optimism rooted deep in the Enlightenment.[32] For Kant holds that it is only the recognition that there is a gap between the needs of reason and the demands of nature that creates the possibility that the two might be brought closer together. We might say that it is this possibility that provides the form of every regulative principle of reason. Kant's point is not simply that it is impossible to know that the needs of reason and the demands of nature coincide but that it is fatal to assume it. Here the connection between Kant's dualism and his assertion of the limits of knowledge becomes clear. The maintenance of an absolute difference between reason and the world stands together with the denial that the world in itself is transparent to reason. If reason is constitutive—capable of knowing the world as a whole—then the world that is given to us must be reasonable. If reason is regulative, it is possible that human action can make it more so.

Recognition of these claims cannot wholly remove our sense of uneasiness about the notion of a regulative principle. The notion remains elusive, perpetually threatening to become empty or absurd. In describing reason's activity in all its spheres, I have tried to exhibit a sense of content that is not cognitive, undermining the temptation to view constitutive principles as the only legitimate ones by sketching a plausible alternative. Yet even the fullest exposition of the idea of a regulative principle would, I think, leave a certain dissatisfaction. To dispel it, we must dispel the consistent temptation to regard constitutive principles as necessary for full content when only regulative ones will do. If Kant is correct, this temptation is transcendental illusion, with which we may struggle but will never fully escape.

Accepting the legitimacy of regulative principles requires not only the acknowledgment of a disharmony between reason and the world that all our efforts have been directed to ignoring: it requires the still more difficult acknowledgment of our absolute freedom in the face of this disharmony. Hence, Kant describes the obstacle to enlightenment as a lack not of understanding but of resolution and courage. Reason's drive toward constitutive principles is just the drive toward a certainty independent of ourselves and our will: therein lies the seduction of objectivity. Every coming of age involves giving up certainty, and dependence provides protection. Every coming of age involves abandoning the illusion that the capacity to make demands upon the world provides a guarantee that those demands can be fulfilled. In the realm of reason, this illusion is called transcendental. But one must be wary of metaphor. Kant's appeal to reason to come of age is not, like so many such appeals, a call to abandon youthful ideals. It is rather a call to abandon a youthful belief in their easy fulfillment; in the knowledge that reason's demands will be clearer, its steps surer, its opportunities for satisfaction greater for having arrived at a true estimation of its powers.

Notes

1. Curiously, this quote is not taken from Kant's own words but from a letter from a certain C. A. Williams, which Kant took the unprecedented step of adding to his own text as an appendix.

2. Förster (1989a) argues that different conceptions are reflected in different periods of Kant's work. While it may be true that Kant's last works maintain with some clarity that the metaphysical conception of the first *Critique* cannot be upheld, Förster also notes that many elements of what he identifies as a post-Critical conception of philosophy can be found in the first *Critique* itself, as will be discussed later.

3. On the "meta-critique," see Beiser (1987, 2–7, 325–26).

4. See my discussion in chapter 3, section I.

5. Kemp Smith tries to systematize a version of this description of the relations between philosophy and metaphysics (1962, 580).

6. It would also, as I argued in chapter 4, involve disastrous consequences, so that it is positively undesirable; but Kant had not developed this argument at the time of the first *Critique*.

7. Yovel raises the question whether there may be a genuine metaphysical urge that is irreducible to practical interests (1980, 290–93). If this is the case, as many philosophers maintain, then Kant's doctrine of the primacy of the practical will appear as a demand for repression. One holding this view will not be surprised that the urge to metaphysics would continue to reassert itself. In the following, however, I have tried to answer the question of the persistence of metaphysics from within a Kantian framework, that is, on the assumption that the drive to metaphysics has a practical origin.

8. Cassirer gives a good statement of this natural view (1981, 145–53). See also Ameriks (1992, 259), and Förster (1989a, 191). Yovel gives what is perhaps the most succinct description of this replacement, which he rightly sees as only part of a larger process (1989a, 140–43).

9. On whether and how the *Metaphysics of Morals* can be regarded as metaphysics, see Bittner (1989). It should also be noted that Kant did not consider the *Metaphysical Foundations of Natural Science* to be the full metaphysics of nature that he often promised to deliver; but see Butts (1986a) for a fuller discussion of the status of that work.

10. Beck's introduction to his translation of the *Prolegomena* gives a concise statement of what post-Critical metaphysics is to be: "The task of the only metaphysics that can be science, therefore, is to elaborate what a priori knowledge we can have; it will be metaphysics of nature if it studies the a priori form of what is (in the world of phenomena) or the metaphysics of morals if it studies the a priori form of obligation, of what ought to be" (1950, xix–xx). The problem with such a statement is not only that it leaves the relation between such projects and the disposition to metaphysics utterly opaque but that it also leaves us with the traditional problem of discovering what significant tasks have been left undone by the supposedly propaedeutic critiques. The *Metaphysics of Morals* is said to be necessary in order to understand the source of moral concepts (VI, 375). Yet this seemed to be the goal of the *Critique of Practical Reason* (see chap. 3, sec. I); the interesting remaining questions seem to be the ones Kant describes as casuistical.

11. For a summary of those insights, see chap. 2, sec. V. Yovel makes a similar point: "Kant seems to have claimed for philosophy what he excluded from the other forms of knowledge. Indeed, there seems to be a major discrepancy between his metaphilosophy and his philosophy of objective knowledge" (1977, 671). In his *Kant and the Philosophy of History*, Yovel writes that Kant's own critical conception should have led him to question the view of philosophy as issuing in a final eternal system of truth: "Or to use Kant's own language, a 'regulative' idea of philosophy must here take the place of the speculative quest for final system" (1980, 287). To my knowledge, Yovel is unique in having made such a suggestion. Saner raises questions that certainly lead in this direction (1973, 226–29); Arendt's remarks remain more general. By the time of his fine article "The Interests of Reason: From Metaphysics to Moral History" Yovel (1989a) seems to believe not only that Kant should have held a regulative conception of philosophy but that he did hold something very close to one. The conception I shall describe in the following has many points of similarity with that of Yovel.

12. See the opening of the *Second Discourse* and the *Emile* for some of Rousseau's own statements about the peculiarities of his own method.

13. For a description of reason as "the permanent judge, and at the same time the permanent defendant" at the endless trial that constitutes critique, see Saner (1973, 255–56).

14. For a good discussion of the three maxims, see O'Neill (1989, chaps. 1–2). For a similar description of critique as a process, see O'Neill (1992).

15. See Yovel (1989a, 137–39). Arendt claims that it is precisely the regulative character of critical thinking that makes it antiauthoritarian and politically significant in a way that speculative philosophy cannot be (1982, 38).

16. On the justification of reason as a reflexive process, see O'Neill (1992, esp. 291) and Yovel (1980, 212).

17. For further discussion, see Walsh (1982, esp. 164).

18. See Arendt (1977) and Henrich (1989). Patricia Kitcher's *Kant's Transcendental Psychology*, (1990) though concerned with somewhat different questions, contains much valuable discussion of matters relevant to Kant's notion of self-knowledge.

19. Of course, the status of those sciences has been notoriously difficult to determine. Questions of the sort of knowledge provided by Freud's work remain acute, and they seem to arise even, if possible, more problematically for the thinkers with whom Kant was concerned. The unsteadiness of the lines between philosophy, psychology, physical science, and literature is expressed by the various hopeful candidates for the designation "Newton of the Mind"; I believe this unsteadiness to be an argument for a more fluid understanding of the knowledge produced by the human sciences in general but cannot argue for this here. It remains true that even a looser conception of what counts as knowledge of the human should be able to maintain a distinction between philosophy and psychology, which is our present concern.

20. For another discussion of the differences between Kant's investigations in the "Analytic" and psychological ones, see Guyer (1989); alternative views are offered by Kitcher (1990).

21. See, esp. VII, 69; passages of the *Fortschritte*; and the *Anthropology*. Curiously, the latter's definition of what Kant calls "pragmatic anthropology" ("where we try to know man in terms of what can be made of him" [VII, 246] suggests that the distinction between philosophy and some sorts of human science will not be of tremendous significance.

22. On mental illness, see Butts's (1984) discussion of *Schwärmerei*; on dinner guests, see VII, 276–78.

23. For a discussion of Kant's use of these claims, see chap. 3, 276–8 sec. I–II.

24. Compare the footnote to the preface of the *Metaphysical Foundations of Natural Science* (19).

25. See, especially, the final footnote to "Orientation" (VIII, 147). Reiss also points out that the famous "Sapere aude!" — which Kant calls the motto of Enlightenment in the opening paragraph of "What Is Enlightenment?" — is correctly translated as "Dare to be wise!" rather than the more common "Dare to know!" (1970, 192).

26. Inexplicably, Kemp Smith translates *Kindesalter* as "infancy."

27. The connection between skeptical philosophy and adolescence is also made by Cavell (1986, 234).

28. The "Discipline" accuses skepticism of a censorship no less problematic than that practiced by dogmatic metaphysics. This is particularly interesting in view of the fact that despite Hume's talk of committing books to the flames, actual censorship in Kant's day was squarely in the hands of dogmatic metaphysicians who banned or published in mutilated form those books they thought would undermine the social order. In denouncing as nonsense reason's pretensions to advance beyond the empirical, Hume, Kant suggests, is proposing a form of censorship (A758/B786–A769/B797). This seems to reflect not only Kant's belief that the skeptic's claim to knowledge is as dogmatic and unfounded as that of the metaphysician but also his awareness that the most effective and pernicious form of censorship may not be one that commits books to the flames but one that subjects them to ridicule, trivialization, and contempt.

29. Saner emphasizes the importance of the discovery of Tahiti for eighteenth-century thought and Kant's decisive rejection of his contemporaries' enthusiasm for it (1973, 235–36). Tracing Kant's references to the (somewhat fictionalized) Tahitians would give us a good picture of his ideal of the human, which combines both a (Leibnizian) demand for perfection with an insistence on egalitarianism. While Kant may not have shared Trotsky's rhapsodic belief that in the truly human society, everyone will be an Aristotle, a Goethe, or a Marx, each would certainly be expected to be an Emile.

30. Compare Yovel's words: "Projecting an ideal of intelligibility which we cannot attain has a definite philosophical meaning. It brings back to our consciousness the finitude of human existence—the fact that, for us, neither the world nor our own reason can be made fully intelligible. Hence we must live with a constant gap between the rationality we legitimately seek and the rationality we can legitimately attain" (1977, 673).

31. For a somewhat different discussion of these questions, see O'Neill (1992).

32. This was given perhaps its boldest expression by Cohen, who wrote, "*Our future depends on* the ability to comprehend in their pure rational difference both nature and morality, 'the starry sky above me and the moral law within me', and not to seek their unification except in the idea of the one God" (quoted in Derrida, 1991, 67; my italics).

References

Following common practice, Kant's works are cited according to volume and page number of *Kants gesammelte Schriften, herausgegeben von der Deutschen Akademie der Wissenschaften* (Walter de Gruyter, 1902). Exceptions are the *Critique of Pure Reason*, where references follow the standard A and B pagination of the first and second editions; and the *Lectures on Ethics* (Hackett 1963) referred to as *Lectures*, translated by Louis Infield (a translation of *Eine Vorlesung über Ethik*, edited by Paul Menzer [Rolf Heise, 1924]. Where standard English translations were available, I have used them with occasional changes; other translations, particularly of Kant's less familiar essays, are my own. For abbreviations of Leibniz's works, see under his name. All italics in quotes are original unless otherwise noted.

Adams, R.M. 1977. "Leibniz's Theories of Contingency," *Rice University Studies*, 63:1–41.

Allison, Henry. 1983. *Kant's Transcendental Idealism*. Yale University Press.

——. 1989. "Justification and Freedom." In Förster (1989b), 114–130.

——. 1990. *Kant's Theory of Freedom*. Cambridge University Press.

Ameriks, Karl. 1992. "The Critique of Metaphysics: Kant and Traditional Ontology." In Guyer (1992), 249–279.

Arendt, Hannah. 1977. *The Life of the Mind*. Harcourt Brace Jovanovich.

——. 1982. *Lectures on Kant's Political Philosophy*. University of Chicago Press.

Bacon, Francis. 1960. *The New Organon*, F.H. Anderson, ed. Bobbs-Merrill.

Bayle, Pierre. 1965. *Historical and Critical Dictionary*, R.H. Popkin, ed. and trans. Bobbs-Merrill.

Beck, Lewis White. 1950. "Introduction." In *Prolegomena to Any Future Metaphysics*, by Immanuel Kant, Lewis White Beck, trans. Bobbs-Merrill.

——. 1960. *A Commentary on Kant's Critique of Practical Reason*. University of Chicago Press.

Beck, Lewis White, ed. 1967. *Kant Studies Today*. Open Court.

Beiser, Frederick. 1987. *The Fate of Reason*. Harvard University Press.

——. 1992. *Enlightenment, Revolution, and Romanticism*. Harvard University Press.

Bencivenga, Ermanno. 1987. *Kant's Copernican Revolution*. Oxford University Press.

Benjamin, Walter. 1977. "Dialog über die Religiosität der Gegenwart." In *Benjamins gesammelte Schriften*, Band II, Rolf Tiedemann and Hermann Schweppenhaüser, eds. Suhrkamp.

Bennett, Jonathan. 1966. *Kant's Analytic*. Cambridge University Press.

Berkeley, George. 1940. *A Treatise Concerning the Principles of Human Knowledge*, G. J. Warnock, ed. Open Court.

Bittner, Rüdiger. 1989. "Das Unternehmen einer Grundlegung zur Metaphysik der Sitten." In Ditfried Hoffe, ed., *Grundlegung zur Metaphysik der Sitten*.

Böhme, H., and G. Böhme. 1983. *Das Andere der Vernunft*. Suhrkamp.

Brittan, Gordon C. 1978. *Kant's Theory of Science*. Princeton University Press.

Buchdahl, Gerd. 1966/67. "The Relationship between Understanding and Reason in the Architectonic of Kant's Philosophy." *Proceedings of the Aristotelian Society* 67: 209–226.

——. 1969. *Metaphysics and the Philosophy of Science*. Basil Blackwell.

——. 1986. "Kant's Special Metaphysics and the Metaphysical Foundations of Natural Science." In Butts (1986a), 127–161.

Burke, Edmund. 1969. *Reflections on the Revolution in France*. Conor Cruise O'Brien, ed. Penguin.

Butts, Robert E. 1984. *Kant and the Double Government Methodology*. Reidel.

——, ed. 1986a. *Kant's Philosophy of Physical Science*, Reidel.

——. 1986b. "The Methodological Structure of Kant's Metaphysics of Science." In Butts (1986a), 163–199.

Cassirer, Ernst. 1945. *Rousseau, Kant, Goethe*. Princeton University Press.

——. 1962. *Leibniz's System in Seinen Wissenschaftlichen Grundlagen*. Georg Olms Verlagsbuchhandlung.

——. 1981. *Kant's Life and Thought*. Yale University Press.

Cavell, Stanley. 1986. "In Quest of the Ordinary." In Morris Eaves and Michael Fischer, eds., *Romanticism and Contemporary Criticism*. Cornell University Press.

Cohen, Hermann. 1910. *Kants Begründung der Ethik*. Cassirer.

Couturat, Louis. 1901. *La Logique de Leibniz*. Ancienne Libraire Germer Bailliere.

——. 1972. "On Leibniz's Metaphysics." In Frankfurt (1972), 19–46.

Curley, E.M. 1972. "The Root of Contingency." In Frankfurt (1972), 69–97.

Danford, John W. 1990. *David Hume and the Problem of Reason*. Yale University Press.

Derrida, Jacques. 1991. "Interpretations at War: Kant, The Jew, The German." *New Literary History*, 39–95.

Duncan, Howard. 1986. "Kant's Methodology." In Butts (1986a), 273–306.

Förster, Eckart. 1989a. "Kant's Notion of Philosophy." *Monist* 72: 284–304.

——, ed. 1989b. *Kant's Transcendental Deductions*. Stanford University Press.

Frankfurt, Harry, ed. 1972. *Leibniz: A Collection of Essays*. Notre Dame University Press.

Frege, Gottlob. 1978. *Foundations of Arithmetic: A Logico-mathematical Inquiry into the Concept of Number*. J.L. Austin, ed. and trans. Northwestern University Press.

Friedman, Michael. 1985. "Kant's Theory of Geometry." *Philosophical Review*, 455–506

——. 1986. "The Metaphysical Foundations of Newtonian Science," in Butts (1986a), 25–60.

——. 1991. "Regulative and Constitutive." *Southern Journal of Philosophy* 30:73–102.

——. 1992a. "Causal Laws and the Foundations of Natural Science." In Guyer (1992), 161–199.

——. 1992b. *Kant and the Exact Sciences*. Harvard University Press.

Gay, Peter. 1969. *The Enlightenment*, Vol. 2: *The Science of Freedom*. Norton.

Gulyga, Arsenij. 1985. *Immanuel Kant*. Suhrkamp.

Guyer, Paul. 1979. *Kant and the Claims of Taste*. Harvard University Press.

——. 1989a. "The Unity of Reason," *Monist* 72:139–167.

——. 1989b. "Psychology and the Deduction." In Förster (1989b), 47–68.

——. 1990. "Reason and Reflective Judgement." *Nous* 24: 17–43.

——, ed. 1992. *The Cambridge Companion to Kant*. Cambridge University Press.

Hegel, G.W. 1974. *Lectures on the History of Philosophy*. E.S. Haldane and Frances H. Simpson, trans. Humanities Press.

——. 1977. *Faith and Knowledge*, Walter Cerf and H.S. Harris, trans. SUNY Press.

Heine, Heinrich, *Zur Geschichte der Religion und der Philosophie in Deutschland*. In Klaus Briegleb, ed., *Sämtliche Schriften*, vol. 5. Ullstein.

Henrich, Dieter. 1973. "Der Begriff der sittlichen Einsicht und Kants Lehre vom Faktum der Vernunft." In Prauss (1973), 223–254.

——. 1976. *Identität und Objektivität*. Carl Winter Universitätsverlag.

——. 1989. "Kant's Notion of a Deduction." In Förster (1989b), 29–46.

Hermann, Barbara. 1989. "Justification and Objectivity." In Förster (1989b), 131–141.

Hintikka, Jaako. 1969. "Kant's Notion of Intuition." In Terence Penelhum and J.J. MacIntosh, eds. *The First Critique*. Wadsworth.

——. 1973. "Kant Vindicated." In Jaako Hintikka, ed., *Logic, Language Games and Information*. Oxford University Press.

Horkheimer, Max. 1977. *Zur Kritik der Instrumentellen Vernunft*. Frankfurt.

Hume, David. 1975. *An Enquiry Concerning Human Understanding*. Oxford University Press.

——. 1978. *A Treatise of Human Nature*. Oxford University Press.

Kemp Smith, Norman. 1962. *A Commentary to Kant's Critique of Pure Reason*. Humanities Press.

——. 1966. *The Philosophy of David Hume*. St. Martin's Press.

Kitcher, Patricia. 1990. *Kant's Transcendental Psychology*. Oxford University Press.

Kitcher, Philip. 1984. "Kant's Philosophy of Science." In Wood (1984), 185–215.

Kitcher, Philip. 1986. "Projecting the Order of Nature." In Butts (1986a), 201–235.

Konhardt, Klaus. 1979. *Die Einheit der Vernunft: Zum Verhältnis von theoretischer und praktischer Vernunft in der Philosophie Kants*. Forum Academicum.

Korsgaard, Christine. 1986a. "The Right to Lie: Kant on Dealing with Evil." *Philosophy and Public Affairs* 15:325–349.

——. 1986b. "Kant's Formula of Humanity." *Kant-Studien* 77: 183–202.

——. 1989a. "Morality as Freedom." In Yovel (1989b), 24–48.

——. 1989b. "Kant." In Robert J. Cavalier, ed., *Ethics in the History of Western Philosophy*. St. Martin's Press.

——. 1992. "Creating the Kingdom of Ends." In *Philosophical Perspectives*.

——. n.d. "The Standpoint of Practical Reason." Unpublished manuscript.

Koyre, Alexander. 1965. *Newtonian Studies*. Harvard University Press.

Leibniz, Gottfried W. 1969. *Philosophical Papers and Letters*, Leroy L. Loemker, ed. Reidel. (cited as L)

——. 1951. *Selections*, Phillip Wiener, ed. Charles Scribner's Sons. (cited as W)

——. 1952. *Theodicy*, Austin Farrer, ed. and E.M. Huggard, trans. Yale University Press. (cited as T)

——. 1981. *New Essays on Human Understanding*, Peter Remnant and Jonathan Bennett, ed. and trans. Cambridge University Press. (cited as NE)

Lessing, Gotthold. 1959. *Gesammelte Werke*. Hanser.

Ley, Hermann, Peter Ruben, and Gottfried Stiehler, eds. 1975. *Zum Kant-Verständnis unserer Zeit*. VEB Deutscher Verlag der Wissenschaften.

Livingston, Donald W., and James T. King, eds. 1976. *Hume: A Reevaluation*. Fordham University Press.

Lovejoy, Arthur. 1936. *The Great Chain of Being*. Harvard University Press.

MacIntyre, Alasdair. 1988. *Whose Justice? Which Rationality?* University of Notre Dame Press.

Maimonides. 1976. *Guide for the Perplexed*, 2nd rev. ed., M. Friedlander, trans. Dover.

Mates, Benson. 1986. *The Philosophy of Leibniz: Metaphysics and Language*. Oxford University Press.

Melnick, Arthur. 1973. *Kant's Analogies of Experience*. University of Chicago Press.

Mendelssohn, Moses. 1979. *Morgenstunden*. Reclam.

Okruhlik, Kathleen, 1986. "Kant on Realism and Methodology." In Butts (1986a), 307–329.

O'Neill, Onora [Onora Nell]. 1975. *Acting on Principle*. Columbia University Press.
——. 1989. *Constructions of Reason*. Cambridge University Press.
——. 1992. "Vindicating Reason." In Guyer (1992), 280–308.
Parsons, Charles. 1969. "Kant's Philosophy of Arithmetic." In Sidney Morgenbesser, Patrick Suppes, and Morton White, eds., *Philosophy, Science and Method*. St. Martin's Press.
——. 1984. "Commentary: Remarks on Pure Natural Science." In Wood (1984), 216–228.
Prauss, Gerold, ed. 1973. *Kant: zur Deutung seiner Theorie von Erkennen und Handeln*. Kiepenheuer und Witsch.
Rawls, John. 1980. "Kantian Constructivism and Moral Theory." *Journal of Philosophy* 77:515–572.
——. 1980–87. "Lectures on Kant's Moral Philosophy." Unpublished.
——. 1989. "Themes in Kant's Moral Philosophy." In Förster (1989), 81–113.
Reichenbach, Hans. 1973. *The Rise of Scientific Philosophy*. University of California Press.
Reiss, Hans W. 1970. *Kant's Political Writings*. Cambridge University Press.
Rousseau, Jean-Jacques. 1979. *Emile*. Allan Bloom, trans. Basic Books.
——. 1986. *The First and Second Discourses Together with the Replies to Critics*. Victor Gourevich, ed. and trans. Harper and Row.
Russell, Bertrand. 1937. *The Philosophy of Leibniz*. London.
——. 1971. *Introduction to Mathematical Philosophy*. Simon and Schuster (published by arrangement with George Allen and Unwin; same pagination as 1919 edition).
Saner, Hans. 1973. *Kant's Political Thought*. University of Chicago Press.
Schiller, Friedrich. 1910. "Über Anmut und Würde." In *Werke*, vol. 7, 85–160. Bibliographischen Institut.
Schlick, Moritz. 1959. "The Foundation of Knowledge." In Alfred J. Ayer, ed., *Logical Positivism*. Macmillan.
Schneewind, Jerome. 1992. "Autonomy, Obligation and Virtue." In Guyer (1992), 309–341.
Scholz, H., ed. 1916. *Hauptschriften zum Pantheismusstreit zwischen Jacobi und Mendelssohn*. Reuther und Reichard.
Shell, Susan M. 1980. *The Rights of Reason*. University of Toronto Press.
Spinoza, Baruch. 1949. *Ethics*, James Gutmann, ed. Hafner Press.
Stroud, Barry. 1977. *Hume*. Routledge and Kegan Paul.
Sullivan, Roger. 1989. *Immanuel Kant's Moral Theory*. Cambridge University Press.
Taylor, Charles. 1989. *Sources of the Self*. Harvard University Press.
Thompson, Manley. 1972. "Singular Terms and Intuitions in Kant's Epistemology." *Review of Metaphysics* 26:314–343.
Toulmin, Stephen. 1961. *Foresight and Understanding*. Harper and Row.
Vaihinger, Hans. 1892. *Commentar zu Kants Kritik der reinen Vernunft*. W. Spemann und Union Deutsche Verlagsgesellschaft.
Van der Linden, Harry. 1988. *Kantian Ethics and Socialism*. Hackett.
Vania, Natalie. 1989. "Doesn't Regulative Systematicity Belong to Judgement, Too?" M.A. thesis, University of Maryland.
Velkley, Richard. 1989. *Freedom and the End of Reason*. University of Chicago Press.
Vorländer, Karl. 1924. *Immanuel Kant*. Felix Meiner Verlag.
Walsh, W. H. 1975. *Kant's Criticism of Metaphysics*. University of Chicago Press.
Walsh, W.H. 1982. "Self-Knowledge." In Ralph Walker, ed., *Kant on Pure Reason*. Oxford University Press.
Westfall, Richard. 1977. *The Construction of Modern Science*. Cambridge University Press.
Wolin, Sheldon. 1976. "Hume's Conservatism." In Livingston and King (1976), 239–256.
Wood, Allan. 1970. *Kant's Moral Religion*. Cornell University Press.

——. ed. 1984. *Self and Nature in Kant's Philosophy*. Cornell University Press.

Wright, Kathleen. 1987. "Kant und der Kanon der Kritik." In Aleida and Jan Assmann, eds., *Kanon und Zensur*. Wilhelm Fink Verlag.

Young, J.M. 1982. "Kant on the Construction of Arithmetical Concepts." *Kant-Studien* 73:17–46.

Yovel, Yirmayahu. 1977. "Systematic Philosophy: Ambitions and Critique." In Dieter Henrich, ed., *Ist systematische Philosophie möglich?* Bouvie.

——. 1980. *Kant and the Philosophy of History*. Princeton University Press.

——. 1989a. "The Interests of Reason: From Metaphysics to Moral History." In Yovel (1989b), 135–148.

——, ed. 1989b. *Kant's Practical Philosophy Reconsidered*. Kluwer Academic Publishers.

Index